A MEMOIR
OF
D. H. LAWRENCE

A MEMOIR
OF
D. H. LAWRENCE

(The Betrayal)

G. H. NEVILLE

Edited by
Carl Baron

WITHDRAWN

Cambridge University Press

Cambridge

London   New York   New Rochelle
Melbourne   Sydney

Published by the Press Syndicate of the University of Cambridge
The Pitt Building, Trumpington Street, Cambridge CB2 1RP
32 East 57th Street, New York, NY 10022, USA
296 Beaconsfield Parade, Middle Park, Melbourne 3206, Australia

First published 1981

Printed in Great Britain by
Western Printing Services Ltd, Bristol

Library of Congress catalogue card number: 81–7656

British Library Cataloguing in Publication Data
Neville, G. H.
A memoir of D. H. Lawrence.
1. Lawrence, D. H. – Biography
2. Authors, English – 20th century – Biography
I. Title   II. Baron, Carl
823'.912   PR6023.A93Z

ISBN 0 521 24097 2

CONTENTS

ILLUSTRATIONS

Between pages 72 and 73

Photograph of Lawrence and Neville's class at
Beauvale Boys' School, 1894
(reproduced by courtesy of Dr Keith Sagar)

George Henry Neville, *c.* 1908
(reproduced by permission of the Neville family)

D. H. Lawrence, *c.* 1908
(reproduced by courtesy of Local Studies Library, Nottinghamshire
County Library)

An Idyll by Maurice Grieffenhagen (1891)
(reproduced by permission of the Walker Art Gallery, Corporation of
Liverpool)

ACKNOWLEDGEMENTS

I am above all indebted to Mr James Neville for his kind invitation to prepare his father's Memoir for publication, and for his patience in awaiting its appearance. I am most grateful to him, and other members of the Neville family, for their willingness to answer questions and supply information: Mrs James Neville, Mrs G. H. Neville; Mrs G. Neville and Mrs Stone; and for much help from G. H. Neville's niece, Mrs Jean Temple. Mr Roy Wilson kindly supplied me with a copy of his father's recollection of Lawrence and Neville.

A debt of special gratitude is owed to Mr David Philips, Keeper of Fine Art at the Castle Museum, Nottingham, for his part in locating the Memoir and arranging to borrow it for the 'Young Bert' exhibition of 1972.

I am also grateful to Professor James T. Boulton of the University of Birmingham, and to Mr Michael Black and Mrs Lindeth Vasey of the Cambridge University Press, for reading the work in draft and making many helpful suggestions.

My special thanks go to Dr Helen Baron for much advice and assistance throughout the preparation of this edition.

C.E.B.

Cambridge
August 1980

EDITOR'S INTRODUCTION

Lawrence: the biographical problem

It is commonly supposed that a great deal is known about the young D. H. Lawrence and his home background in Eastwood near Nottingham; and by comparison with many other writers, there are very full records. Many of his friends wrote memoirs or were interviewed for their reminiscences; a number of letters have survived; and Lawrence himself, in *The White Peacock* and principally in *Sons and Lovers*, has given versions of his early life. But these abundant materials can still leave readers with a puzzled sense that no coherent shape of a personality and life emerges from them. The psychology of the young man remains a mystery for which no convincing account has yet been given. The present volume cannot solve that mystery, which could only be tackled in a full-scale biography, but it offers some new leads towards a solution.

The White Peacock, as the first in a series of works of art very directly engaged in the interpretation of their author's life, might be expected to give a cross-section, at a valuably early stage, of Lawrence's inner life. Readers of this first novel are often struck by the strange complexity of the author's character, which is intimated through prose that, whatever aspect of it one looks at – whether its narrative, its descriptions, its tones, its characters – expresses extraordinarily complicated and varied inner pressures. This sense of the bafflingness of Lawrence's literary products was gestured at in a variety of ways by his earliest critics and reviewers, as when, for example, some reviewers thought that *The White Peacock* was written by a woman. It is so baffling in its intimation of its author's character that we realise that any fresh help in making sense of his psychology is welcome.

The works by Lawrence most widely read are his four outstanding novels, *Sons and Lovers*, *The Rainbow*, *Women in Love* and *Lady Chatterley's Lover*. I suggest that it has become a critical challenge worth taking up, to understand whether and in what ways these very different novels are exploring the same fundamental material as *The White Peacock*. The biographical challenge, distinct from but related to the critical one, is to establish whether in essence all Lawrence's main problems were present before he ever put pen to paper. In other words, although at different periods of his writing life he draws upon immediate or recent experiences, we need to ascertain whether nevertheless some possibilities of his personality and relationships might not have been fixed already, before he began to write, and before he met the people who could later fill out those basic predispositions. It seems to me that *The White Peacock* expresses pressures, needs and psychological patterning in imaginative form in direct line with his later handling of those same patternings when realities and experiences had taken the place of needs and fantasies.

These suggestions are hypotheses only; but so much writing about Lawrence takes for granted that his life consisted of very different phases, that the possibility of an underlying fixity needs raising. While it is to the greatest focal points of artistic truth in Lawrence's writing that we should look for the controlling elements from which to establish the shape of his inner life, even so a would-be biographer of his early life needs to make sense not only of *Sons and Lovers*, but also of *The White Peacock*, because in its curious way it is a more spontaneous, expressive work.

Whatever sense one has of the way in which *The White Peacock* relates to the later writings, it does convince one of the desirability of unearthing as much as possible about Lawrence's early life and environment. This is where G. H. Neville's Memoir is important. For, although it is a modest effort and nothing like so well written as Jessie Chambers's minor classic *D. H. Lawrence: A Personal Record*[1] – and indeed there are some bad misjudgements of taste in it, such as the excruciatingly sentimental verses of his own that Neville places at the end – nevertheless it does offer much that is new. First, it provides some facts that are not in the other life-records. Second, it is a

2

conscious and sustained effort by someone who knew Lawrence well in his youth to interpret that life for us. Third, it exposes for our contemplation the character of Neville himself, who was one of the two main male friends of Lawrence's youth. And finally it is important because Neville's own life-story and personality can now be clearly seen to have constituted significant raw material for Lawrence's art.

Neville's life and character

George Henry Neville was born just over a year after Lawrence, on 7 October 1886, in Eastwood. His family was a little more affluent than Lawrence's, as is illustrated by their move, when Neville was seven, to 43 Lynn Croft. It took the Lawrence family two moves and fifteen years to reach Lynn Croft, with its 'handsome' bay-windowed houses.

Neville's father, James Neville, was a miner who later became a dairyman; he in turn was the son of another James Neville, a miner. It was this first James Neville who had moved from Staffordshire to Eastwood. Neville's father first married Sarah Ellen Baker, a widow of about thirty with three children, and after her death in 1918 he married another widow, also with a family. James Neville and Sarah Ellen had five sons of their own in addition, of whom George Henry was the second. The Nevilles became a numerous family in Eastwood, and it is not uncommon for people who crop up once or twice as minor figures in the Lawrence life-records to be more or less distantly related to them. Later on, the Nevilles became a well-known family in Eastwood; from 1924 they ran the garage and taxi service, and owned the ambulance and the fire-engine in the days before the Town Council had its own fire-engine.

Little is known about Neville's father, but members of the family describe him as a man whose domineering nature could on occasion run to cruelty towards his family, even to Neville's mother. His sister, Hannah, lived with them and he treated her as a servant. It may be of importance, in considering G. H. Neville's attitude to women, that for his father they were very definitely second-class citizens.

Another important figure in Neville's immediate family was his one elder brother, William Baker Neville. His remarkable career, which is very similar to that which Lawrence's elder brother Ernest once seemed to be launched upon, can best be expressed in the words of the obituary in the *Eastwood and Kimberley Advertiser* for 23 April 1948, which provides some flavour of the outlook and career prospects available to young men of G. H. Neville's and Lawrence's age and circumstances:

> From pit-boy to general manager of the London Co-operative Society briefly records the remarkable life's story of the East-wood boy, Mr R. William Baker Neville, J.P., who passed away . . . at his Buckhurst Hill (London) home, at the age of 63.
>
> Son of a miner (the late Mr James Neville) of Eastwood, the elder member of a large family, he commenced his working career in practically the only available industry in the district in those days, and became a ganger at High Park Colliery, but following an early accident underground, he was found employment as an office boy on the surface. Being of a studious nature and withal ambitious, he continued his studies under his old schoolmaster, Mr William Whitehead, and secured a position on the clerical staff of the Langley Mill and Aldercar Co-operative Society, where he attained a position of some responsibility. In 1912, he obtained an important post with the Royal Arsenal Co-operative Society, London, where his unusual capabilities were quickly recognised, and in a few years he was appointed secretary and chief executive officer of that important concern. In 1937 the Greater London Co-operative Society claimed his services, and at the head of that big concern – the world's largest retail Co-operative Society – he saw in ten years the sales raised from £14,000,000 a year to £25,000,000 . . .
>
> He was elected President of the Co-operative Congress at Margate in 1939, and was a permanent magistrate for London County. He served on many important Government Committees . . .
>
> From his earliest days Mr Neville was a Bible Student and very devout in his religious beliefs. He was always deeply attached to the Beauvale Methodist Church, where he became organist and Sunday School teacher, and served on the local preachers' plan . . .
>
> The funeral service was [attended by, amongst many others] the Right Hon. A. V. Alexander, M.P., P.C., Minister of Defence . . .

G. H. Neville himself took in 1899 the alternative route to

4

self-betterment of a scholarship from the local school at Beau-vale to Nottingham High School. There an excellent staff was led by the headmaster James Gow, a Doctor of Literature and former Fellow of Trinity College, Cambridge, whose next headship was of Westminster School, and who also acted as chairman of the Headmasters' Conference (i.e. the association of public school headmasters). For both Neville and Lawrence attendance at Nottingham High School meant the temporary immersion in a socially superior world.

At that time, at the turn of the century, bright working-class boys who had won scholarships to schools such as Nottingham High School had very little opportunity for taking responsible jobs in the professions because of the prohibitive cost of higher education. So, just as Lawrence had to find himself work as a clerk at a Nottingham factory, Neville worked briefly for a local tailor. But both managed to ensure themselves some further educational qualifications by becoming pupil, or 'uncertifica-ted', teachers at local schools, Lawrence at the British School, Albert Street, Neville at the Gilt Hill School; and by attending, one day a week, a teachers' training centre near Eastwood, at Ilkeston. But in 1905, at the end of that training, whereas Lawrence succeeded in winning one of the twelve scholarships awarded throughout England which enabled him to go to University College, Nottingham to take the Certificate in Education, Neville had to find a teaching job. He worked for a short time as a certificated teacher at the Gilt Hill School, before moving in 1907 to a better post about fifty miles to the south-west at Amblecote, Stourbridge, on the western outskirts of Birmingham in Staffordshire. In 1908, Lawrence went to a teaching post in Croydon.

Despite this separation their friendship continued, and they went on holiday together every year until Lawrence left for the continent in 1912. Neville had married in 1911, and from the beginning of 1912 he and his newly formed family lived at Armitage, Rugeley, Staffordshire, moving once or twice within Armitage before settling in mid 1914 in the house in which they remained until Neville's death in 1959.

George Neville's later career can be summarised briefly. He left teaching in 1916 and took employment with the rationing department of the Food Office. After the war, he joined Henry

Boot and Sons, Sheffield, acting as an agent for council-house construction work. In 1924 he attempted to form his own company, Building Supplies, Birmingham, Ltd, but the venture collapsed within a few years. After this Neville took employment with Coralite Construction Ltd in Manchester. This employment kept him away from home all week travelling, and sometimes for two continuous weeks; a lifestyle which lasted for about a year. Meanwhile he had two sidelines: one was travelling round to public houses selling cut-price whisky, and the other was journalism. He wrote a series of articles in the *Staffordshire Advertiser* from 1919 (with breaks) to 1929. In the mid 1930s Neville hauled whey, at first with his eldest son as driver, and later using a hired coal lorry; and in the latter part of the decade, he did accounting work. Finally in 1939, his brother William Baker Neville succeeded, through the good offices of his politician friend A. V. Alexander, in finding Neville a post as a regional disposals officer.

The character sketch of G. H. Neville given by his relatives shows a man of considerable energy and many talents, but also of a domineering and authoritarian temperament.

His house was always overflowing with books, and he wrote poems, plays and sketches as well as a great many newspaper articles. He played the violin and was a good enough singer to give solo recitals of the kind noted in the *Staffordshire Advertiser* for 20 September 1919, when at a dinner for returned soldiers and sailors given during the Peace Celebrations in Armitage which he had helped to organise, 'Mr G. H. Neville rendered "The Perfect Day" as a closing item, and by request gave "Because" as an *encore* . . .' He was a moderately accomplished painter, and an enthusiastic gardener, especially knowledgeable about herbs. He was an active sportsman, playing both football and cricket, and a very keen angler; he owned two guns and was a fair shot. He was a regular supporter of the Parish Church of St John the Baptist where he painted and lettered the rolls of honour which were installed in the church, and he was a respected member of his community to whom people turned for counsel, and for help in such matters as accounts and tax-returns.

There is, however, general agreement among members of his family that he was a regular drinker, visiting his local pub every night; that he was not infrequently involved in relationships with women; and that he had a tendency to violence. For example, one Sunday lunchtime when he had been drinking he struck and scarred his twenty-one-year-old son with a carving knife. He caused one or two scandals in his village over women. After one such entanglement a young schoolteacher had to be shipped off to Canada and her irate father, an army major, horse-whipped Neville all the way from church to home; but Neville was strong enough or proud enough – or both – to walk the quarter of a mile ignoring the blows.

The same fierce pride was evident in his generosity towards his family, to whom he liked to give handsome presents despite, or perhaps because of, the help they occasionally had to give him in his lasting financial difficulties, which continued even after he had secured a good job in 1939. His family also report that he could be argumentative and dogmatic, and it may be that it was a tendency to be outspoken in his opinions that led to his series in the *Staffordshire Advertiser* being abruptly terminated in 1929 by its editor, who wrote a curt note to him saying that his articles had given offence in some quarters and he was no longer welcome as a contributor.

Neville and Lawrence

Neville's newspaper articles have the added interest in the present context that he sometimes worked into them fragments of autobiography. They were mostly lengthy interviews with local farmers giving detailed descriptions of their farms, and they incidentally reveal that Neville had a good deal of miscellaneous knowledge not only of agriculture but of poetry, architecture and local and general history. In his personal reminiscences he very occasionally mentioned Lawrence, as when, writing on 24 November 1928, on the dissolution of the manors in his locality, he begins:

> Today I have been living in a land of enchantment. I remember many years ago, when I was out on a long tramp with my boyhood chum, now D. H. Lawrence the novelist, and, coming upon a beautiful ruin, I started rhapsodising as usual. Lawrence stood it for a while, and then, turning to me, he said, 'You are a sentimental little beggar, you know.' He had the advantage

7

of me in age by a matter of two years [actually one], and spoke from the lofty pinnacle on which that placed him. Incidentally, if you would like to know more of both of us, read his first novel *The White Peacock*. If to love these old world things . . . is to be a sentimentalist, then I thank God for it.

When Neville described the young Lawrence as his special friend, he was not exaggerating. It is a very striking feature of the surviving records how much of Lawrence's youth was spent in the company of girls. Professor Jonathan David Chambers spoke for all the memoirists when he said, 'Lawrence had flocks of girls around him wherever he went: he went shopping with them and helped them to choose their hats and frocks.'[2] Neville himself and Alan, the elder brother of Jessie and J. D. Chambers, were the marked exceptions, and the two chief male friends of Lawrence's youth. In a letter of 30 July 1908, Lawrence appears to have been defending himself against a charge that all his friends were girls, and, in a context in which he takes pains to stress his physical strength, he says: 'Do not suppose I have no men friends. I could show you two men who claim me as their heart's best brother; there is another, home for the vacation, who has been with me every available moment – till I am tired, I confess . . . I have worked a long fortnight in the hay, with my friends, men, three men, whom I really love, in varying degrees.'[3] These three men were Alan Chambers, George Neville and probably Richard Pogmore.

In this same letter Lawrence describes, in a brief narrative vignette, how he and his friends slept out one night under a haystack and were disturbed by a tramp. Lawrence says of Neville: 'It took all my friend's excellent English and refined accent to convince him that we were not of the great fraternity.' Later, Lawrence used the incident as background material for the short story 'Love Among the Haystacks'. Neville also refers briefly to this event in his Memoir.[4]

Three months later, in October 1908, Lawrence left Eastwood for his first serious teaching job in Croydon. The friendship Neville and Lawrence had developed at Beauvale School, Nottingham High School and Ilkeston Teacher Training Centre was continued by correspondence, and particularly by their summer holiday trips together for the next three years. Unfortunately, not a single letter from either one to the other has survived, but their activities can be pieced together from references in Lawrence's letters to other people and from memoirs.

In the summer of 1909 a holiday party was formed, comprising Lawrence, his mother and his sister Ada, Alice Hall and her father and mother, Frances and Gertrude Cooper, and Neville. They went for a fortnight to Shanklin, on the Isle of Wight. Neville gives some reminiscences of this holiday in his Memoir.[5] It was also the holiday that gave Lawrence the knowledge of the Isle of Wight which a year or two later he could draw on when recreating and interpreting in *The Trespasser* the experiences that Helen Corke and her music master, H. B. Macartney, suffered there together – by an odd chance – in the same summer.

A year later Neville was on holiday again with Lawrence. This time they went alone to Blackpool, to a large, high-quality boarding-house near the north pier, kept by a relative of Neville's, Mrs Kate Swarbrick. This is the holiday which Lawrence recast in *Sons and Lovers* – characteristically he has sought accuracy in atmosphere and character but tinkered with details of times and names:

> At Whitsuntide he said he would go to Blackpool for four days with his friend Newton. The latter was a big, jolly fellow, with a touch of the bounder about him. Paul said his mother must go to Sheffield to stay a week with Annie, who lived there . . .
>
> The two young men set off gaily for Blackpool . . . Four days were clear – not an anxiety, not a thought. The two young men simply enjoyed themselves. Paul was like another man . . . He was having a good time, as young fellows will in a place like Blackpool.[6]

In his Memoir, Neville has left an account of their holiday: the violinist who entertained them, the various girls who were there, the young Yorkshire widow Clara, who made a dead-set at Lawrence.[7] By chance, we can fill out the record here, for William Baker Neville's brother-in-law, Ernest Wilson, wrote a recollection of Lawrence, part of which reads:

> Most of us leaving school at the age of thirteen years started work in the local collieries for economic reasons, but those with outstanding ability and good home circumstances could carry on their education. This is what happened to Bert who went to Ilkeston Teachers' Training Centre. He travelled

there by train from Eastwood. It was at this centre that he struck up a friendship with another local boy George Henry Neville who also lived on Lynn Croft.

The remarkable nature of this friendship was that whilst Bert Lawrence was so shy and retiring, George Neville was a lively and mischievous boy. Could it have been that Bert Lawrence found in George Neville an outlet for his subdued boyishness? Or did George Neville have an influence on Bert in bringing him out of his retiring nature? The latter I feel is possible, for their friendship lasted many years.

As young men they came to stay for a holiday in the same boarding-house as my wife and I were staying. This was at 77 Talbot Street, Blackpool. Bert was now a man of twenty years of age [actually in 1910 he was twenty-five] and not at all shy and retiring. In fact he was as lively in his associations as George Neville although he still was a man of long lean appearance, hollow cheeks and untidy hair-style.

I also noticed that his temperate habits which his mother had tried to foster in him, had almost gone . . . Just prior to leaving the boarding-house, D.H. drew figures of men firstly very thin and secondly corpulent with appropriate words on the food they had enjoyed.[8]

Lawrence returned to discover that his mother had fallen fatally ill with cancer at the home of her sister and brother-in-law, Ada and Fritz Krenkow, in Leicester. Although Mrs Lawrence's death in December 1910 signalled the break-up of Lawrence's youthful world, the gradual confirmation of that break-up – Lawrence's leaving the teaching profession, determining to live by his pen, and the crucial decision to go abroad and stay abroad – was still some way in the future.

So again in the summer of 1911 a holiday party formed itself, and again Neville was there. The party went to Prestatyn, in North Wales, from where Lawrence wrote to his Croydon schoolmaster friend, A. W. McLeod:

I've been out bathing both mornings – alone – 'on a wide wide shore' – amid a disagreeable peevish pack of seagulls – felt quite primeval and near to Nature: and swallowed a most ghastly mouthful of deadly brine: the sea is very choppy.

This is quite as good as a Charles Garvice novel – hope you appreciate it. What are you doing? Vale . . .

The 'love', à la Garvice, shall come later.[9]

This time Louie Burrows, to whom Lawrence was engaged, was also a member of the party, and it is evident from her papers now at the University of Nottingham that she and Lawrence were contemplating spending their honeymoon later at the same guesthouse. However, Jessie Chambers noted:

> I heard later that Lawrence was never still for a minute, that he ran up and down the crags like a man possessed; that he absolutely refused to be left alone with Louie and insisted on Ada accompanying them wherever they went.[10]

After returning to their teaching jobs in September 1911, Lawrence and Neville were out of contact for several months until Lawrence suddenly learnt from Neville that he had married, and already had a son. In telling him this news, Neville appealed to Lawrence to go and stay with him, now at Bradnop near Leek in Staffordshire, and he duly spent a week with Neville in March 1912. This was the last time the two friends were together, for Lawrence had already met Frieda Weekley and was to leave with her for Germany at the beginning of May. Lawrence was then twenty-seven, and Neville twenty-six.

As far as is known, Lawrence and Neville had no further contact. It seems likely that Neville read the novels that Lawrence was writing while he knew him, but it is not clear whether he kept up with Lawrence's subsequent books as they were published. It may be that after Lawrence's death in 1930, when his mind was turning to Lawrence, he read a number of his works. Certainly he had Lawrence in mind in 1928. For in his Saturday column in the *Staffordshire Advertiser* on 24 November 1928, he reminisced about his 'boyhood chum' in the words quoted above; and in his next article, of 1 December 1928, he noted a recent journalistic piece of Lawrence's with a wistful interest. His topic for the series was 'The Dissolution of the Manors' and for this week, Drayton Manor:

> As I introduce Peel to your notice, I am studying a print of Noble's magnificent marble bust of Sir Robert Peel, which stands in the National Portrait Gallery. It is a truly noble figure; a magnificently handsome man (not the 'Valentino' handsome man as referred to by my friend D. H. Lawrence by a strange coincidence, in one of our leading Sunday papers,[11] the day after I referred to him in the 'Advertiser').

Whether or not Neville's interest had lapsed in the intervening years, it was certainly fortunate that he was thinking of Lawrence in the late 1920s, for this doubtless enabled him to feel prepared, as the obituary notices came out in 1930, to set down some of his own memories.

The writing of the Memoir

A number of motives seem to have prompted Neville to write this account of Lawrence. Foremost amongst them was the appearance in April 1931 of a book which gave widespread offence, John Middleton Murry's *Son of Woman*.[12] Murry provoked Neville by his knowingness about Lawrence's early life. Neville felt he could authoritatively refute the false biographical construct that Murry had confidently derived from the fictional representation in Lawrence's writings. Neville's declared aim was to give the world a pleasanter, happier Lawrence than could have been imagined by those readers of *Son of Woman* who absorbed uncritically its portrayal of a tortured neurotic. Indeed Neville maintains that no one else would have interpreted the quotations from Lawrence's writings as Murry does, and it is a feature of his Memoir that his very different version of Lawrence draws on no quotation from Lawrence's writings (apart from 'Myself Revealed'[13]) other than those given in *Son of Woman*. He had also undoubtedly been influenced by the interest shown in Lawrence's life and works consequent upon his death in March 1930, for many magazines and provincial papers offered obituary assessments which produced a correspondence in reply. In addition, one or two of his surviving letters to editors of journals show that Neville was at least partly motivated by pressing financial needs to make a little money out of his recollections of Lawrence.

Although his Memoir went unpublished at the time, he was one of the very first to write out such recollections. He originally sent a letter about Lawrence's background to *The London Mercury*, which was printed in March 1931; it is not clear whether he had already written more of the Memoir than this or expanded it later from his letter. In the mid 1930s he offered a typescript of the present work to a publisher, but it was not accepted. Edward Nehls incorporated the *London Mercury* piece into his *D. H. Lawrence: a composite biography* in 1957.[14] Harry T. Moore interviewed Neville when preparing his own biography of Lawrence, *The Intelligent Heart*, 1954 (revised and reissued as *The Priest of Love*, 1974), and he reported:

> George Neville was cordially helpful, though now and then it was plain that he was not telling all he knew.[15]

Now that Neville's complete Memoir has come to light, it is clear that even here, despite his strong desire to set the record straight, there were certain things that he was not prepared to include. He differed in principle from Lawrence about using people's life stories as material, and plainly had a strong conviction that private life should be kept private; so in some sense he seems to have had to overcome a reluctance in himself to write the Memoir at all, because he felt he was trespassing on the Lawrence home. It may be that there is some pattern to his discretion: where he is notably silent is about his own life-story. Also, although in attempting to rebut Middleton Murry he was addressing himself to the general public, there are clues in the Memoir and associated papers that he was particularly keen to win recognition for Lawrence in his largely hostile home-town of Eastwood. Neville's conviction was that Lawrence's genius could be compared with Shakespeare's, and that for generations of future readers Eastwood would become a place of pilgrimage comparable to Stratford-on-Avon, and indeed that Lawrence had assimilated that Nottinghamshire–Derbyshire environment into his art in such a way as to confer a peculiar and lasting interest upon it.

Unlike some of the other people who knew Lawrence in his youth and who were interviewed by Lawrence scholars for their recollections, Neville (like Jessie Chambers and May Chambers[16]) is not engaged in a naïve exercise of memory but in a conscious and sustained effort at interpreting character: he therefore selects from his recollections incidents which illustrate his interpretation. This characteristic has advantages and disadvantages. One disadvantage is Neville's tendency to transmute his material into saga or myth. For example, it is widely supposed by commentators on Lawrence that his group of Eastwood friends called themselves the 'Pagans'. But if we look at the records, we discover that Neville adopted this term in his letter to *The London Mercury*, and that he alone of that group used it. This tendency, reinforced in places by romanticising tones, should warn the reader against assuming the literal accuracy of Neville's account in matters of detail. On the other hand, that *London Mercury* piece is the sole source of the story that the factory girls at Nottingham attacked the sixteen-year-old Lawrence when he was working with them, and attempted to debag and expose him – an incident which sticks in the mind of all students of Lawrence's character, and must be an important fact of biography. The factory girls in *Sons and Lovers*, we can conclude, have been greatly humanised. (Lawrence did use such an incident in his art, in the short story 'Tickets Please', where the motive for the girls' assault is reversed from the real-life situation Neville describes, and is made not a provoking primness but a provoking predatoriness.)

It would be inappropriate to anticipate in this introduction the contents of the Memoir itself, but since a number of items warrant discussion I have included amongst the notes of a factual kind, giving necessary dates and references, some longer notes and some appendices. But one specimen may perhaps be given here of Neville's interpretative effort. A central strand in Neville's argument is his interpretation of the impact that the Haggs Farm, the home of the Chambers family, had on Lawrence. Neville reports that the tone of the Lawrence family home was genteel and very proper. One of the aspects of this gentility was an extreme reticence on any matters connected with sex. Neville makes plain that, while there can be no doubt about the Chambers family's respectability, nevertheless the necessary tasks of farming made reproduction, animal mating, and the like, perfectly ordinary topics of discussion. Neville believes that Lawrence was so astonished, embarrassed and finally profoundly impressed by this feature of farm-life that there and then, while still in his teens, he made up his mind that this was to be the main topic which would concern him as a writer.

Lawrence makes some play in *The White Peacock* with social discomfort caused by explicitness about such facts of farming. Of course, if Neville is correct that Lawrence was impressed in this way and determined to write on the theme of sex, despite – and this is Neville's other main contention – its being profoundly alien to him to do so, certain critical questions might follow, such as whether the unease which some readers have felt with the opening pages of *The Rainbow* derives from an over-emphasis on the writer's part comparable to the defensive hardness of the over-sensitive or squeamish.

But Neville's sense of what Lawrence was like largely matters in so far as it helps us understand more clearly what Lawrence thought about Neville. It is this – what Lawrence thought about Neville – that is the real interest, because here is an unexplored tract of the raw material of Lawrence's art. The remainder of this introduction will therefore be devoted not so much to introducing the Memoir that follows as to complementing it with suggestions as to its further critical and biographical significance.

Don Juan and Peter Pan

It is ironic that Neville should have chosen to be so discreet about himself, when Lawrence had indiscreetly poured out some of the central facts of Neville's life-story in a letter to Edward Garnett in 1912, which was eventually published.[17] This potted biography of Neville records in a narrative form Lawrence's response to the news of Neville's marriage. The letter is dated 8 March 1912:

> And Neville – my very old friend, the Don Juanish fellow I told you of – went and got married three months back, without telling a soul – and now boasts a son: 'Jimmy, a very fine lad.' – He writes me eight pages, closely packed, this morning. The girl is living at home, with 'Jimmy' in Stourbridge. The managers asked George – Neville – to resign his post, because of the blot on the scutcheon. He said 'he'd see them frizzled first.' In the end, he was removed to a little headship on the Stafford–Derby border – has been there six weeks – alone – doing fearfully hard work. Don Juan in hell, what ho! He implores me to go and stay a week with him. I suppose I s'll have to. This has upset me – One never knows what'll happen. You know Georgie has already got one illegitimate child. It's a lovely story, the end of it: the beginning was damnable. She was only nineteen, and he only twenty. Her father, great Christian, turned her out. Georgie wouldn't acknowledge the kid, but had to pay, whether or not. That's five years back.

Editor's introduction

Last October, I am told, the girl got married. Before the wedding – two days or so – she went to Neville's home with the child, and showed it to Georgie's father and mother.

'I've come, Mr Neville, for you to own this child. Who's the father of that – ?' pushing forward the small girl.

'Eh bless her, it's just like him', cried old Mrs Neville, and she kissed the kid with tears.

'Well Lizzie,' said Neville to the girl, 'if our George-Henry says that isn't his'n, he's a liar. It's the spit and image of him.'

Whereupon Lizzie went away satisfied, got married to a collier, and lives in Cordy Lane. She, with one or two others, will rejoice over George's final nabbing. Isn't it awful!

All this, by the way, is quite verbal truth.[18]

Here Lawrence's attitude to Neville's 'story' is largely satirical, but the facts of illegitimacy and the evidence that Neville felt nothing for the children he fathered struck deep into Lawrence's imagination and powerfully affected his preoccupation with the nature of masculinity. Whether or not Lawrence's satire is a defensive covering over of distress, he had moved a long way from the unrelieved anguish with which he appears to have received the news five years earlier, in the spring of 1907. For Jessie Chambers records:

On an evening of that same spring (when Lawrence was in his twenty-first year) his sister cycled up to the farm. She had come to tell me something that shocked us all very much. A friend of theirs was in deep disgrace – in A[da]'s conventional phrase he had 'got a girl into trouble'. On the following evening Lawrence came himself, looking white and upset. As soon as we were alone he asked me if I had heard about his friend – they had been High School boys together. He seemed relieved that I knew. He said his mother had told him about it that morning. He was very distressed. His mother had said how terrible might be the consequences of only five minutes' self-forgetfulness. And it seemed to add to the tragedy that the young people had only seen one another on Sunday evenings after chapel – so Lawrence said. He told me these things in a voice that sounded sick with misery, and I felt very concerned, wondering why he should take it so to heart. Then he startled me by bursting out vehemently:

'Thank God . . . I've been saved from that . . . so far.'

I was puzzled, feeling in the dark about the whole business,

16

and very sorry for Lawrence's distress. He seemed relieved after he had told me about it.[19]

Lawrence presumably meant that he had been spared 'temptation', not that he had happily been spared unwanted children. He was twenty-one at this time, and Neville, following Lawrence himself, is insistent that Lawrence was a virgin until he was twenty-three. It is certain that Lawrence had not yet embarked on the sexual experimentation that Neville reports him to have later determined upon: he had not even participated in the regular and accepted teenage social activity of 'spooning' which he so vividly describes in Mr Noon.

One of the reasons why Lawrence was sick with misery at this news is that he was himself still in a state of almost pre-pubertal boyishness. Elsewhere in his Memoir Neville makes plain that Lawrence's absence from boys' sports such as cricket, football and swimming, had left him at this time without much acquaintance with men's bodies or such knowledge of sex as may be gleaned by mixing with teenage boys; and Neville also shows that he had a limited conception of the female body. Lawrence himself left a striking testimony to his innocence when he wrote to his sister Ada in July 1911 (that is, when he was twenty-six) that Neville had told him by letter about his injury from a cricket ball, and Lawrence asked his sister what the word 'scrotum' meant.[20] But readers of The White Peacock must feel throughout the novel that despite the flirtations and indeed marriages and begetting of children, there is notable failure to convey any sense of adult sexual experience.

This crucial point about Lawrence's retarded development can best be brought out by listening to the tones of voice in his letters across the period 1907 to early 1912. First, from a letter to Blanche Jennings, 13 May 1908:

Hail, Blessed Damosel, you are a genius: you have invented the letter which does not begin with a kiss, a letter altogether un-Judas-like. I have an aversion to kissing people straight off – I have somewhat of a distate for being caressed (except on occasions). So you have had the blissful courage to shed that formality – that 'Dear –,' – that 'My dear –' greeting which is like being kissed by one's Auntie in the street. You are delicious. To rip straight off with 'Really David, if I went in for dignity –' is nearly as good as if a parson should arise in his pulpit and say right out, with no prayings and slobber 'Sit up – put your hearts in your pockets out of the way, and prepare your wits. You're going to think tonight about a few little things.' You won't endear me any more – nor I you. Bonum![21]

However much we allow that Lawrence's writing during this period is partly literary experimentation, and however much we allow for the seventy-odd years which have passed since Lawrence wrote this, we surely feel it to be the prose of a lively sixteen-year-old (or thereabouts) rather than that of a man of twenty-two. It is a representative specimen of Lawrence's prose at this time, which for all its partial sophistication of thought, is curiously boyish: its tones are oddly pre-sexual.

A second extract, from a letter of 1 November 1909, gives a mixture of boyish and maturing tones:

> I think no youth was ever more verbose than I: it is amusing to remember. But I am waxing vastly more reticent: I cannot write letters now: the only ones I accomplish are those to my mother. – But tell me what you think of the verses, will you? – if it is worth while. Do you take the *Review*? – in October's, the verses of Rachel Annand Taylor were exceedingly good: did they rile you? What do you think of Ford Madox Hueffer's 'A Call'? I think it has more art than life. I have been up to see him twice – he is really a fine man, in that he is so generous, so understanding, and in that he keeps the doors of his soul open, and you may walk in: you know what I mean: I likewise have a habit of admitting whosoever will into my intimacy, a habit of which the south, and school, are curing me.[22]

Written a mere eighteen months after the previous quotation, this passage manifests the new tones which began to make themselves heard towards the end of October 1908, when Lawrence had made some real adjustment to living away from home.

And then, a world away in maturity (15 May 1912):

> Can't you feel how certainly I love you and how certainly we shall be married. Only let us wait just a short time, to get strong again. Two shaken, rather sick people together would be a bad start. A little waiting, let us have, because I love you. Or does the waiting make you worse? – no, not when it is only a time of preparation. Do you know, like the old knights, I seem to want a certain time to prepare myself – a

sort of vigil with myself. Because it is a great thing for me to marry you, not a quick, passionate coming together. I know in my heart 'here's my marriage'. It feels rather terrible – because it is a great thing in my life – it is *my life* – I am a bit awe-inspired – I want to get used to it. If you think it is fear and indecision, you wrong me. It is *you* who would hurry who are undecided. It's the very strength and inevitability of the oncoming thing that makes me wait, to get in harmony with it. Dear God, I am marrying you, now, don't you see. It's a far greater thing than ever I knew.[23]

This was a Lawrence that Neville and many of his other Eastwood friends never knew.

Lawrence's slow emergence from his tenacious and retarded adolescence cannot be fully traced from the imperfectly surviving records. However, it seems clear that his leaving home to go and live in Croydon, the death of his mother, and his meeting and eloping with Frieda Weekley, comprise his principal *rites de passage* from boy to man. It is worth dwelling upon this, I believe, largely underestimated fact of retardation a little longer. Jessie Chambers tells us how acutely painful to him were Lawrence's first weeks away from home:

> On his second day in Croydon Lawrence sent me a letter that gave me a shock. It was like a howl of terror. People were kind, he said, but everything was strange, and how could he live away from us all? He dreaded morning and school with the anguish of a sick girl. Finally he said he felt afraid for himself; cut off from us all he would grow into something black and ugly, like some loathsome bird . . . . In a postscript he told me not to say anything of this to his mother, he had written to her that everything was all right and he was getting on well. I burned his letter immediately lest anyone should see it. I had known that it hurt him to leave us, but I came nowhere near to guessing how much.
> The phase of acute homesickness soon wore off.[24]

Biographers have, I believe, been misled by the flirtatiousness in *The White Peacock*, a novel which has in large part a Midlands setting, into supposing that such in actual life were relations between Lawrence and the girls in his group, in the years immediately preceding his leaving home. It seems to me, on the contrary, that Lawrence's own flirting with girls comes from his Croydon years and is fed back onto the scenes of *The White Peacock*, thus disguising his own protracted and unusual boyishness. It is only with a hypothesis of this kind in mind that the original impact upon him of his friend George Neville's misdemeanours can be fully felt. It was the brutal intrusion into his world of the adult world into which, while his dominant and possessive mother sustained a mutual relationship more intimate than was compatible with ordinary adolescent development, he was avoiding or being prevented from entering.

Neville and 'The White Peacock'

An index of the impact that Neville's news had upon Lawrence is that he made the 'story' central to his first effort at writing a novel. In the 1930s Jessie Chambers told the French Laurentian scholar, Emile Delavenay: 'In speaking of *Women in Love*, did I say that Gerald Crich is only a development of Leslie Tempest in *The White Peacock* and that the character of the latter was founded in the first instance on D.H.L.'s school-friend, G. H. Neville.'[25]

In the fifty-eight-page fragment which has survived of an early version of *The White Peacock*, at that stage called 'Laetitia',[26] the key feature of the story is that the character Lettie, the Laetitia of the title, has had an illegitimate child by Leslie Tempest; and Lettie (and with her, one can fairly say, the the author) is bewildered to find that Leslie has no feelings of fatherhood or responsibility of any kind for his child and its mother. In this early version, Lettie, now married to George (not yet Saxton but Worthington), gives birth to Leslie's child, conceived before she was married. When asked by a friend why she did not marry Leslie Tempest if he was the father of her child, Lettie replies that she does not love him. In the course of the story Lettie goes out at night to meet Leslie and he is accompanied by a lady who is obviously ignorant of the whole affair. Later Leslie sends Lettie a cheque for £500.

Although thought about this fragment must necessarily be speculative, it appears inescapable that Lawrence's first venture as a novelist centrally comprised imaginative exploration of Neville's behaviour.

No doubt Neville discussed directly with Lawrence the episode which led to his early disgrace, and it may be that he misled Lawrence about the payment. For in having Leslie Tempest make over £500 to Lettie, and in using the phrase in his 8 March 1912 letter to Edward Garnett, 'Georgie .. had to pay whether or not', Lawrence may have been writing in the belief that Neville himself paid a maintenance allowance to the mother of his illegitimate daughter. Members of Neville's family tell me it was his elder brother, William Baker Neville that made what was apparently the standard payment of ten shillings a week to support the child (who, I am told, died at about the age of twelve).

However, Lawrence's development is rarely simple. Although there is a big difference between his horrified reaction of 1907 and his sardonic comments in the letter of 1912, Lawrence could handle aspects of the episode with humour even in 'Laetitia' written only a year or two after the event. For there is a scene of manifest ridicule and some comedy in which the child is christened by a big Yorkshire clergyman called Mr Clements. This scene prefigures in some detail one in the short story, 'The Christening'; and in both of them the tyranny of a certain chapel type of religion is the target for Lawrence's satire. He was noted in his youth as a mimic, particularly of the local clergymen, and in a number of his writings comical confrontations take place in chapel. Perhaps the papering over of realities of behaviour by the solemn pieties of chapel touched a comic spring in Lawrence's temperament.

Although in the transformation effected by successive re-writings of *The White Peacock*, Lawrence removed the illegitimate child, he did leave some traces of the original 'Neville material'. In the twelfth chapter Lawrence hints at a night of pre-marital intimacy between Leslie and Lettie. But here Leslie Tempest's Neville-like 'independent, assertive air' is crossed with a Lawrence-like nervousness and anxiety.

Apart from his 'story', Neville and incidents from Lawrence's friendship with him, appear in the novel in a variety of forms. There is, for example, a direct portrait of Neville in the description of Leslie Tempest. This sportsman with 'crisp hair of the "ginger" class', who is shown as casually moving from one admiring girl to another, had that fine, lithe physique, suggestive of much animal vigour; his person was exceedingly attractive; one watched him move about, and felt pleasure. His face was less pleasing than his person. He was not handsome; his eyebrows were too light, his nose was large and ugly, and his forehead though high and fair, was without dignity. But he had a frank, good-natured expression, and a fine wholesome laugh.[27]

It should not escape notice that 'Mother liked Leslie'. An older member of the Neville family, who herself remembers Lawrence, believes that despite his mischievousness and 'bounder'-like character, George Neville was acceptable to Mrs Lawrence simply because he so very obviously liked her son.

It would, of course, be mistaken to attempt to sustain any simple identifications of characters or incidents in life with those in the novel. For example, Lawrence's initial discomfort at the raw facts of farm-life is reflected in *The White Peacock*, but in the novel it is Leslie Tempest who is nettled by the young farmer's explicitness, and clearly some characteristic Laurentian transpositions have taken place. The exchange is recognisably based on the experiences of Lawrence at the Haggs which Neville has described,[28] but the atmosphere in Lawrence's use of the experience in the novel is quite different from that in the appropriate section of Neville's Memoir. Lawrence has exploited the demonstrations of squeamishness to enhance his picture of Leslie Tempest's social superiority, while at the same time initiating the subdued speculation that his response somehow makes him less of a man than the nonetheless potentially boorish George Saxton.

A further transposition is suggested by George Neville's assertion that a bathing episode in his own friendship with Lawrence is rendered in the novel as one between George Saxton and the narrator. Indeed such is the evidence in the Memoir of sentimental affection between Lawrence and Neville, and such are the hints of Neville's jealousy of Lawrence's friendship with Alan Chambers, that one might wonder if these relationships did not find artistic expression in Lettie's coquettish playing-off of George against Leslie.

Neville's experiences were certainly not confined, in Lawrence's artistic treatment of them, to *The White Peacock*. Just as he seems to have developed the basic facts of 'Lizzie's' pregnancy by the irresponsible youthful Neville into the triangular situation which he made central to his first conception of *The White Peacock*, so he appears to have returned to this biographical material and made a modified form of it the culmination of the first version of 'The Sisters', the work that eventually led to *Women in Love*. For in the six pages of the first draft of 'The Sisters', numbered 291–6, which have survived (in the words of Professor Mark Kinkead-Weekes):

> Gudrun, pregnant with Gerald's child, confronts Gerald and Loerke in her lodgings in England. Gerald now wants to marry her, but she suspects it may be only because of the baby. Loerke has already offered himself.[29]

It is of some importance that, however rewritten, the basic material for *The White Peacock* and the basic material for *Women in Love* may have had the same origin in Lawrence's experience. An appreciation of this would help us to determine in what senses Lawrence developed as an artist.

Neville and 'Mr Noon'

Lawrence based two works closely on Neville's life. They did not come out until 1934 and 1940 respectively, and then in publications probably sufficiently obscure for Neville not to have noticed them. These works were the unfinished novel *Mr Noon* and the comic play *The Married Man*.[30]

Lawrence's diary-entries and correspondence indicate that he began *Mr Noon* on 7 May 1920, worked at it concurrently with *Aaron's Rod* throughout 1920 and 1921, and was hoping in mid 1921 to complete it before the end of the year. The first section of a comic novel of that title was published posthumously in 1934 in a volume of Lawrence's short stories, *A Modern Lover*, and reprinted in *Phoenix II*. It was thought that this was all of the novel that Lawrence had written until the recent exciting discovery of a manuscript of the much more extensive though still unfinished novel, which has been acquired by the Humanities Research Center of the University of Texas at Austin.

As has long been known, in the published section of the novel, the adventures of Gilbert Noon the schoolmaster who goes 'spooning' with Emmie Bostock after chapel – not that he attends chapel – were based on George Neville. The young couple in the novel carry their spooning a little far in the greenhouse at the Bostock home, where her father Alf Bostock discovers them; and although Gilbert Noon manages to escape, Mr Bostock eventually succeeds in identifying him, with the result that he is summoned to a special investigation of his conduct by the local education committee and forced to leave his teaching job. This part of the novel ends with Emmie Bostock, 'ill' in bed with stomach pains, being visited simultaneously by her bank-clerk fiancé Walter George Whiffen and by Gilbert Noon.

Whether Lawrence actually wrote *Mr Noon* in the 1920s or whether, as seems to me most likely from abundant internal evidence, he was rewriting in the 1920s material which had been drafted in about 1912–13, is a question still to be solved. My subjective impression is that the story was first drafted when Lawrence had schools and schoolteaching at the front of his mind, and that phrases, images and references are immediately comparable with his language in letters and other writings of about 1912, including the play *The Married Man*. With a critical edition of the full text of *Mr Noon* soon to be published, it is pointless to speculate at any length now.

There is a deposition in the Nottingham city archives by Mr S. Bircumshaw, a contemporary of Lawrence's and Neville's, identifying some of the characters in the novel as named persons in Eastwood. This is not the place in which to pursue these possible interrelations of life and art. But plainly this story corresponds in its main features, if not in its narrative detail, to the thumbnail sketch of Neville's amorous career that Lawrence had offered Edward Garnett. It is not clear whether Emmie is pregnant or whether Lawrence is simply making play with the idea of her possible pregnancy, but this makes no difference to the essential similarity in the triangular situations here, in 'The Sisters', and in 'Laetitia'. No one, so far as I am aware, has yet given thought to assessing the significance of what Lawrence *excluded* when redrafting his novels. It would be worth framing a theory as to why Lawrence decided to remove the triangular relations between Leslie Tempest/Lettie and child/George Worthington, and between Gerald Crich/

pregnant Gudrun/Loerke from *The White Peacock* and *Women in Love*, especially if it transpires that this material only found a home in the comic play *The Married Man* and the comic novel *Mr Noon*.

There are many curious links between *Mr Noon* and Lawrence's other writings and it will be a delicate task to assess what if any critical or biographical significance they yield. They do however reinforce the conviction that Neville's behaviour represented equivocally to Lawrence an alien masculinity which he both envied and disliked. One example is the likeness between a passage in the so called 'Burns novel' fragment of late 1912[31] and the spooning chapter of *Mr Noon*. A more significant link is with *The Rainbow*. In the chapter 'Spoon' in *Mr Noon* Lawrence gives a long description of Gilbert Noon's after-chapel kissing with Emmie Bostock. Readers no doubt consult their own experience to judge whether this is a masterpiece of realism or effective humorous fantasy, or whatever. One or two general features of the situation are made play with: it is a dismal, rainy night and Emmie Bostock has an umbrella. Mr Noon's spooning becomes suggestively intense and, 'With a sudden lacerating motion she tore her face from his, aside.'[32] There is a similar episode, very differently handled, in *The Rainbow*. There, Will Brangwen, in revolt against his marriage, goes out one evening to pick up a girl at the Nottingham Empire with the intention of seducing her. His plan is going quite well. Once again, the general features of the situation are the same: the evening is dismal and it is raining, and Jenny, the factory girl, has her umbrella with her; and Will Brangwen presses suggestively onwards with his kisses when, 'with a sudden horrible movement she ruptured the state that contained them both'.[33] What Lawrence appears to be attempting here in *The Rainbow* is to assimilate a Neville-like, somewhat predatory, sexual adventure into the larger context of Will Brangwen's marital relationship. It may be that Lawrence was trying to show the relatedness, even the compatibility, of what had previously seemed to him quite different kinds of sexual experience.

Neville and 'The Married Man'

The Married Man is the work that Lawrence most closely fashioned about George Neville's character and circumstances. It was written not very long after his week's stay with Neville in March 1912. From the inclusion in the play of versions of recent incidents which he also recounted in his letters – the visit to Neville, a dance near Eastwood at which Lawrence reports himself to have behaved in a 'fast' manner, and Frieda Weekley's visit to William and May (Chambers) Holbrook's farm – we can see that Lawrence was setting out some of the main elements of his current life for provisional analysis. Clearly his play did not cost him any substantial creative effort, but the circumstances of Neville's entrapment by marriage gave Lawrence the opportunity to reflect upon the change in life which he too was undergoing: from a single state to involvement in a stable relationship. Lawrence and Frieda's subsequent life, travels, fights and the like are so well known that we may be in danger of always reading his life backwards, and thus of forgetting how climactic and precarious were his circumstances in early 1912.

Lawrence, it will be recalled, fell ill with pneumonia in mid November 1911 and was very seriously ill through to January 1912, when he spent a month at Bournemouth for convalescence. This was the point at which he determined to resign from schoolteaching, a resignation which took effect from 5 March; and this, too, was the period at which he recognised his incompatibility with Louie Burrows. He broke his engagement with her at the beginning of February. He had moved from Bournemouth back to Eastwood after a few days at Edward Garnett's home, The Cearne, in Kent, in early February. He is presumed to have met Frieda Weekley, even if in some sense he had been acquainted with her earlier, on or about 17 March. He stayed with Neville 25–31 March and *The Married Man* was written by 23 April, at which date he reported to Edward Garnett that he had 'just written a comedy – middling good'.[34] Lawrence went abroad with Frieda on 3 May.

In the play the convalescent Billy Brentnall, a bank clerk, is visiting his old friend George Grainger, a doctor. Grainger, it transpires, has married a few months previously a girl called

Ethel who has subsequently had a child by him. For this misdemeanour he has been compelled to leave his home town and take a temporary job in a small village. Grainger meanwhile is showing himself more than reluctant to face the responsibilities of his married condition and, living away from his wife, has been pursuing a number of the local girls; two in particular, Annie Calladine and Sally Magneer. The fact that Grainger is married is unknown to all except Brentnall, who, during the course of the play releases the fact to the two girls; and as a result George is compelled to undergo a confrontation scene with Annie and Sally who charge him with his behaviour in the presence of his wife. Reluctantly, he chooses not to continue running away from his evidently unhappy wife but to live with her and the child.

The details of the plot serve to bring out the dilemmas of the young men, who want to flirt with young women but to avoid being tied by marriage or a single relationship, and the dilemmas of the young women, who enjoy the company of young men but resent the risk of exploitation and unmarried motherhood. The young men are each forced to acknowledge the responsibilities of their relationships: George Grainger, that he is a married man; Billy Brentnall, that he is an engaged man; and Grainger's friend Jack Magneer, that he ought to be an engaged man. The evident dilemmas beneath the surface of the mannered comedy are observed upon, though hardly resolved, by the Frieda-like figure of Brentnall's fiancée who appears like a *dea ex machina* and, at the end of the play, calls upon the other people to recognise their real feelings honestly and to act honourably upon them whatever they are.

The play can properly be described as largely fashioned about G. H. Neville's life and circumstances, many superficial details of which are faithfully reproduced. George Grainger is based on George Neville, who had a brother-in-law called Grainger. The dates of Grainger's marriage and the birth of his son, only slightly adjusted, fit the historical facts exactly; indeed Grainger's wife and son are given the names of Neville's wife and son in real life. Neville's landlady at Leek was called Mrs Plumb, and Grainger's in the play, Mrs Plum. Billy Brentnall is based upon Lawrence, whose nickname, often used by Neville in the Memoir, was Billy. Elsa Smith is based upon Frieda, whose daughter was called Elsa. The names of places between the West Midlands and Eastwood, again slightly adjusted, fit perfectly Neville's circumstances and Lawrence's journey.

Three letters of this period illustrate with more depth how Lawrence transformed, if not life into art, at least fact into fiction. The first is to Edward Garnett of 24 February 1912. The interest of this first extract is that, with its would-be rakish slang and pride in 'shocking' behaviour, it can stand representative of something that Lawrence and Neville had in common which features particularly in this play:

> My sister and I were at a bit of a dance last night at Jacksdale –
> mining village four miles out. It was most howling good fun.
> My sister found me kissing one of her friends goodbye – such
> a ripping little girl – and we were kissing like nuts – enter my
> sister – great shocks all round, and much indignation. But –
> life is awfully fast down here.[35]

In the play, the comedy of this situation is compounded by the fact that it reveals Brentnall's undisclosed engagement just at the moment when he has divulged Grainger's undeclared marriage:

> *A* LADY *in motor cloak and wrap appears in the doorway. The men,*
> *slightly tipsy, bend talking to their partners, who are engrossed. No*
> *one notices the newcomer.*
> BRENTNALL. It is, on my honour. You believe me, Sally?
> (*She looks him earnestly in the face, as they dance the forward step.*
> *When they come together for the waltz, he kisses her.*)
> You believe me?
> SALLY (*almost in tears*). Yes.
> BRENTNALL. It is true. Poor Sally. (*Kisses her again. They begin*
> *to laugh.*) . . .
> ADA. Oh!
> GRAINGER. What?
> (*They break apart.* JACK *and* BRENTNALL *keep on dancing, the latter*
> *kissing* SALLY. GRAINGER *goes unsteadily to the doorway.*)
> THE LADY. I called to see Mr Brentnall – but don't disturb
> him, he looks so happy.
> GRAINGER. Does – does he know you?
> THE LADY. A little. (*She laughs.*)
> GRAINGER. Billy! Billy!
> BRENTNALL (*looking up*). What now? (*Sees the lady.*) No![36]

More of the background can be seen in a letter written by Lawrence to May Holbrook on 27 March 1912 from Bradnop, Leek:

I am here since Monday – shall be home again — D.V. on Saturday evening. It's a truly rural sort of place. Diddler [i.e. George Neville] and I dodge about at evening. His school has 51 kids – a girl for the infants. It's pretty – Derbyshireish – grey stone – fields dark green. I gave the little clods a lesson on color yesterday afternoon – they gorped like frogs . . . In the evening Diddler took me a tat-tah, and of course got lost. We wriggled over a river on a rail. It's very Switzerlandish, just over the Long Shaw. Later we called at a farm, where the old woman reigns supreme in a fur shoulder-cape, and the old man, deaf as a post, blorts like a bullock occasionally, nearly making you jump out of your skin. Mrs Titterton is the masterful sort. She gives me to understand she would mother me: manage me, that means. She mothers her own three great sons to such an extent that they will never marry. She keeps them in order, but they're very happy: live good and healthy animals. Jack runs the rig in Leek occasionally. A woman throned is really – !

I'll bring you *Man and Superman* on Sunday. I suppose J[essie] will be at the cottage. The play was very good. I said nothing to Mrs Weekley about coming over. Will discuss it further with you.[37]

Another element in Neville's situation which Lawrence revealed neither to Edward Garnett in his letter of 8 March (quoted above) nor in that to May Holbrook quoted here – though he may have expected May to take some hint from the phrase 'Diddler and I dodge about at evening' – he disclosed in a letter of 2 April to his ex-fiancée, Louie Burrows:

Last week I was in North Staffordshire with Neville. He is married – did you know? – last November, on the q – t. His baby was born in January. He had to leave Amblecoate. They gave him a tiny temporary place in the country near Leek, where I stayed with him. His wife is with her parents in Stourbridge, some 50 miles away. He lives 'en bachelier'. Which is quite a story![38]

In *The Married Man* Lawrence selects from the experiences described in these letters. Jack Magneer in the play is clearly based on Jack Titterton, but Lawrence avoids any exploration of the possibilities contained in the sentence, 'She mothers her own three great sons to such an extent that they will never marry.' Instead he draws on Neville's life 'en bachelier', Jack's 'running the rig', and his own transition from hectic flirtation to a single stable relationship, to dramatise half-comically the moment at which young men face up to becoming married men. In the play Billy Brentnall and Elsa Smith are presented as having attained a joyful wisdom in their handling of these difficult matters, whereas George Grainger is left, despite shedding a few sentimental tears, in a state of sullen and angry resignation to his reponsibilities. In life, however, we learn from Jessie Chambers, Lawrence expressed himself as much more sympathetic to Neville's predicament:

> He had been travelling all day and was nearly worn out with the cross-country journey from the Staffordshire border. The trains had been slow and the connections bad . . . he fell to talking about his friend who had married not long before and had got a baby son.
>
> 'Fatherhood's a myth,' Lawrence declared. 'There's nothing in it. I asked [Neville] how he felt about it, and he said he felt nothing, nothing at all. He has no feeling whatever towards that infant. There's no such thing as fatherhood,' he concluded slowly, as though the words tasted sweet on his tongue.
>
> My sister and I were silent. Lawrence's perversity was no new thing to us. We were acquainted with the history of the young man in question, and could not help reflecting that his fatherhood involved someone's motherhood, a myth less easily disposed of. Lawrence knew quite well what we were thinking, and enlarged upon the theme characteristically. 'The average man with a family,' he went on, 'is nothing but a cart-horse, dragging the family behind him for the best part of his life. I'm not going to be a cart-horse.'
>
> My brother-in-law twinkled at him, chuckling softly.
>
> 'You're nothing but a rake, Bert, a positive rake,' he said.
>
> 'Nay, dunna say that, Bill, dunna say that,' Lawrence replied comically.[39]

Presumably the play was written with sufficient, even if slight, distance from his visit to Neville to license Lawrence in his optimistic handling of Billy Brentnall and Elsa Smith's engagement and attitudes.

It is known from Barbara Barr's account that her mother

Frieda Weekley took her and her sister Elsa to May and Will Holbrook's farm one weekend in the spring of 1912 when Lawrence was there.[40] When Elsa Smith in the play says that Will Hobson drove her over to find Brentnall at the Magneer's farm, we see how Lawrence was binding together in both geography and time the disparate episodes of his life at that period. But it is interesting to note that Neville's wife, as she has informed me, never met Lawrence. So, in bringing Grainger's wife into a scene with the girls whom Grainger had been pursuing, and at the same time bringing Frieda/Elsa Smith out of Nottingham as far as Will Holbrook's farm, and then on from Will Holbrook/Hobson's farm to the Bradnop world, Lawrence has taken the liberty of fiction to create a climax out of matters which were never so clearly shaped in life.

The Married Man is not a play of much merit. Lawrence was generous in describing it as 'middling good', and it was only published posthumously. Its interest is that of a fictional diary. For example, it offers the nearest thing outside Neville's Memoir to a quasi-transcript of the bantering and rakish tones which we may presume dominated the exchanges between Lawrence and Neville when they were alone together. It conveys the would-be witty slang which Lawrence adopted at this period of his life, a slang which Neville himself, on the evidence of the Memoir, never wholly outgrew. Its deeper interest lies in its revelation of those matters, of manliness, marriage and fatherhood, which Lawrence was preoccupied with; though we have to look elsewhere for his successes in forging them into art.

The Memoir below shows Neville presenting *his* version of his attitude towards his marriage. He presents himself as marrying in what would be supposed by an uninformed reader to be normal circumstances, and Lawrence he presents as determining to go abroad when Neville's companionship has been withdrawn. Readers of the play and Memoir may well feel that neither 'art' nor 'autobiography' does or can quite give real historical truth, but *that* must be divined by the contemplation both of the works and the life-records in a single perspective.

EDITORIAL NOTE ON
THE NEVILLE PAPERS

The surviving papers represent four main stages in the composition of G. H. Neville's Memoir. First there are a few manuscript fragments, which represent Neville's first thoughts; two are separate fragments of section 1, 'Early days' ms. 1 (eleven pages) and 'Early days' ms. 2 (four pages), and the other is six pages of pencil notes towards the eighth part of section 2. Then comes a continuous draft of the whole Memoir without the introduction, of which section 1 has been typed. At this stage section 2 is in manuscript ('D.H.L. and his parents' ms.) but there are also the first three pages of an improved typescript ('D.H.L. and his parents' ts.). Thirdly, the next stage is a carbon typescript of the continuous manuscript, complete with introduction. Finally there is a later typescript of the complete work. Both of these typescripts show pervasive revision and improvement. I have followed the most improved, later, typescript, and corrected any errors by reference to the first typescript and the manuscript.

In addition to this main material there is the manuscript and (improved) typescript of a talk on Lawrence, entitled 'D. H. Lawrence of Eastwood, Notts. – early days', which uses material from the first two sections of the Memoir, and appears to have been written in the 1950s.

In places the early stages of the first two sections or the typescript of the talk contain material different in fact or in emphasis from the final typescript of the Memoir, and I have drawn such material into the notes.

The part of the Memoir which was published in *The London Mercury* for March 1931 is here entitled '1: Early days'.

A MEMOIR
OF
D. H. LAWRENCE

INTRODUCTION

I am aware that I am sitting down to a very difficult task; to the task of making some people believe what they do not wish to believe, and trying to convince others of something they think scarcely possible. And it is a task which is more or less forced upon me by circumstances, and a task which, in my own mind, I feel certain ought not yet to be attempted; not for publication at any rate, because it is not possible, so far as I am concerned, to write the full story of Lawrence and those all-important early days, while there is the certainty that people yet alive, and, I hope, truly happy, would be hurt in one way or another. Lawrence, himself, would have said, in those same early days, that it did not matter whose feelings were hurt, or whose happiness was jeopardised, so long as the result added to the sum of human knowledge. Whether he would have said the same in his latest years is, to my mind, very questionable.

I have also a certain worried feeling with regard to my ability to perform the task and to do full justice to so important a subject, for Lawrence is an important subject, argue as you will. I am not skilled in the art of book-writing, and, though I have done a great amount of work as a free-lance journalist, it has been, for the most part, of the 'pot-boiler' variety, and under a *nom de plume*, which I adopted when I first commenced writing, in the days when one was not always safe in expressing certain views over one's own signature.[1] But, in this part of the Midlands,[2] I have gained something of a reputation in the matter of telling my story straightforwardly and intelligibly, and so I trust that what I lack in the art of book-writing may be compensated for by the story I have to tell, the truths I have to utter, the fairmindedness I hope to shew, and the ultimate end I hope to achieve, which is to try to shew you a 'different' Lawrence.

There must be a certain consciousness of 'betrayal' in a work of this description. I shall have to tell you of events that happened, and things that were said, in the sanctity of the home – in the Lawrence home, where I was always regarded almost as one of the family[3] – and to reveal such things must needs bring something approaching a sense of desecration, but I have no fears on that score, for I shall hope that, throughout my work may permeate the spirit of love which has always been with me, and which I am not ashamed to confess still glows warm in my breast, and increases in warmth as my spirit goes back to those early days, when Lawrence, and I, and the rest of the 'Pagan' brotherhood[4] – if I may use the term to include our group of both sexes! – were building for the future.

It may be possible that I must needs shew a little bias towards Lawrence; it would only be natural if I did, but I hope it will not be so. I want to tell you what I may of the story exactly as I now see it, looking back through the years, and then regarding the present day, and leave you to judge for yourselves, after studying the Lawrence I have to show you.

And may I crave your sympathy in my task? I think you will give it to me, acknowledging that I am tackling a very big task somewhat unwillingly, but recognising that, in the circumstances, it has to be done, so that mankind may be able to pass fair judgement upon Lawrence; and that cannot be done until much of the information in this book is given to the world. I claim your sympathy, too, as a man fighting for the dead friend of his youth, and as one striving to give to posterity a sweeter Lawrence than has yet been presented.

1

EARLY DAYS

It is an amazing thing that so little should generally be known, and so much mystery be made, of the early life and circumstances of David Herbert Lawrence, in view of the fact that there are so many persons living today who could each contribute quite an interesting 'something' to the story of those early days. The majority of us who formed that little band of comrades – we have been called 'Pagans' – of whom you have read in *The White Peacock* and *Sons and Lovers*, are still living, and each of us could tell a story of Lawrence; and what a different story from what might be expected in many quarters![1]

I am acutely conscious of the fact that it would be wrong to attempt to deal with the early life of Lawrence by giving a bare recital of the simple facts. Each of the outstanding incidents of those early years should be considered carefully because of the impression it, individually, made upon this hypersensitive character. I have no hesitation in saying that one of the deepest impressions made upon Lawrence's young nature, affording an explanation of an attitude towards his father that must have appeared inexplicable to many people, was made when he discovered the true circumstances in which his mother and father were married;[2] and I have still less hesitation in expressing the opinion that the 'Little Woman' (Lawrence's mother) never made a greater mistake than when she related those circumstances to us. His cynical attitude towards some women dates from an incident that occurred shortly after the death of his brother 'Ern', whom the whole family idolised.[3] This attitude was further 'burnt' into him by the 'blistering' his young soul received during the time he was working as foreign correspondent to a firm of manufacturers in Nottingham.[4] The girls at the factory appear to have taken a sheer delight in searing his youthful innocence. You may be of the opinion that such a remark is a queer one to be made in respect of D. H. Lawrence. It is; but believe me, it is a true one.

Briefly, the story of those early years is as follows: Arthur Lawrence, a young collier, a member of a family of miners from Brinsley,[5] one of the numerous mining villages lying in the Eastwood district in Nottinghamshire, a dashing and good-looking youth, fond of dress and the gayest possible time, used to follow the custom of many youths of the district and run down to Nottingham most weekends by one of the cheap market trains which always ran on Wednesdays and Saturdays.

I have never known quite definitely how the meeting came about; but I believe it was at one of the numerous 'dances', or 'dancing classes', held in the city on Saturday nights, that he first met 'Lydia', the daughter of a tradesman carrying on business in the Peashill Rise district of the city, and a member of a family in quite good circumstances. Lydia promptly fell in love with the handsome, dark and curly-haired young collier, and no doubt the love was mutual, for Arthur Lawrence most certainly sincerely loved his wife. It is certain that there was considerable opposition from her people,[6] but Lydia had that strain of stubbornness which she transmitted, in a marked degree, to each of her sons, and to David Herbert in particular, and her little toss of the head and irritating 'sniff' that I remember so well, were answer to all objections.[7] She married Arthur Lawrence. There were five children, the names in order of birth being George, Emily,[8] Ernest, David Herbert and Lettice Ada.

When I was seven years of age, my family moved into a house that father had built in the Lynn Croft[9] district of the Parish of Greasley, and all the children of our family began to attend at the Beauvale Board Schools. Here it was that I first made the acquaintance of Lawrence, who was one year my senior, and one standard higher in the school. He was a thin, pale, weakly lad always scrupulously clean, neat and tidy, with no energy for our oft-times over-robust games, and no apparent inclination to attempt to join us. A book and a quiet corner were always his delight and he would much more often be found with girl companions than with boys. He had a high-pitched, girlish voice, which always rose in pitch with the least excitement, a feature which he retained to early manhood, as he retained also that impatient toss of the head he got from his mother, and that unruly lock of hair that always would persist in drooping to one side of his high forehead.[10]

Throughout the whole of his schoolboy years, he was known as 'Bert', and this was the name used by the whole of the members of the family. Occasionally, I have known a misguided woman, thinking to address him in a way which might be construed as shewing liking, or sympathy, call him 'Bertie', and this he positively hated, though I do not recall an instance when he allowed his resentment to shew itself.

At this time, the Lawrences were living in 'The Breach', a typical agglomeration of colliery houses, spoilt by its abominable 'middle lane', a feature which D. H. Lawrence never forgot,[11] and always held as a sin committed by the colliery company responsible for the erection of such an unsavoury, unhealthy, and unnecessary blot on the earth, spoiling what were otherwise quite good houses at that time.

Ernest Lawrence, who received his early training in an office at Langley Mill,[12] a neighbouring town just over the Derbyshire border, had made splendid progress, and succeeded in obtaining a position, with plenty of prospects of advancement, in a very large London office.[13] He was an exceptionally good son, whose main thought appeared to be to do his best to help his mother and the other members of the family, and he was particularly anxious that his younger brother, Bert, should have if possible, a better educational start in life than he himself was able to get. Our old schoolmaster, Mr William Whitehead, suggested that Lawrence ought to try to obtain one of the scholarships which the Notts. County Council had recently commenced to offer, and he specially coached Lawrence for the examination. I remember the news coming through that Lawrence had been successful and was the first boy from that school to win such a scholarship. Dear old Whitehead positively beamed with joy at the success of his first entry in the County competitions.[14]

Just before he was twelve years of age, then, we find young Lawrence attending Nottingham High School, where Dr James Gow was Head,[15] and by this time, the Lawrences had moved to the Walker Street house, a move which they regarded as quite a distinct social advance.[16] The following year, I had the honour of following in the footsteps of Lawrence, and the 'Beauvale Yell' celebrated the fact that Whitehead's candidate had again been successful.

Then followed our High School days together, starting from home shortly after seven o'clock in the morning, and returning just before seven at night, with always a pile of lessons to do later,[17] though we younger ones could always depend on a little real help from Lawrence with any knotty points during the tiresome train journey. Even in these days, Lawrence had that little, troublesome, hacking cough that used to bring his left hand so sharply to his mouth – a cough and an action that he never lost.

During holidays we always tramped; tramped, many times, the live-long day, and at least one day in every holiday we contrived to spend tramping in the Derbyshire dales. It was chiefly during these tramps that we gathered our knowledge of the life of the fields and woods, and I think we gathered, pressed, and mounted specimens of every plant, shrub and tree to be found for miles around.[18] Lawrence was never very keen on the collection of insects, though he had a very profound knowledge of the insects of the locality, and the mounting and dressing of the specimens in this case fell entirely to my lot.

High School days over;[19] and neither of us could follow our own inclination and become pupil teachers, because we had not sufficient 'backing influence' to gain us admission. Lawrence started to work at the factory in Nottingham, where he stayed for about twelve months,[20] when he contracted pneumonia and for a considerable time his recovery appeared to be very improbable. As he slowly improved, it became very obvious that he ought not to attempt to continue his arduous duties in Nottingham. He still longed for the teaching profession, and so, after considerable 'effort', he was able to begin duties as a student at the Albert Street Schools, Eastwood, where Mr George Holderness was in charge.[21]

The Education Act of 1904[22] made entry to the teaching profession quite a different matter from what it had been previously, and, in the following year, I had passed the entrance examination and was a student teacher at the Greasley Gilt Hill Schools, and, on certain days, joined Lawrence on our journeys to Ilkeston, to attend the local centre for preparation for further examinations. [23]

These were the days that saw the real gathering together of the 'Pagans'. The group was composed almost entirely of student teachers, of whom Lawrence and I were the only male members, with the occasional addition of Alan, the elder brother of 'Jess', to whom Lawrence, many years later applied the name of 'Princess'. [24]

It was at this period, too, that Lawrence began seriously to apply his mind to sketching, in which branch of the arts he had, as yet, been but a somewhat dilettante dabbler, and I think it was at this time also that he made up his mind that some day he would make his name as a writer. Let there be no misunderstanding about that; Lawrence even in those early days, knew that he had the capacity for literary greatness and had thoroughly made up his mind to achieve it.

The Little Woman had never appeared to be quite comfortable in the Walker Street home after the death of 'Ern' and a move was next made to the Lynn Croft house, [25] chiefly owing to the influence of 'Franky' and 'Grit' of the 'Pagans', whose father owned the property. They remained in this house until the Little Woman laid down the wearisome burden of her life, to the torture of the soul of Lawrence.

Student days over and his intermediate examination passed with flying colours, Lawrence was given a position as assistant master at the Albert Street Schools, but he realised that, to be in the profession without attendance at a training college was a very serious handicap. The Little Woman shared his opinion, and, though it was obvious that it would mean a very great struggle to bear the expense, they decided that the sacrifice must be made, and they commenced saving every possible penny towards sending Lawrence to college. Thus, the following year [26] saw Lawrence beginning his studies at Nottingham University College Day Training Section. As we all expected, too, he came through remarkably well and had an extraordinary success in the college finals.

It was during this University training period that the friendship between Lawrence and the 'Princess' reached its highest point, and Lawrence and I had a standing arrangement that, on Saturday evenings, after I had played cricket or football, as the case might be, I would look round at his home. If he was not there, he would be at the farm – the home of the 'Princess'. The reason for this was that he was very seldom certain as to whether he would be going to the farm or not. If he settled down to write or sketch and the work progressed to his satisfaction, he would stick to it, very often until it was completed. But when the story did not develop to his liking, the Little Woman would say, 'He's gone up there again, George. He lost his patience, crammed his papers into his pocket, snatched up his cap and went.' Usually, I would sit down for a chat, or perhaps, if Ada chanced to be there, or any of the 'Pagans' had called, we would indulge in a little singing – usually folk-songs or glees – until I thought Lawrence would be almost ready to start from the farm, and then I would be off to meet him on his way back.

I have seen it stated that the 'Princess' lived in the same village as Lawrence. This statement is entirely wrong. To go by the road from the Lawrences' home to the farm was a good three miles, but there was an unwritten permission for the family from the farm, and their friends, to take the cut over the fields beyond the reservoir and through the woods, which reduced the journey to about two miles. If I reached the fields before meeting him, our old High School whistle call,[27] sent out into the darkness at intervals, prevented us from missing each other in the darkness, and, at the same time, told the keepers, who were always on the alert, that the trespassers were not the poachers against whom they had continually to guard.

Sometimes I got as far as the farm, where I would usually find Lawrence and the 'Princess' with their heads close together and the crumpled papers spread out in front of them; but the papers soon disappeared with my arrival.

The explanation of that is to be found in the fact that the 'Princess' was the only one of all the 'Pagans' who did anything at all to encourage Lawrence in his writings. We were all enthusiastic on the subject of his sketches and paintings, but we all realised the danger of a literary career for him. The 'Princess' however, helped him by her encouragement and assistance, and received some nasty remarks from some of the other 'Pagans' for her pains, but she was proof against all such pettiness and her dark eyes would continue to gleam brightly and her lips to smile that everlastingly inscrutable smile of hers, as though she were saying to herself, 'Wait! You will see who laughs in the long run.'[28]

College days over, Lawrence obtained a post as assistant master at the Addison Road School, Croydon.[29] I was at Stourbridge at this time, and the correspondence between Lawrence and me consisted chiefly of personal items, family news, and always arrangements for the next holidays, when we would again be at home together. He was still writing short stories and poems and discussing them with the 'Princess' in correspondence, and even part of *The White Peacock* was written at this time.

The 'Princess' has the credit for 'launching' Lawrence. I am quite certain that she would be the first to admit that he required no 'launching'. What did she do? She merely made surreptitious copies of manuscripts Lawrence had lent to her, or sent to her to read and correct where necessary, and, without consulting Lawrence on the matter, she sent these copies on to the *English Review*. Hueffer recognised that here was something for which he had been seeking – genius – as he himself expressed it when he and Lawrence met personally a short time later. And since then, so far as I am aware, the genius of Lawrence has never been questioned.

Success made his double task too heavy, and once more his over-taxed body cracked under the strain he was putting on it and his ever-constant enemy – pneumonia – again almost claimed him. The Little Woman once more had the dreadful experience of being called to the bedside of a son in the London area, and of making the journey full of doubts as to whether she would be able to reach him in time. In the case of 'Ern' she had been too late, but David Herbert had retained the vital spark of life, and the unremitting care of the Little Woman and the others forced back the grasping hands for the time being. After a period of recuperation, Lawrence made up his mind that it was impossible to continue as a teacher and continue a literary career at the same time. He gave up his profession to follow his star.[30]

Shortly before the publication of *The Trespasser*, Lawrence was staying with me in a little village in the hills dividing Derbyshire from Staffordshire,[31] and we spent much of our time on our walks over the hills, attempting to find a more suitable name for the story, but without coming to any definite decision. Ultimately, I believe, Messrs Heinemann settled the matter for themselves.[32]

While I was away in the daytime, Lawrence was busy with the final bringing into shape of *The Rainbow*[33] and, at the time, I predicted trouble over the bedroom scene; but Lawrence was adamant. Later, when the trouble actually developed, and there appeared to be a chance of avoiding the trouble if Lawrence would consent to re-write that chapter, he not only maintained that attitude but declared that he would much rather destroy the whole manuscript than alter one jot or one tittle of it 'for the sake of such a set of fools'. That was a flash of the real Lawrence.

Now, though I was just as well aware, as was Lawrence, that the incident therein portrayed was absolutely true to life, and had indeed occurred, I advised the line of least resistance and suggested a certain method of rewriting the chapter, by which it appeared to me that the main feature could be kept, while the trouble would be avoided. Lawrence, however, would have none of it. The book must stand or fall as it was. It fell; and today, book-lovers all the world over are seeking copies of the American edition and paying extravagant prices to obtain them. Is there anyone who dares to assert that they are doing this because the book is indecent? I would suggest that the book could be published today without question.

'Teufel', he said to me when I tried to insist – the name was given to me by his idolised brother 'Ern' – 'Teufel, the real knowledge of the world consists of the related experiences of the men and women who have lived in it. To each human being separate experiences, thoughts, and emotions come, and it is a duty which each one of us owes to the world, to add our own contributions,[34] just as we know them, whether they be the result of our own experiences or as related to us by others.' It did not occur to me at the time that Lawrence was propounding to me his lifetime creed, but I know now that it was so, and I want to prove that he was true to his creed, aye, true unto death.

I objected that living persons might be affected, hurt in their feelings, damaged in their reputations, upset in their homes, disgruntled in a thousand and one different ways.

And now the old, impatient Lawrence flashed to the surface again as he replied, 'Just the same old Teufel! You always were such a sentimental devil – more's the pity. Think of the stories you could write if only you would let yourself go. Don't you see that we must each of us be prepared to take the responsibility of our own actions! How can anyone complain so long as the narrator tells the truth? And suppose their puny feelings are hurt, or, what is probably nearer the mark, they get a pain in their pride, what does it matter so their lesson is given to the world and they shall have taught others to avoid the mistakes they made?' You will note that Lawrence referred to one type of experience only. There you have the line he marked out for himself. There you have the line he followed; and in following that line, he had to show that truth, as we know it, must reveal much more of ugliness than of beauty. In the upshot *The Rainbow* fell; and in falling, placed Lawrence in the very forefront of the novelists of his day in the considered judgement of those who read him rightly and are qualified to judge. From that time Lawrence lived his life before the world and there is no necessity for me to stress facts already so well known.

'Have you heard anything of poor old Bert lately?' That was always the question my sister asked me during the later years of his life and her method of alluding to Lawrence well illustrates the general attitude towards him of those who had any knowledge of him at all, who knew his lovable nature, who appreciated his real genius, who understood the splendid fight he made, both through circumstances and against a physique never at all robust; and all this, even though some of them may have considered that the line he had marked out for himself was a wrong line, or, at least, a misguided one.

Strong in his own strength, Lawrence forged on to his destiny – mental and bodily distress, exile, and death; and in his death, he must have made the great discovery that death had brought to him more love and lovers than ever he had known in life, and that their numbers were ever increasing throughout the world. May this be balm to his spirit and cause him to rest in peace.

Frankly, by this work I hope to increase still many times more the number of those lovers and to combat a tendency lately exhibited in some quarters, to decry Lawrence in a manner that most certainly would never have been attempted while he still lived. And to do so I am convinced that I have only to shew that right to the end Lawrence was true to himself and the line he had marked out for himself, and almost too true to the principle that a man should give his experiences to the world, for mankind to gather what knowledge may be available from them.

2

LAWRENCE AND HIS PARENTS

In an article entitled 'Myself Revealed', published in the *Sunday Dispatch* on 17 February 1929, Lawrence dealt with the subject of his parents in the following manner: 'My father was a collier, and only a collier, nothing praiseworthy about him. He wasn't even respectable, in so far as he got drunk rather frequently, never went near a chapel, and was usually rather rude to his little immediate bosses at the pit.'

'My mother was, I suppose, superior. She came from town, and belonged really to the lower bourgeoisie. She spoke King's English, without an accent, and never in her life could even imitate a sentence of the dialect which my father spoke, and which we children spoke out of doors. She wrote a fine Italian hand and a clever and amusing letter when she felt like it. And as she grew older she read novels again, and got terribly impatient with *Diana of the Crossways* and terribly thrilled by *East Lynne.*'

'But she was a working man's wife, and nothing else, in her shabby little bonnet, and her shrewd, clear, different face. And she was very much respected, just as my father was not respected. Her nature was quick and sensitive and perhaps really superior. But she was down, right down in the working class, among the mass of poorer colliers' wives.'[1]

Just as the following 'Revelation' of himself is merely a somewhat horrible distortion, so his description of his parents is an absolute travesty of the real facts. But by this time, Lawrence had taken up the attitude that he, too, was of the working classes, that there was a general desire to keep him there, and that, 'Damn them! He would remain there.' His attitude in this article is reflected in an attempt to portray an early family life spent in the most squalid of circumstances, and with scarcely a redeeming feature.

47

What would be the natural impression received by the ordinary reader from a description of that kind? To them, Lawrence's mother becomes a somewhat disreputable figure – the woman who has 'come down', and has been content to 'slide under'. The home is the home of the typical drunken collier, disturbed repeatedly by the drunken brawlings of the father, with poverty apparent everywhere, because the father was wasting in drunkenness that which was needed at home. Is not that the case? Nothing could be further from the truth, and in saying so, I speak from an intimate knowledge of the homes of colliers of every type, grade and condition.

Then there is the picture of himself: 'I was a delicate, pale brat with a snuffy nose, whom most people treated quite gently, as just an ordinary delicate little lad.' The truth is that he was an exceedingly 'nice' little lad, certainly delicate, whom most people treated as being a little 'superior', which, also, he most certainly was.

But even while shocking all of us who knew him in his youth, Lawrence cannot deny to his mother certain attributes, which, in themselves, directly contradict the remaining portions of his description, and one is glad to find that he could not allow even a developed attitude entirely to eradicate that feeling of adoration and admiration that he had for his mother when he was a youngster, and indeed, I have always believed he kept it so long as she lived. And I think my belief is proved by his poem on her passing. [2]

Please do not for one moment imagine that those terms I have used – adoration and admiration – are too strong. To Lawrence, especially in his early days, the Little Woman was the whole world. She was his Earth, his Heaven, his Hell.

And his father? His father was just a necessary factor so long as it was necessary for him to have an existence. And that was all; quite definitely that was all. Poor old man! As a matter of fact he was full of a consuming love for his wife and all his children, and for Bert (D. H.) in particular, but his wife had been coldness itself to him for many years, and the children were always so near to their mother that their father could never get anywhere near to them in a spiritual sense; and he never did.

But it is unfair to the memory of Arthur Lawrence that he

should be handed down to posterity as 'just a drunken collier'. I have not the least hesitation in saying that he was not a drunkard.[3] So far back as I can remember, which goes back to the time when D. H. Lawrence was twelve years of age, Lawrence *père* was, comparatively, a very temperate man. From the point of view of his earnings his first thought was always for his home, and he never had enough money left, after that, for any drunkenness. He never neglected his work. Up at approximately 5.30 every morning, he would be away to the pit, over a mile away, swinging his crippled leg in the later years, hail, rain, or shine, winter or summer, year in and year out; and there was never one to wish him luck as he went, and never a joyous greeting on his return. Do you wonder that he liked to join a few cronies in a favourite corner when he could afford to do so?

I remember going round to the Walker Street house one Friday night (pay night) and finding the Little Woman sitting quietly weeping by the table, with a few coins spread out in front of her. It was one of the very few occasions on which I remember the high courage of the Little Woman to have faltered.

'Whatever's the matter?' I asked.

'What am I to do, George?' she questioned through her tears, and then continued, indicating the coins, 'Fourteen and threepence to keep the five of us for a week and pay the rent.'

'But, good gracious!' my youthful indignation flared out, 'He surely got more than that. He never misses his work. He couldn't go five days and get only that much.'

'He's been every day, but they were all quarters or halves, and the amount is right. Here's his packet – seventeen and threepence. He had to have a little bit for himself for a bit of tobacco and a glass of beer, or course.'

I have lived that scene again many times. How often the Little Woman cried and wondered how she should lay out the meagre earnings I know not, but I do know that the memory of that scene has often been a guide to me when I have been dealing with working men.

Drunken! Depraved! It is not fair. There was nothing he loved better than to get rid of the dirt of the pit, and he was one of the very few colliers I knew, in those days, who always insisted on his back being thoroughly cleansed when he was washing, on his return from work.[4] The Little Woman usually performed this service for him, but when I have been there, and she has been busy, I have scrubbed his back for him many a time.

Then there was the week-end, when Arthur Lawrence went up town to meet his cronies. 'Not respectable', says D.H., but I venture to suggest that you would have been pleased at the sight of him; well-washed, his curly hair and beard most carefully combed, black broadcloth coat with tails (a near relative to a morning coat!), beautifully white polo collar (washed and ironed by the Little Woman's own hands) narrow black tie, black soft hat, walking stick, and always with a somewhat jaunty air, he would go to spend his little hour at the 'Wellington', the 'Nelson' or the 'Miners' Arms' and then, possibly, back to the 'Three Tuns' (quite near the house) before proceeding home.

Old Lawrence belonged to that race of men for whom, under the proper circumstances, a glass of beer is quite a good thing. It gives them an uplift, improves them, bucks up their ideas and brightens their outlook. The existence of such a type of man is hardly sufficiently recognised. A couple of glasses of beer will make them cheerful. Arthur Lawrence was like that. He would arrive home in the very best of humours, full of amusement over something that had touched his imagination during the evening, and only anxious to regale us all with an account of it from his point of view. And there was a peculiar point here: if any of the rest of the 'Pagans', or anyone else besides myself and the family happened to be present, the old man would go over to his little armchair on the far side of the fireplace, at the foot of the staircase, and commence to tell his story *in the most perfect King's English, with an affected voice and accent*, entirely forsaking the local dialect he usually employed. But before he had proceeded far in this strain, he was generally interrupted by a shriek of laughter, led by D.H., well seconded by the Little Woman who would then instruct him to hold his tongue or go to bed, which latter he would usually proceed to do, after expressing his feelings by removing his shoes and tossing them, but not at all violently, into the nearest corner, or under the table. I look back with pleasure on the fact that, whether he spoke to the others or not, I never remember an occasion on which he went to bed without giving me the same greeting: 'Goodnight, George! Goodnight me lad!' He was no drunken reprobate; in fact, in my opinion he was quite a bit above the average collier of that district in those days.

David Herbert Lawrence, in his early years, thought very bitterly of the wrong his father had committed by marrying his mother; and I was never able to get much further by pointing out that his mother had also married Arthur Lawrence. The answer to that was that he married her under false pretences, which, to some extent was true, for it is undoubtedly the fact that, up to the time they were married, Lydia Beardsall was under the impression that Arthur Lawrence had some kind of a staff job at the collieries, was an official of sorts, permanently employed and at a fixed salary.

It was not for very many years afterwards, and then not until he came personally into contact with a somewhat parallel case, that he began dimly to recognise the wrong that the Little Woman had done to his father by remaining with him when she had reached the conclusion that she had no feeling left for him, could make no response to his warm, impulsive nature, but that, having 'made her bed', she must be prepared 'to lie on it'.

At the time referred to, Lawrence went to live with a couple who had degenerated into a similar state of existence.[5] I well remember Lawrence telling me of it, and I still have a very vivid impression of the picture drawn for me by an expression he used. Both the man and the woman made a confidant of Lawrence, and he said the man had told him that his wife had no more warmth for him than a bag of mud would have had, while the woman took every possible opportunity of describing to him the wickednesses and infidelities of her husband – in all probability more imaginary than real. My advice to Lawrence, on the occasion referred to, was short and terse: 'If I were in your case, I should get out of such a damned hole – and the sooner the better.' I wish he had taken that advice!

There was a good deal of truth, however, in Lawrence's statement that a good many of his father's troubles, and consequently the troubles of his family, were of his own making;

almost of his own seeking.[6] And in making this statement, Lawrence does not appear to have recognised what a very close application it has to his own case. The trouble with the old man was that, if he thought he would like to say a certain thing, he would say it, entirely regardless of the place he was in, or the members of the company present; just "ffend or please', to use the local expression. This propensity of his was very well known, and many times, during week-ends he was 'primed' by someone with an axe to grind, with the result that, in the following days Arthur Lawrence would be airing somebody else's grievance, pointing out how scandalously genuine workers were treated when they refused to 'kow-tow' to the 'little tin gods of under-bosses', and getting himself ill-thought of for no reason. I have known him come home with such a tale of ill-treatment supposed to have been meted out to an acquaintance, possibly a fellow-worker under the same company. The Little Woman would sit in absolute silence until he had finished, and then, inevitably, would come that quick, perky, sideways tilting of her head, with the distinct sniff we all most feared, and then she would ask, 'And what has all this to do with me, Sir? Or, for the matter of that, with you either?'

Then off he would go into a tirade against those little over-men, pointing out that, if they were allowed to treat certain individuals in such a manner, without protest, it would not be long before everybody else would be subjected to the same treatment. He would tell 'em. He would show 'em . . . and so on, only, at last, to be pulled up by the Little Woman saying, 'Hold your tongue, Sir, or be off to bed. You make me tired with your everlasting maunderings. Why should you imagine you can fight other people's battles? You cannot even fight your own. And you're suffering now, and we are all suffering from your previous stupidity in needlessly taking on other people's battles, instead of looking after your own and ours.' And then, more often than not, she would remind him of how much he had earned in the last few weeks, which gratuitous information would immediately drive him off to bed. But, somehow he appeared to be unable to help it, or to have no power to fight against it, and in this matter, D. H. Lawrence was most truly his father's son: it was ever impossible to persuade him that a proposed course of action was not for the best, or that something he proposed to say, or even had said, was either wrong or at least would have been better left unsaid.

In this connection, I am very forcibly reminded of a discussion I had with him in March 1912. I had raised the matter of the very pointed references he was making, in his writings, to living individuals, and of the fact that, for the majority of his characters he was using the names of actual people we knew well, though, in fairness to Lawrence, I think I ought to say that the character as portrayed by him is usually just about as near being diametrically opposed to the character of the actual holder of the name as it possibly could be. The immediate question was the feelings of the relatives of the poor devil of a musician and music master about whom you read in *The Trespasser*, and who had actually sought a way out of his troubles by committing suicide, though I had also referred to some very unkindly remarks that had reached me as to other references in *The White Peacock* and *Sons and Lovers*.[7] Lawrence would not hear of any argument, and, knowing him so well, I knew it was quite useless to attempt to convince him, but I have a very, very vivid recollection of what I said to him on that occasion. 'Bert, old man!' I remember saying, 'believe me, if you will persist in placing all your friends and acquaintances in your own particular pillory you will finish up without a friend in the world.'

And then listen to Lawrence himself, writing from a more or less voluntary exile, in 1929: 'But something is wrong either with me or with the world or with both of us. I have gone far and met many people, of all sorts and conditions, and many whom I have genuinely liked and esteemed. People, *personally*, have nearly always been friendly . . . And I have *wanted* to feel truly friends with some at least, of my fellow-men. Yet I have never quite succeeded . . . And whether I am a worldly success or not I really don't know. But I feel, somehow, not much of a human success.'[8]

Old Arthur Lawrence was happy in his later years. Though D. H. Lawrence may have had no love for his father, yet he saw to it that his father was free from the shadow of want; and whether people admired the works of his son or not, old Arthur enjoyed the reflected glory which came from the fact that he was the father of D.H. And don't forget my earlier statement that old Lawrence had a genuine love for his son!

Let us return, for a little while, to the collier's home in which Lawrence spent his youth, of which I am certain you have so wrong a mental picture, and where I spent so many happy hours. I will write of the Walker Street house. There were six houses in the row, which joined up, at the town end, with a much larger house, belonging to Mr Frank Mellor, who was a departmental manager at the Lynn Croft pottery of Messrs Bourne. Each of the six houses had a bay window to the front room or 'parlour', into which the front door opened directly from a tiny walled and railed enclosure; an apology for a front garden. So far as I remember, no one ever attempted a garden. There was one entry or passage to each two houses, with a common back yard and garden path to each two houses also. Though I say 'garden path', the small amount of ground provided was by no means worthy of the name, but Arthur Lawrence always kept his little portion tidy, and sometimes succeeded in growing a little of something. Behind the houses was the local Baptist Chapel, with a high boundary wall between, so that there was no outlook at all from the rear of the premises. There was a magnificent stretch of country to be viewed from the front windows, but as it looked out immediately over the chimney pots of 'The Breach', lying in the valley below, the landscape beyond was robbed of much of its charm for the Lawrences. The house consisted of scullery, living-room and parlour on the ground floor, with three bedrooms, the staircase running up with 'winders'[9] from the living-room. The pantry or larder was under the stairs and received only borrowed light from the living-room. The scullery had the usual complement of pots and pans, together with the set-pot,[10] sink, table and mangle. The living-room was furnished with the little armchair previously referred to for Mr Lawrence, a low rocker for the Little Woman, always on the side nearest the window, a dining table, sofa, dresser with well-filled bookcase above, sewing machine, a few Windsor chairs and rug in front of the fire, usually home-pegged from cloth snippings,[11] the tiles[12] of the floor being otherwise bare and always scrubbed to a scrupulous cleanliness. The walls were adorned with photographs and one or two carefully selected prints. The parlour had a suite of quite good quality, upholstered in heavy green repp, there was a useful cottage piano, a carpet, with stained surround for the floor, and a skin rug before the fireplace. The pictures were photographs and engravings – though most of them were replaced with paintings later – and the ornaments were neither so numerous nor so flamboyant as to become too obvious.

Upstairs all was neatness and snowy whiteness, with sufficient furniture for comfort and necessity. The hallmark in the whole place was orderliness, neatness and cleanliness – the hallmark of the Little Woman. And there was never any deterioration; but there was a constant improvement, a little addition here, repairs there or a replacement somewhere else, until, when they moved into the Lynn Croft house, they had a home of which I believe they were all honestly proud; and with good reason.

But perhaps the most convincing proof is in the fact that the 'Pagans' of *The White Peacock* and *Sons and Lovers* truly loved the Lawrence home, almost as though it were their own. And there was not a 'Pagan' who would have enjoyed squalid surroundings for a single instant.

You will naturally ask wherein, then, lay the root of the undoubted bitterness that lay at the bottom of Lawrence's feelings for his father. It was in the fact that Arthur Lawrence was just mean. Not mean, particularly in the small sense of coppers, but mean in soul; his sacrifices were not willing ones. He got no joyous thrill from any form of self-denial for the sake of his wife and children. What sacrifices he made were forced upon him by his wife, and he found them nothing but irksome. Often, she had to resort to subterfuge – after having forced such sacrifices – to see that the children got various things they needed. Especially was this so in the matter of clothes, and I call to mind two instances, both in this connection, both of which left a very vivid impression on me. The second one has something of a humorous side and so we will take that one first.

Not long after the family removed to the Lynn Croft house, I called there immediately after lunch one Saturday to leave a message for Bert. There was a small outer door, and then, about nine feet up the path, a large screen-door. This slipped from my fingers and closed with a loud bang. As I went quickly up the path, I glanced through the side window of the living room and saw Ada making a wild dash out of that room, into the hall, with a pile of hat-boxes.

I went in, laughing, and asked, 'Why rush 'em away like that? Why not let me have a word as to whether they suit?'

'It's you, George, is it?' said the Little Woman, 'We thought it was father.'

'What if it had been? If Ada wants a new hat, I don't see any reason why she shouldn't have one. She earns 'em herself now, doesn't she?'

The Little Woman's head went up, with the sniff we knew so well, and I knew that I had said the wrong thing, in spite of the fact that Ada's dimple was shewing plainly and her eyes sparkling with the fun of an adventure. 'You don't know everything, George Neville,' Mrs Lawrence admonished me, and continued, 'I'll tell you something my mother said to me a long time ago – "Lydia," she told me, "it is necessary to deceive a *good* husband with one eye, but a *bad* one with two."'

I was always considered amongst the crowd as being more or less incorrigible, and so I suppose it was only in keeping with that reputation when I grinned largely and asked, 'And the rushing away of the hats – do you call that a one-eyed deceit or a two-eyed one?'

The only reply I got was a 'Huh!' accompanied by our sniff, and a look which told me quite plainly that she understood that I recognised myself as something of an idiot to be asking questions the answers to which I already knew well. But in spite of that, I felt then, though only quite a youth at the time, the same feeling that, many times intensified, I feel today, that I would like about a quarter of an hour with the Little Woman's mother and with all other mothers who have given such and similar advice to their daughters, in order that I might attempt to give them an idea of the trouble, strife and misery they have caused to the very souls which it should have been their first duty and pleasure to protect from evil. It is the teaching of the Devil.

The other incident – a much more dreadful one – directly concerned Lawrence and his father.

Lawrence called me a sentimental devil; perhaps I am. And

I freely confess that, as I write of this incident, I have a feeling that I ought not to do so; that it ought to be regarded as a regrettable incident, to be closed and forgotten. But in these days, so many people are attempting to probe and pry into the secrets of the life of D. H. Lawrence – people whose only object can be to exploit and commercialise his memory, for they would never be satisfied to publish such puny material or such wild and extravagant guesses unless it were so – that, in justice to him, since a large section of the literary world is in process of forming its judgement on the real character of D. H. Lawrence, I suppose I ought to reveal some, at least, of my knowledge of him, and, indeed, I have his own ruling as an excuse for revealing all my knowledge if I cared, or dared, to do so. In passing, let me say here that our literary people would be well advised to suspend their judgement on Lawrence, take very little notice of any so-called life of Lawrence, because, since so many people yet living are involved, there is no person dare attempt a real life of Lawrence. And the real life of D. H. Lawrence is less easy to obtain from his works than would be the life of George Bernard Shaw.

On a certain Saturday afternoon, during the time Lawrence was attending Nottingham University, I had promised to accompany him to the farm. I went round to the Walker Street house,[13] tapped at the door, gave my usual call and walked in. The Little Woman was resting in her rocking chair. "Lo, George! He's just changing. He won't be long. Sit down. He's a bit longer than usual today; he's got his new suit and I expect that's the reason.'

'He's got it then? I'm so glad. Is it all right?' I asked.

'Don't know. I've not seen it on yet. It only came this morning.'

It had involved great sacrifices on the rest of the family to send Bert to college, and I know that he had been a little ashamed at the necessity of making his clothes last so long, as it was absolutely necessary that he should do; they were thread-bare and darned to the last extremity, though always neat and tidy, before they could possibly be discarded. I was, indeed, glad for his sake, to hear that it had been found possible for him to have a new suit.

He came downstairs with a pleased smile, lifted his hand in

57

his very familiar gesture and pirouetted before us. 'Well! How do I look?' he laughingly asked, and added, 'I know you will want to express your opinions.' Really, we quite understood that he was anxious to have our opinions.

'Of course!' laughed his mother, and now her head went up, her eyes shone and her whole face lit up, as it always did when he shewed extra pleasure as the result of some of her efforts.

It was a grey flannel suit, the first such suit he ever had, and it was, in my opinion, more befitting his style than any other garment I had ever seen him wearing. I was just expressing this view when Mr Lawrence walked in. Mrs Lawrence immediately busied herself with some little thing, while Bert pretended to be seeking a book in the bookcase. I suppose I ought to have known better, but I have never liked chopping off a sentence because somebody has come into the room, and I still have a very deeprooted objection to anyone else doing it on my entrance. I therefore continued what I was saying and, having finished my remarks, I turned to Arthur Lawrence, wished him 'good afternoon' and asked him if he did not agree with my remarks.

'New suit, eh! And wheer did that cum from?' he asked.

'It came from the Co-op of course', snapped the Little Woman.

'Is it peed for?' was the next question.

'Yes it is *peed* for', she retorted, and I remember the expression, and the infinite scorn of her tones as she mocked his dialectical 'peed' for 'paid'; one of the very few times I ever heard her use any of the local dialect. But its very use, the accent, and the scorn were very regrettable, for they lashed old Lawrence to fury – the only time I remember seeing him in anything approaching an actual rage.

'Yer can mock me, an' be off-hand wi' me, an' turn yer nose up, but if it is peed for it's my money as peed for it; an' it's a damn shame. 'Ere I ain't got a copper even ter get mesen a drink, an' 'e can 'ave owt 'e wants. What's 'e want wi' new suits? An' if 'e does why can't 'e goo out an' earn 'em? Not get you ter rob me for 'em.' He shouted this harangue in quite a loud voice, thumping the table at intervals, by way of punctuation.

During the progress of this tirade, Bert had signalled to me that we should be off, and I stood ready to go, but old Lawrence was between the open door and the bookcase, flinging his arms about, so that it was impossible to pass.

'Arthur Lawrence', said the Little Woman quietly, 'you just sit down and hold your tongue.' Never had I known that quite, admonitory 'Arthur Lawrence' to fail; and it is possible it would have been just as efficacious as usual, but Bert broke in, 'How dare you say such things to my mother? And what sort of a beast do you call yourself to be anybody's father and act like that?'

'Beast now is it?' he bellowed. 'Beast! I ought ter 'a bin a beast an' knocked some o' the damn silliness out o' some on yer long sin'. Beast is it?? 'Cos I speak raight out an' say tha'rt not worth thee salt. Too damn lazy to work like anybody else's kids an' get owt for theesen, an' then tha' 'as the damn cheek ter call me "Beast" when I say owt. Fer tew pins I'd . . .' and with the action he raised his right fist and stepped towards Bert, who, taut and white with passion, raised his fist and stepped forward also. And there they stood, breast to breast, teeth exposed and all but snarling, glaring into each other's eyes, just as you have seen the untamed things of the wild. Poor Little Woman! She rushed towards them, crying, 'Hold your tongue, Sir, and you, Arthur Lawrence, I say sit down', but I took her by the shoulders and placed myself in front of her. Then I thrust my two arms between them and with the right arm forced the father back, while the left arm held off the son. Old Lawrence put up a small struggle, but I then seized his collar tightly and gently shook him. 'Enough of that', I said, 'enough from both of you. And now, listen to me: I'll knock down the one who strikes first, without the slightest hesitation; and I mean just that.'

That settled it, for I had something of a reputation in the fistic art in those days, and old Lawrence went to his chair. I told him a few real home truths, including the fact that he might consider himself very lucky that I had not been in Bert's place, that had it been my mother of whom he spoke I would have licked him unmercifully, and then I turned to D.H. and told him that he ought to be ashamed of himself, 'For, after all, he *is* your father', I concluded.

'My God! Yes. He is. Come on, let's go.' He kissed the Little

Woman, gently stroking her hair as he did so, and we set out.[14]

Down the fields towards the Breach we went, Lawrence slightly in the lead, as always, when anything had upset him, tearing away at top speed, as though able to counteract his mental pain by physical effort. Through the Breach by the middle passing, along the Bottoms, over the bridge crossing the little stream he stormed on, but pulled up panting and coughing half-way across the meadow.

'What the devil do you mean by telling me I ought to be ashamed of myself?' he chokingly asked.

'Come along to the stile and sit down, and then I'll tell you', I replied, and then added, as we went along, 'but don't try talking to me like that, Bert, because I'm not having it; and don't forget that, if you don't want another row.'

We reached the stile and sat down.

'You can think yourself lucky,' I told him.

His whole form stiffened suddenly as he blurted out a favourite expression, 'Good gracious! Why?'

'Because, had you been dealing with my father instead of your own, you would have been dead now, unless your legs had managed to save your neck, big as you are', I told him.

'That's different', he retorted. 'Your father wouldn't have been such a damn beast. He *is* a beast, a beast to mother, a beast to all of us', and he was growing passionate again.

'Steady on!' I used a common local expression. 'I agree he was pretty bad today, but you haven't quite considered it all yet. You will think more about it later on. And in any case he *is* still your father, the author of your being, your parent, just as much as your mother, and . . . '

'I didn't ask him to be my father. I had nothing to do with it. He took the responsibility of bringing me into the world and is too mean to stand the responsibility for what he has done. What does he want? He wanted me to go to school till I was thirteen and then go out and start to "bring summat in" no matter whether I was fit for it or not, as so many other colliers' children have to do. He's like all those others. What do they care about their children? They come by accident, and with no consideration on the part of the parents, and, so far as the parents are concerned, nothing matters so long as, at about the age of thirteen, they start to "bring summat in".'

'I know all about all those things', I told him, 'but that is beside the question. I'm not talking about the responsibility of those who brought us into the world. That's their funeral – and ours, too, sometimes, I agree. But at present I'm talking about us, and the fact that we *are* here, in relation to those parents. You can't threaten your father and go to chapel tomorrow night. From a sporty point of view you should never do it, and, worst of all, you know, or ought to know, that your father is physically incapable of thrashing even a good strong schoolboy in these days. If *you* weren't ashamed for yourself, I was ashamed for you. Anyway, had you struck him I should certainly have knocked you down as I threatened; and that should tell you what I think about it. Besides, you are probably expecting to have children of your own some day, as I am. Would you like to look forward to the time when one of your own boys will threaten you?'

He had been watching me with a constantly changing expression as I harangued him, but, as I came to the latter portion of my speech I knew that at last I had struck the right note; knew that in his vision he was seeing or had seen his children smiling upon him, and I knew that into that visionary existence no frown had ever been allowed to obtrude. And now his eyes flamed into mine with that love-light, that dancing love-light that I knew so well, his arm came across my shoulder and his high-pitched little laugh rang out. He held me close as he said, 'Teufel! I'm afraid we shall never quite agree on some points; but I know just how you feel, *and I wish to God I could feel like it*. I can't, so let's leave it at that. I'm ever so sorry you were upset. There! Will that do? And about those children of ours – what are we going to do about them?'

He held me closer for a few seconds, laughed again as he released me, and sprang from the stile saying, 'We're late, and making it worse by loitering.'

'I know, but a minute or two more won't matter much. About those children – let's resolve that, if ever we *do* have any children of our own, we will try to do at least a little more for them than was ever done for us.'

He stood for a few seconds, thinking. Suddenly he snatched off his cap and said, 'Amen to that!' He paused and then added, 'And now let's go. And we must not waste any more time.'

61

We hurried along, and not for quite a time did I realise that I had neglected to remove my cap when Lawrence sealed his share in the resolution.[15]

He was always like that, sunshine and shadow, but the shadows mostly came from without in those days. And his sunshine was a beautiful radiance, beautifying all things that came in contact with its effulgence, and causing one largely to forget the shadows.

Never, from that day to this, have I mentioned the incident to a soul. It was the end. Sometimes, before that day, I had observed, without any comment, that Lawrence was forcing himself to make an effort to be kinder to his father. I think the probable reason was that his mother had been talking to him on the subject, for I remember that one evening when I remarked on the fact that old Lawrence was pottering about in the garden and I had suggested that I should go out and talk to him for a little while, she had said to me, 'Aye, do George! You know, I feel a bit sorry for him sometimes. He *does* seem a bit lonely', and there was the sound of a great sadness in the low, slow, quietness of her voice. And as the thought had occurred to her, I feel quite confident that she had discussed it previously with Bert, or would discuss it with him later. She discussed almost everything with him; she discussed too many things with him for his peace of mind in my humble opinion, but, on the other hand, much of the wonder of the works of D. H. Lawrence would have been impossible had those discussions not taken place.

It was the end. Whatever spark of feeling for his father Lawrence may have retained up to that day, or whatever small amount of interest, respect, or – call it what you will! – he had been trying to cultivate, was gone, and for him, after that time, he had a father simply because his father was there and immovable. He was never himself in his father's presence, and we all knew it. Bert was never his sister's joyous 'Billy' or 'Alice Beatrice's' rumpled 'David', while his father was present, and even 'Grit's' awful 'Birtie' (pronounced very strongly accentuated in the best Birmingham manner!) would fail to rouse him, though at any other time 'Grit's' punishment would have been immediate and severe.

Oftentimes one of the 'Pagans' – and I have even known the

Little Woman do it! – would slip a few coppers into the old man's hand surreptitiously, and suggest that he went to get a drink. He always went; and, later on, I think he understood and went gladly.

The pity of it! And yet I knew the old man loved the lad. I knew it by the questions he would ask of me when I talked to him in the garden. I knew it by the way he would pick up a jar or something his son had been decorating, hold it, and gaze at it when he thought no one was observing him. I have seen him stroking the lad's cap, and I remember most vividly of all how, when Bert was at the worst during that attack of the dreaded pneumonia which was the primary cause of his entry into the teaching profession and I used to be sitting with him from somewhere about seven until round about ten in the evening, the old man would come into the bedroom in stockinged feet, and with his slippers in his hand would stand behind the screen awaiting my signal. If I signalled 'asleep', he would come softly to the foot of the bed and just look and look at the poor wasted figure, while the tears would trickle unheeded down his face and hurry off his beard. If he heard the ravings of his delirious son, he would just stand quietly behind the screen, cry quietly for a time, and then move softly away to his bed. Often I did not hear him go.[16]

I thought much on this incident later, and particularly after the 'hat' episode of which I have told you previously. Why didn't old Lawrence know that Bert wanted a new suit, and that he was going to have one? Why shouldn't he have known that Ada proposed to purchase a new hat for herself? And, obviously, there must have been a hundred other 'Whys?'

When it was decided that Bert could not carry on at the Nottingham factory and might become a teacher, with practically no prospects as to salary for at least two years, I can solemnly affirm that old Lawrence not only agreed, but was heartily in support. So far as I know, he was never consulted as to Bert's going to college; but I am certain that had he been consulted he would never have opposed it. Some of these 'wise old saws' cut much more deeply than their inventors ever dreamt that they might.

What of the Little Woman? Need I write of his love for her?

Or of his love for his sisters? He never had much chance to shew his love for his brother George, but he idolised his brother 'Ern'. His sister Ada (Lettice Ada for the information of some of you!) has told you something[17] of his love and care for them, of his sharing of their joys and sorrows, and I doubt not that Emily ('Injun Topknot' as Lawrence sometimes teasingly used to call her, referring to her brilliant hair!) would be only too willing to verify Ada's claim.

You must have gathered from his works that his love for his mother was something unusual. But do not allow yourself to be led astray by any statements claiming that Lawrence was so great a lover that he loved all the world.[18] He did nothing of the kind. There were people and things for which he had the very greatest detestation; people he would do anything to avoid meeting – I could still name most of them and you might name some of them from his works! – and things with which he would never willingly come into personal contact.

But Lawrence was always passionate and intense. 'Intense' I would put down as the keynote to his temperament; but generally Lawrence tries to hide this feature or portrays it in a different light.

Lawrence, so far as his mother was concerned, was an unwanted baby. God knows whether his father ever wanted him, or whether he was just an accident arising from a physical contact which must, by that time, have become a mere process of carnal satisfaction to Arthur Lawrence and probably a contact unsatisfactory and even distateful to both. There would be the constant 'battle of wills' during the period preceding his conception – possibly during part of that period too! – and then, even after birth, he was still unwanted. Is it strange that his nature was 'unusual'? Is it any wonder that he was less robust than the preceding children? Then came the dawn of love for him; and his mother cherished him the more fiercely because of the previous denial of love. Arthur Lawrence was not of the 'family man' type. There was no constant seeking for the dawn of recognition in his baby's eyes for him, and thus he missed one of the most lovely sights it is ever given to man to see. But the mother caught that dawn of recognition, fostered it, kept it to herself and hugged it to her bosom, and the years brought to those two a wonderful love, ever growing stronger and stronger, never weakening as other loves came along, always willing to pour itself out for the welfare of the beloved, and strong enough, on the mother's part, to stand aside when necessary. There has been a kind of suggestion that there was something carnal and almost bestial in this love of Lawrence for his mother.[19] The bare idea is madness. The Little Woman was something by way of being a saint, in spite of any mistakes she may have made. She was decidedly Puritanical in her morals and teachings, in spite of her reading of what were then fairly 'advanced' novels. The incident referred to, in this connection is only used by Lawrence to intimate the period of his life at which he became, knowingly, 'sex-conscious', and ought to be used only to refute the other suggestion, i.e. that he 'may have been sex-precocious'.

It was in the thousand-and-one 'little ways of love' that the greatness of their devotion exhibited itself. Each seemed to be the axis of the other's orbit, so that no movement was possible without its relative effect upon both of them. In his early youth, Lawrence had no other interests to distract his attention from his mother, and therefore his affection never wandered, and in wandering weakened as is so often the case, the term weakened being used in the sense that it is weakened by division; and there is usually a weakness in division in spite of the fact that, in some cases, division is essential if strength is to be obtained.

But nothing was allowed to divide or distract the love of these two, and it was, to me, one of the most wonderful things on earth. Lawrence could always demonstrate his love; I always envied him that faculty.

There was no atom of selfishness in their love, on either side. It may be assumed, indeed it has been assumed, that the Little Woman harmed Lawrence to some extent by imposing her love upon him, to the exclusion of other and more natural loves. It is not so. She discussed with me, quite a number of times, the possibility of his marrying and settling down, and there was never any shelving of the subject, any grasping opposition, or any hostility, either veiled or open. In fact, I am quite convinced that, had Lawrence been able to content himself with such a course, it would have been a source of great satisfaction to his mother. In that I judge from the attitude of my own mother, and what she said to me on the subject.

The Little Woman had a mighty love for 'Ern', but when 'Ern' wrote home to say he had decided to become engaged to a certain lady and would like to bring her home, his mother wrote back expressing her pleasure at the news, sent the suggested invitation to the lady, and soon had all of us busy on 'preparation' for the visitor. I know it would have been the same in the case of D.H. I know it was so when, eventually he *did* become engaged, *and I know exactly the reason the engagement was broken*, but this is not the time or place to deal with that question. Suffice it that, in welcoming her prospective daughter-in-law as she always did, the Little Woman quite disproved the suggestion as to the selfishness of her love for D.H.[20]

Enduring to the end, too, was that love. Ada wrote to tell me of her mother's passing and to send me a photograph of the Little Woman, taken on the tiny lawn at the back of the Lynn Croft house, in the days of that last illness.[21] 'Poor old Bert!' she wrote, 'he has suffered tortures during these long weeks of her illness. He looks awful.'

If there is any finding of each other in another existence, on another plane, in another dimension, or anywhere else, after this life, those two are together. But one of the greatest arguments that I can imagine against the possibility of spirit-contact with the departed, is the fact that Lawrence records no manifestation as between himself and his mother. And in saying that, I am disregarding a spirit manifestation which occurred in my own family.

Lawrence is sometimes accused of a certain coarseness. Life, in the raw, is coarse, at times exceedingly so, and it will generally be admitted that Lawrence got right down to the raw. But there was no coarseness in Lawrence himself, and I can say with the utmost truth that in all the years I never once heard him tell a story anything approaching the ordinary 'smutty' club-story, which is so familiar in these days, and which is indulged in, either as raconteur or as listener, by members of both sexes; and it is surprising how soon the listener develops into the raconteur in this connection. Even people with the worst possible memory develop enough effort to 'get off' a story as to be in the swim. Lawrence never would have it. I recall that a certain youth who was attending High School during our years had a whole fund of stories he certainly ought not to have had at his time of life. His people kept many horses and I take it that he collected his stories from the grooms. He appeared to consider himself as socially somewhat superior to us and it was something unusual for him to travel in our compartment. Physically, he could probably have broken Lawrence in two parts.

Soon after I commenced at Nottingham,[22] this youth came into our compartment one morning and commenced to roll off some of his really wicked stories. Lawrence tried to stare him out of countenance, but it was useless, and, since he continued with his yarns, Lawrence finally sprang to his feet, his face white, horribly distorted and more passionate than I would have believed possible, leaned over his tormentor and hissed, 'Shut up, you filthy little beast. Who wants to hear the muck from your stables? If there is any more of it, I'll knock your head through that pane; and I hope you cut your throat in going through.'

I do not think that another word was spoken on the whole journey; everybody was too astonished for speech. Lawrence sat white, panting and glaring in his corner, and I believe, to this day, that if it had been necessary he would have been willing to die in the attempt to carry out his threat. I know he would have made the attempt.

There was no coarseness in his home. The worst language I ever heard Arthur Lawrence use was a 'damn' or a 'devil', and he was immediately pulled up for that. I recollect that once, in giving a verbatim report of what someone else had said, he repeated the term 'bloody fool', and received an awful lecture for his pains. In later years I heard D.H. use much worse terms (judged by the standard of those days!) than I ever heard used by his father.

I have racked my brains to try to find any instances of anything approaching coarseness from the Little Woman, but only on one occasion can I find an instance of anything of the kind; and even that was done deliberately, in order to make as deep an impression as possible. It achieved its object I assure you. I had received previous warning that something might happen, but the shock was no less to me in spite of that.

'Franky' had developed a habit of using the word 'pip' with annoying frequency. The Little Woman had expressed to all of us her distaste for the term, but I think we all regarded it as just a foible on her part. I know I thought very little of it, in spite of the fact that the Little Woman had told me that if 'Franky' persisted she would tell her something quite plainly.

One night we were foregathered at the Walker Street home. Bert and I were either writing or sketching at the table, Ada sat with Eddie[23] on the couch, while 'Beat' had her usual place (when it was not required by the Little Woman!) in the rocking chair, drawn out of the corner so that her feet might be nearer the fire.

In lounged Franky – she always lounged! – spick, span and immaculate as usual, followed by her sister 'Grit'. There was the usual chorus: 'Hello, Franky! Hello, Grit!' And then the Little Woman's quieter, 'Well, Franky! How *are* you?'

'Oh! I've got the pip', and I know we all smiled because it was just the answer we all expected; all of us, that is, save the Little Woman herself.

Never before had I seen her rush to the attack so speedily. 'Frances', she began, and now her little body was arched forward, her head was a little sideways and protruding and her finger was raised in a gesture of admonition. 'I've told you before that I don't like that expression, and now I tell you that it is an expression that no lady ought to use; it is only used in ignorance and I will not have it used in my house.'

Poor Franky was non-plussed and the rest of us were astonished. 'I'm very sorry Mrs Lawrence, but . . .'

'And so you ought to be', interjected the Little Woman.

'But really, Mrs Lawrence, there's nothing in it. It's only just a sort of a saying. It doesn't really mean anything.'

'Doesn't it. That's all you know', was the snappy rejoinder. 'I told you it is only used in ignorance. Tell me do you know what "pip" is?'

Franky slowly shook her head. The Little Woman sniffed and tossed her head. Then she looked hard into Franky's eyes and said, 'I thought not. Well! "Pip" is a disease that canaries have', and then, after a pause, she slowly added, 'under their tails.'

Then there was a frightfully embarrassed silence, but the situation was saved by 'Beat'. When amused, she had a natural faculty for going off into shrieks of laughter, a habit which she used to attempt to counteract by pushing her handkerchief into her mouth, as quickly as possible, on the first symptoms of an attack. A sort of combined habit, too, was one of throwing out her feet until the whole of her body was just straight and stark.

When she finally grasped what the Little Woman had really said, she was much too late with the handkerchief, but in the struggle to get it to her mouth in time, combined with the spasmodic assumption of the straight line on the part of her body, she lost her balance and her shriek of laughter became a real howl of fear as the rocker went over backwards. By the time we had picked her up, straightened her crumples and recovered from our general hilarity, the constraint had gone, and the 'Pagans' were again at their ease in the beloved headquarters – the Walker Street house.[24]

And the Little Woman's object was achieved; I never heard a 'Pagan' use the expression again,[25] and it certainly was never heard at headquarters.

I have tried to make you see something of the surroundings of Lawrence in his early days, and to give you an idea of the atmosphere in which he developed that attitude towards his parents which has so much puzzled the world. I have attempted to keep down this portion of my writings to those features which have some direct bearing on his attitude towards his parents while at the same time giving as nearly as possible, a true impression of his home.

Personally, I think very little of Lawrence's attitude towards his father; many a man has hated his father with far less cause than Lawrence had. And I have never thoroughly satisfied myself that it was really hatred in Lawrence's case. See how he tried to hold the balance between his father and his mother. That is not hatred. If, finally, he decided that the ultimate responsibility rested with his father, he was probably right; in any case, he most certainly meant *all* fathers, and was not applying the decision particularly to his own father, who was just the medium for his conclusions. His care for the welfare of his father and sisters after the Little Woman's passing shewed no hatred. Lawrence, as I said before, was always intense, went to extremes – in everything – and you will often find him using exceedingly strong terms when much milder ones would, for you or for me, fully have met the case.

It is wrong, definitely wrong I repeat, to assume that the character of D. H. Lawrence was tremendously affected by his attitude towards his father or his mother. It was built up slowly and gradually by a series of incidents or happenings, some of them apparently trivial at the time, but which, on an intense nature such as his, had an enormous cumulative effect.

I have not the least hesitation in saying that the decisive point in the life of D. H. Lawrence was reached when he first commenced to visit at the 'Haggs' – the farm of his early stories (but not the one therein portrayed!) [26] – and that the life of the farm played a bigger and much more essential part in influencing his development than did his father, his mother, or his home.

3

THE EFFECT OF THE FARM

Lawrence would be somewhere about seventeen years of age when he commenced to visit the 'Haggs' farm.[1] The 'Princess' or Jessie as we will now call her, had known Lawrence and his people for some little time previous to that, and had undoubtedly talked of Lawrence and his home in glowing terms to her parents and the rest of the family. Whether she had been able to say much in favour of the other members of Lawrence's family, or of the other members of the group of 'Pagans', I am much inclined to doubt. It should be understood that she had been calling at the Walker Street house occasionally for some little time before he went to the farm, and, by reason of the fact that he was the only member of the 'Pagans' in whom she was very deeply interested, and the fact that she shewed this feeling rather too plainly, she was by no means as popular as she might have been.

Actually, she was transgressing the unwritten law of the 'Pagans' that no member should shew undue preference for any other member. For any group, disintegration always lies that way.

After the very unusually circumscribed limits of the sphere of the early days of D. H. Lawrence, one can scarcely imagine the awakening, one might say the shock of the awakening, to an entirely new realm. At the Haggs the order of his own home was entirely reversed. At the Walker Street house, the little universe revolved around the Little Woman, and through her in a secondary way, round Bert. At the farm the father of the household was the God Almighty of his little world; the Alpha and Omega; the Sun, Moon, Stars, Earth, Heaven, the Seas and all that in them is. As we would say in our modern slang, he was IT. In the little circle of the farm, all things moved to do his will. The mother, the sons and the daughters[2] were, not figuratively, but quite literally, his handmaidens. I well remember how this feature puzzled Lawrence in those early days. He was, at first, a little inclined to despise the other members of the family for what he called their 'bow down and worship' attitude towards the father, whose immense ignorance of all those things that mattered to Lawrence caused him to have an undeservedly poor opinion of the farmer, in those days. Lawrence, too, was a little nettled at the farmer's good-humoured reception of the exposition of his (Lawrence's) abysmal ignorance on all those subjects which he (the farmer) found interesting; Lawrence's lack of knowledge was a continual source of amusement to him, and he would chuckle with glee at every *faux pas*, to Lawrence's great chagrin. Having recovered from his chuckles, however, he would go to a good deal of trouble to correct Lawrence's ideas, and Lawrence always gave him credit for that and hid his chagrin as best he might for the sake of the knowledge to be gathered afterwards.

There was nothing of the tyrant about the father, and he was certainly well beloved by the whole of his household. It was simply that he was head of his house, and strong enough in character to maintain his part by the very force of that character.

At the farm, subjects which in Lawrence's young life had always been strictly taboo were treated as simply coming into the natural order of things. Soon after Lawrence commenced going up there I went to meet him one night on his return journey and found him mightily disturbed. It appears that all the family were gathered round the fire in the low-ceilinged living kitchen when the father had come in from his evening tour round the animals and had informed Alan, the eldest son, that one of the cows (mentioning her by name: Old Somebody! – they had names for all the animals up there!) was ready for the bull, and had instructed Alan to take her on a visit to a neighbouring farmer's prize bull on the following morning.

Poor Lawrence! I can imagine what a tingling of the skin he would experience as his blushes came. He blushed very readily in those days. I know that, if he had a book or paper in his hands – and it would have been very unusual if he hadn't! – he would hide his face in it. But what had amazed him most of

From the photograph of Lawrence and Neville's class at
the Beauvale Boy's School, 1894. Lawrence above
and Neville below

George Henry Neville, *c.* 1908

D. H. Lawrence, *c.* 1908

An Idyll by Maurice Grieffenhagen, 1891

all was that Alan had simply answered 'Righto, father!', the mother had continued with what she was doing, Jessie had carried on her conversation with him, while the rest of the children had taken absolutely no notice at all, even charming little, black-eyed Molly refraining from asking any of her usual questions.

'You've never had much to do with a farm before, have you?' I asked him, knowing the answer well enough, of course. As he shook his head, I continued, 'It's all in the day's work to them you see. They *have* to know all about such things; have to be watching out for them; have to control them. Everything on the farm must be made to produce, or more strictly to reproduce, in order that the farm shall pay; and the farm pays best where production or reproduction is most carefully controlled and made to come in at the right time. And Old Somebody had to go to the bull before she could produce milk. I expect he was sending his cow to a good bull because he wants to keep the calf.'

'How do you mean – before she can give milk? She's giving milk', Lawrence said.

'Yes. But if she doesn't have another calf, she will stop giving milk. What they call "dry off" ', I told him.

He was silent for a while, apparently weighing it over carefully, and then he said, 'But we're getting away from what I was talking about. What I was pointing out was that he came in and spoke about it openly. Why! Even Jessie just took it as a matter of course.'

'Oh, that!' I answered. 'Of course she did. To her, and to all of them, it *was* just a matter of course. I expect they've heard it, or something similar, scores of times. From their earliest days, they see the ordinary processes of Nature on the farm, just as we see them everywhere else throughout the world, but much more intimately and frequently, and they grow up quite naturally to understand such things.'

'Do you mean they let the children see these things!'

'I mean that if the old man had been using his own bull on that cow, I'll bet it would have been a kind of exhibition for the whole family, had they been interested enough to go and look, which I don't suppose they would be; to them the sight is probably too common to be interesting. Further, I'm willing to bet that, if her father had told Jessie that the lads were busy, and asked her to take that cow to the bull, she would have answered just as Alan did, but perhaps less boisterously, and would have done as he had requested and thought no more of it.'

This roused him up. 'I don't believe it', he said vehemently.

'Please yourself!' That was quite a usual invitation of mine when we differed. 'But can you tell me why she shouldn't?'

'Pah! You know that well enough. It's not a job for a woman.'

'Not if a man's available, I agree. But what about the farms run by women? Widows in particular? Look at those we know.'

This poser kept him silent for quite a time and he returned to the subject in quite a different manner. 'But do you really think that it is the usual thing to talk about natural processes in such an open manner?' he asked.

'I don't *think* anything about it: I *know* it is', I told him, 'and you'll find that out for yourself before you have been going up there long. In fact, you've found it out now, only, just because it doesn't suit you to believe it, you won't believe it. I suppose you prefer to think Jessie an angel?'

'Don't be a damned little fool', he snapped, and that finished off the subject, as I knew it would.

Months later, he recalled our conversation, and then went on to detail to me quite a number of incidents that had proved my contention to be right. All matters appertaining to the farm were discussed quite freely before the whole family; whether the old sow should be served this time in view of the fact that it would mean little pigs to be cared for during the winter months; if the gilt had made enough progress in the matter of growth, or whether it might not be better to wait until next time; the selling of the stock ram and the date by which another must be obtained to improve the lamb-crop and bring in lambs at the right time; what kind of a stallion to use on 'Old Bonny' this year; the future of the fillies; the study of the most suitable bull for the cows and the reasons for and against certain types; even the crossing of the sheep-dog; the handling of calves at birth; dealing with foals and lambs; the best methods of helping cows at the time of delivery; all these and more were subjects he had heard discussed from time to time, quite freely openly and without restraint, save on his part, for he had as yet very little knowledge on the subjects and had not quite overcome his innate aversion for the public discussion of such matters.

Leaving the farm, he went on to speak of Nature generally, and I gathered that at this period he had formed the definite conclusion that the chief law of the natural world was: Reproduce, Reproduce in abundance; and you cannot over reproduce.

I am quite confident that it was during this period that Lawrence was entering into the first stage of his lifelong enigma of 'sex'. And he approached it from a most unusual point of view. It must be remembered that he had never 'knocked around' with any crowds of fellows, never played football or cricket, and I think I am correct in saying that at this time he had never indulged in a bathe; one does not go bathing alone, unless it is obligatory, and I had never managed to persuade him to accompany me when I went off for a swim. And there had been no one to give him any real introduction to matters of sex, save what I had done, and what he had gleaned from his mother, in response to questions that really only touched the surface, when it was the depths he wished to plumb.

I was infinitely in advance of him on the subject, in a hazy sort of way, though a year younger, chiefly by reason of my sporting and other activities, which took me where knowledge, even though hazy, must be gleaned; and because of the fact that one evening in my early 'teens', my father had asked me to accompany him on one of his walks and during the progress of that walk he had endeavoured to give me an insight into sexual matters, but unfortunately had laid more stress upon his accompanying warnings than upon the matter itself. Warnings, which are the equivalent to 'orderings off', are apt to prove more of an incentive than a deterrent; it is the old, old story of the mystery and its solution. But Dad did his best, according to the light and knowledge given to him, and it was infinitely better than leaving a lad to discover everything for himself, as so many parents did, and still do.

I duly retailed it all to Lawrence, but I fear it made very little impression. Possibly I laid too much stress on the warnings, and, of course, they were quite useless to him because, since I am quite sure he had never even known temptation, in matters of sex, at that time, any warnings on the subject naturally fell on deaf ears.

It may be asked how I can be so definite in my statement as to Lawrence's condition, sexually, at that time. It is a perfectly natural question; and the answer is just as perfectly simple. The reason I am so positive on this subject is that, when he did finally determine to set out on his sexual quest, Lawrence informed me of his intention of doing so. But more of that anon.

In process of time, Lawrence had forgotten his original shyness at the farm and could discuss subjects of sex appertaining to the farm quite freely. Not with the female element, at first, of course, but with the father and Alan. Some considerable time elapsed before he could bring himself to take any part in such a discussion *en famille*, but gradually he became able to do so without the least embarrassment.

Looking back through the years, I have an idea that he was becoming imbued with a somewhat erroneous point of view from his experiences and observations on the farm. It is certain that from somewhere he developed a personal ideal, vision or state which had for its foundation the utter dominance of the male. If my idea be right and he did develop such an ideal at this time, it is perfectly clear proof that he was very much lacking in the practical application of his observations. In nature, and on the farm, there can be no male dominance in matters of sex relationship, for such relationship is only possible under given conditions; and those conditions are usually particular and personal to the female. The male is the seeker, the competitor. The intrinsic difference lies in the fact that, in the male, there is the ever constant urge, the subconscious readiness, while in the female, the urge appears only at certain definitely fixed periods. That fact should have been impressed upon him at his very introduction to the subject, when the father announced that 'Old Somebody' was ready for the bull. But the introduction was so sudden and unexpected that it is possible that his shocked senses did not at that time grasp the significance. In any case it certainly should have followed automatically later.

I am supported in this idea by a very significant fact, of which I thought nothing at the time, but which I now give a very important place in the story of Lawrence's development.

We had done a considerable amount of sketching and painting together, chiefly confining ourselves to flowers, fruit, still life, small landscapes and, in my own case, seascapes, with ships or boats, of which I was rather fond, while Lawrence did not care much for that side of it, always preferring a Dutch scene, with a windmill, to the sweetest yacht afloat.[3] Neither of us had undertaken figures, and for my part I had no wish to do so.

Calling at the house one Saturday evening, I was surprised to find him at home.

'Thought you were going up to the farm', I greeted him.

'I was; but I got started on this confounded thing this afternoon and stuck at it till it wasn't worth while bothering. And I can't get it right. Look at it', and he held it at arm's length, with that queer, self-conscious titter that he always used when decrying his own work. 'Isn't it awful?' he asked. It was; and I very candidly told him so, and more.

The significance of the incident lies in the subject; it was an attempt to make a copy of Maurice Greiffenhagen's wonderful picture, *An Idyll*.[4] You know the thing well enough. Lawrence had the woody background and the poppy-spangled foreground with wonderful effect, the colours brighter and possibly better contrasted even than Greiffenhagen's own. Incidentally, Lawrence was always like that; he saw colours always about three shades brighter than any of the rest of us. We had quite a number of arguments on the subject, and on several occasions, I remember asking him to lend me his glasses for a moment so that I might test as to whether it was their use which intensified colours to him.[5] The glasses made no difference to me, and he would sometimes get very much annoyed when I told him that he always insisted on putting Irish greens into English scenery. It is a fact that my representation of a given scene had a habit of appearing quite drab by contrast with his, though it might appear passably well when seen alone.

To go back to the *Idyll* copy; there is no doubt that his figures were awful. 'They're not human figures – they're scarecrows', I told him. His titter rang out into a laugh, through which he tried to say, 'I know', while his mother added, 'You're right, George! They *are* scarecrows'.

He held it out again at arm's length, laughing heartily, laughing as he often did, until the tears rolled from his eyes, and then, with a movement swift as light, the paper was torn through the middle, crumpled into a ball, and hurled into the fireplace. 'Come on. Let's go for a walk', he invited, and away we went for a ramble.

But Lawrence stuck to his Greiffenhagen. I could not tell you how many attempts he made. I know we were all very tired of it, and I know that at long last I lost my patience with him. It was on a Friday evening, bath night for Lawrence, and the Little Woman and Ada had gone to market as usual, leaving Bert in sole possession, to get his bath. I went down to the house about the usual time and found him fresh from his bath, hair all rumpled, feet bare, just trousers, shirt and coat on, working away on his everlasting *Idyll*. I looked at it and snatched it up. 'If you are going to draw figures, why the devil don't you try to draw MEN sometimes, and not always such damn scarecrows?' I asked him.

He laughed merrily and asked, 'What's the matter, Teufel?'

'Matter? I should think it is "What's the matter?" when you are foreverlasting putting such awful caricatures of men onto paper and then tearing them up. Where are you getting your ideas of men from? Look at his back. Why! It's worse than your Dad's – more scraggy. What have you been doing? Taking your Dad's as a copy? or trying to get a squint at your own in a mirror?'

I never asked him for confirmation, but I have always been quite certain that I had guessed the truth – he had been trying to get ideas by attempting to see his own back in a mirror, and it will readily be understood that only a distorted appearance could possibly be obtained that way.

Be that as it may, since I had started on the job, I meant to carry on. I went quickly to the back door, locked it, came back into the room and commenced to unfasten my shoes.

'What on earth are you going to do?' he asked.

'Shew you what a man's back is really like – if he *is* anything of a man', I told him.

He sat watching me, and he was dreadfully puzzled at what

was to him an entirely new view point so far as I was concerned. But as my bare limbs began to come into view his
eyes began to shine and they positively glittered when at last I
stood naked before him and said, 'There now! For God's sake
have a good look at a man with a decent shape while you have
the chance. Here! See some *muscles* – not lengths of rope.
Watch 'em rise and fall, see 'em ripple if you like!' I was
expanding and contracting, flexing and putting in a certain
amount of showmanship I had picked up at gymnasium and in
training, and then I concluded, 'And now have a look what a
fellow's back ought to look like when he was grabbing a girl in
that fashion.' I seized a chair and hugged it, turning my back
to him so as to give him as nearly as possible a view similar to
that of the male in the picture.

I maintained the pose for a time and there was a deep
silence in the room. As Lawrence spoke no word, I turned to
see what he was doing, half-expecting to hear his querulous
tones upbraiding me because I had moved just as he was
getting his impression lines on to paper. Instead of that he was
leaning forward in his chair, his elbows resting on the table,
the cup of his hands supporting his face, upon which was an
expression of perfectly rapt adoration. That is a very strong
expression to use, but it is the only one that will express to you
what I wish to convey. Lawrence adored strength and beauty
with a kind of envious adoration; and in the same way he
adored practically all personal characteristics he did not
himself possess.

I laughed into his eyes and asked, 'Now what's the matter?'

He broke his pose very slowly, still watching me half-
wonderingly just as you have seen a baby following the
movements of its mother with wide, speculative eyes, and
finally gasped out – and 'gasped' is to be interpreted quite
literally – 'I had no idea. Good gracious! You're positively a
pocket Hercules.'

'Rubbish! There are plenty of fellows at the gym who can
shew a better set of muscles than I can', I denied, but he could
not comprehend it. He did not wish to discuss the matter.
What he wished to do was to slip back into his rapt pose again,
and just drink his fill, his very first fill, of the sight of that
beauty of form which he could always see in the human body,

but which so far as I know he was never able to express on paper or canvas. He never had a chance to achieve it in himself.

But that would have been to allow my own defeat, and I would have none of it.

'Wake up, me lad', I adjured him. 'I have not stuck myself here to imitate a statue, even of a "pocket Hercules", just to be gazed at. I've done it so that you can take a quick sketch or two so that you may be able to get a bit nearer to a MAN with that damned *Idyll* of yours. And your mother and Ada will be back before long, probably bringing some of the others with them as usual.'

Unwillingly, grudgingly he took up his pencil and I know now that he only did so because he was quite well aware that had he refused to do so, I should have dressed again, without the least hesitation. He sketched, but not in his usual fiery manner – often with quite unbelievable speed – but slowly, apparently carefully, but really unheedingly, for his mind was not on his sketching; he was just using that as an excuse for more gazing. At last I told him so, and commenced to dress, much to his disgust and chagrin. He said I had spoilt the best of his sketches. I told him it served him right, and that he had been long enough over it to have done 'forty-eleven' sketches, and that in my opinion, he had not been attempting to sketch honestly.

It is useless to speculate now as to how far that discussion might have led us. It was cut off abruptly, for there was the sound of footsteps, a rattling of the back door and Ada's voice calling.

'Just one minute. Sorry!' we called and scrambled through our dressing.

'Whatever have you been doing all this time?' asked Ada, peering at us, eyes blinking in the gas-glare.

'Arguing, instead of clearing up', was Lawrence's laconic reply. 'It's all right. It'll only take a minute. Give me a hand with the bath, George.'

While I had been scrambling into my clothes, Lawrence had been completing his dressing and rushing the sketches out of sight. Thus I did not see them. I asked him many times to let me see them, but he always decried them and said they were too bad to shew anybody. Several times afterwards he asked me to pose for him again, but I never consented; and usually I annoyed him by telling him that what he ought to do was to run over to Nottingham Castle or the School of Art and sit and gaze at the statues because in that case it would not matter in the least how long he gazed.

One definite result was achieved however; his *Idyll* studies improved considerably, and he allowed at least a few of them to remain in existence.[6]

About this time, he began to turn his attention to the female form. It was in connection with these sketches that Lawrence made his only actual physical assault on me. He began on faces, and we 'chivvied' him because his women always had incipient moustaches. He shewed a decided preference for the flaming, Spanish type, and we teased him by telling him that his sketches always shewed what woman he had in his mind. It was the one to whom he was later on engaged.[7] She was with us at Centre, with Lawrence at college, and quite often used to run over to see the Lawrences or the family at the Haggs.

A little later, but generally when he was alone, he proceeded to busts, back views of the nude, etc., and then to whole figures.[8] One night when I called he had apparently just completed a sketch and was sitting at the table holding the sketch out in front of him, examining it critically.

'What's that?' I asked.

He giggled. 'Gracious! Don't try to tell me it's so bad that you can't even tell what it is', he said.

'I don't mean that. I mean, what's it intended to be – a real woman or just a statue?' I explained.

It was a sketch of a woman, standing gazing, naked, to meet the naked future, her carelessness of the future expressed in the ease of her attitude, the hands lightly clasped behind her uptilted head and calm carelessness in her eyes. A good sketch!

'It's a living, breathing woman, full of life, youth, hope and devil-may-care', he told me.

'Oh! Is it really? Then why not make her real instead of being spoilt by your own artificiality, as it is?' I asked.

He turned sharply and glared at me. 'What the devil do you mean by that?' he asked, almost viciously.

'Lend me your pencil and I'll shew you', I offered.

Without speaking, he handed the pencil to me, and swiftly I dashed in the shadings under the armpits and on the body.

Lawrence's frown was meanwhile growing deeper.

'What on earth is that for?' he asked.

'That', I told him, 'is just the difference between your living, breathing woman, full of life and the statue I mentioned. That's HAIR!'

His speed took me entirely by surprise. He fairly leapt out of his chair, and was pummelling at me as he gasped, 'You dirty little devil. It's not true. It's *not* true, I tell you.'[9] But he finished his effort breathless, for with the half-instinctive movement of the boxer I had gone in, buried my face in his chest, wound my arms around him, and then, instead of making it a clinch, I had put an old wrestling grip on him and began to compress his ribs. He still continued his pummellings, but they were less than the puny tappings of an infant.

'Stop that, and don't be a fool', I demanded.

'It isn't true; and you *are* a dirty little devil', he retorted jerkily, but he ceased his pummelling and struggling.

'Have it your own road, but don't try striking me again when I loose you, or I shall not play with you next time.'

I released him and he sank wearily into his chair and rested his head on his hands.

'What's the matter with you? Why did you do such a fool's trick as that?' I demanded of him.

'Beast. It isn't true', was all the answer I got.

'Don't be such a baby. Why should I tell you what is not the truth? 'Course it's true; and more than ever true in the case of a woman like that one – a woman who's got Nature enough in her to grow a little moustache.'

He looked at me, half-wonderingly, but not the least convinced. 'How do you know?' he asked.

'I *do* know; never mind how. I'm only telling you for your own good. I don't get anything for telling you – except a silly attempt to punch my head. Serve you right if I'd given you a good licking.'

He got up and began to gather his materials together. 'I'm sorry, Teufel, old man', he said. 'It was stupid of me, I know. But I don't believe you.'

'That's all right. There's no harm done. Please yourself',
I answered him, and dropping the subject entirely, we decided
that a long walk would best blow the effects of the 'breeze' away.

The farm, then, as the centre of the world of Nature for
Lawrence at that time, was having its all-important effect upon
his development. He was realising that in the end the great
fundamental pivot of living progress, development, increase,
and the basis of any kind of communal existence is sexual
relationship. I doubt if it ever occurred to him in those years
that it is really the control of sexual relationship which he
ought to have substituted. Be that as it may, it is certain that
he now entirely deserted his purely descriptive stories[10] and
began to dabble in sex questions. He dabbled; and disgusted
himself because he felt that he was attempting to write on a
subject of which he had no real knowledge.

He complained to me on the point, one evening when we
were walking over the fields towards Coneygrey Farm.[11] We
had been discussing a book we had both been reading. I am
not quite certain on the point, but I believe it was *Esther
Waters*.[12] He (Lawrence) wanted to write on matters of sex;
but he wanted to go deeper, so very much deeper than anybody had ever gone so far. Generally they were only 'surface
skimmers', or coarse and even filthy. Coarse and filthy in so
far as they merely wrote for the filthy-minded, without having
any serious lessons to impart. He visualised sexual relationship
as being the most beautifully wonderful thing on earth. Quite
obviously he had idealised it. I was able to visualise Lawrence
as going to his first woman as one going to a sacrament. From
his point of view 'sex' was the only subject worth writing about,
but he had a feeling that he really knew nothing at all about it;
one could not really *know* anything about something one had
never experienced.

'Why bother about it then?' I asked him.

'Why bother about it?' he repeated. 'Haven't we agreed
that it is the most important thing in our existence? Don't I
tell you that I have made up my mind that it is the only thing
worth writing about?'

'Even so – why bother about it at this stage? You're only
young yet. You don't *have* to write. You do very little with what

you *do* write, except hand them over to Jess. There is still plenty
to learn. And the personal experience will come in time.'

'And I am to wait till it comes, you suggest?'

'Why not? It can be time well spent; and in any case, you
can do no good by seeking. You will do a lot more harm than
good.'

'But why shouldn't I? Lots of other people do.'

'And most monkeys imitate. You are not supposed to be a
monkey.'

'That's only evading the issue. Other fellows can have a
woman. Why can't I?'

'There isn't any reason on earth, save the conventions, so
far as I know; when you want one.'

'But I've told you I do', and Lawrence positively flared this
statement at me. And now I blazed back at him in return:
'It's a damned lie; you haven't done anything of the sort.
What you have done is to insult yourself and every woman on
earth. If you wanted a woman, because, being a healthy, red-
blooded sort of a chap, you had begun to feel a real urge
towards women, I would say nothing at all about it. It would
be natural; but even then I should probably say that it's best
to wait until she comes without seeking. But what you told me
was that you wanted a woman merely as an experience; so that
you might be able to write better from your chosen point of
view. That wouldn't assist you to write; you would be relating
an experience from an imitation instead of the real thing. And
you would certainly be insulting your chosen woman and
desecrating your own manhood.'

He broke into that confounded high-pitched titter of his as
he threw an arm round my shoulder and said, 'Behold! Teufel,
the Preacher!'

'Preacher be damned!' I denied hotly. 'You know I wouldn't
preach; and I wouldn't throw any bricks either. But I *do* tell
you that your attitude is right-down wicked, not from any
religious point of view but just from a straight man-to-man
aspect.'

'Well! Let's leave it alone and think about it', he suggested,
to which I replied, 'You can do the thinking. It is not at all
necessary for me to do any on that point. I've said what I
had to say. The rest is up to you.'

From that time I feared for Lawrence. For a real red-blooded man 'on the prowl' I should have had less fears; he would eventually anchor himself, somewhere, sooner or later, by reason of his very necessity. But for a Lawrence, with his very expressive nose and tell-tale lower lip and chin, sexual adventures, merely for the sake of experience, could only spell disaster.

It was a very long time before he reverted to the subject again. He never again discussed the probability; but in a queer and roundabout way, he announced the accomplished fact. We were both at home for holidays as usual and taking one of our customary rambles in Derbyshire. Lawrence had just returned from a short stay with friends in a neighbouring county.

At midday we sat, eating a sandwich, in Alderwaslea Park, right on the hills to the west of Ambergate, a beautiful spot overlooking the still more beautiful valley of the Derwent, when Lawrence said quite suddenly, 'I had an awkward experience while I was away, George.'

'What do you mean, awkward?' I asked him, my mouth full.

'Well! Embarrassing perhaps I ought to say.'

'Go on, then! Tell me if you're going to do.'

'The first night I was there, we went out into the woods, and somebody suggested that we should try to get an owl's nest. We climbed a lot of old trees, and kept on until it was almost dark, but we didn't get a nest.'

'Nothing very embarrassing about that so far as I can see', I commented as he paused.

'There isn't; it came next morning. I was wearing this flannel suit, and when I came down to breakfast, L– (mentioning the name of the elder daughter of the household)[13] said to me, '"Oh, Bert! What a mess your coat is in. It is covered all over with green off those trees. Take it off and let me brush it for you."'

'She fetched a brush. I took off my coat and handed it to her and she stepped through the french window and onto the lawn and began brushing vigorously. I remained talking to the others, when, all at once I saw the whole of the contents of the inside pockets go pitching out onto the lawn. You know how awkward young women are at handling men's clothes. I didn't know what to do. There was L–, bending over as low down as she could get, to obtain as good a look as possible. Stiff and still she stood there, feet apart, her left hand extended holding the coat, the brush stretched away from her in the right hand. I stood there suddenly frozen and didn't know what to do.'

'But why all the fuss? Was there anything that really mattered?' I asked him.

'I should just think there was. Besides a letter or two and a few papers of no importance, there was somewhere about a half dozen rubber protectors, just in their transparent flimsy slips; and they were all scattered about on the lawn in front of her', was his astonishing answer.

I sat up and stared at him, scarcely believing. 'And could they see them from the house?' I asked.

'I don't think they could see what they were, though of course they could all see what had happened', he replied.

'Well! You must be a blithering idiot', I told him. 'Fancy carrying the things loose in your pocket like that! They might come out at any time. You might pull one out with a letter or paper at the most awkward or damning time. But in any case, what were *you* doing with them?' I demanded.

'You have to play safe, you know', he answered.

'Do you? So that's it! Still imitation – and running somebody else's soul into sin along with your own.'

'What do you mean?' he questioned, sharply.

'I mean just the same as I did last time we discussed the subject, only those things tell me that you have taken the rottenest way of getting your experience. Instead of getting away and buying yourself a woman, my guess is that you're trading on somebody's regard for you, when there is not the least regard on your side. Now tell me what you did.'

'I rushed out through the window, gathered all the things together, and rammed them back into the pockets anyhow.'

'And what did L– say?'

'She never said a word; but she knew. I know she knew. And she was frightfully embarrassed. You know how she blushes? Almost like a beetroot. It was really lucky in a sense that she had upset them all, because her people put her unease down to embarrassment because of her clumsiness.'

'Well! All I've got to say is that you were a damned sight

luckier than you deserved to be. If the old man had seen them he would have broken your neck; and you know it. And now shut up about it.'

When I reached the really rude, it was quite well understood that any persistence might make me very rude indeed. Abruptly then, the subject was dropped, and we never again referred to the incident. And this is the only time I have ever mentioned it. I do so now to prove the point previously raised, as I then promised to do.

Thus, then, I fixed approximately, for all of us, the time of Lawrence's entry into his sex-adventures. I give you, from his own lips, his reason for undertaking such entry. I assure you that there was no accident about it; it was, quite definitely, deliberately decided upon; and I acquaint you of the fact that Lawrence made his decision in spite of the warning of the man he loved, the man of whose sincere love Lawrence was well aware, and whose love was one of his greatest delights.

I am stressing this point because I am convinced that it should be regarded as the pivotal point of his life, the pivotal point of his teachings, and the point which decided the course of all the rest of his life. I am making no attempt here to discuss Laurentian philosophy. My object is to give you a number of facts which will enable you to reach your own decision, or should at any rate, assist you in doing so.

But I *do* want to make it abundantly clear that, if you believe Lawrence to have been crucified into sex, it was purely self-crucifixion.[14] Except for the fact that I know he refused to be persuaded, refused to see any danger, I should have preferred to call it voluntary martyrdom or self-immolation, having something analogous to the case of the scientist who studies, say, leprosy among lepers for the ultimate good of the human race. But be that as it may, it is probable that the findings of Lawrence, rightly understood and properly taught and applied, may eventually prove of infinitely greater service to mankind than is the individual work of any of those science-martyrs.

4

STAGES ON THE JOURNEY

In this section, I propose to introduce a few of the outstanding events in the early life of D. H. Lawrence, either with the idea of giving you an opportunity of tracing their possible or probable effects upon his development, or of shewing you features which he himself has either belittled or even entirely neglected or ignored.

Up to the time of his commencing to work, Lawrence had a most beautiful conception of women. He saw them all through the glass of his mother. Not *as* his mother of course; there was none like her. Women, to the young Lawrence, were as ministering angels,[1] because all those he knew served in that capacity.

True, as we went about the district, we saw other types, heard other types, and had other types thrust upon us in many ways. But Lawrence always had an excuse for them. Who knew what awful troubles had been forced upon them! How could they be true to their womanhood in the environment in which they were compelled to exist? They were not responsible; it was the fault of those ultimately responsible for such conditions and environment. These and any number of other excuses he would always find; but the women were not at fault.

It was always a pleasure to see him greet a woman he knew, and particularly so if the woman happened to be someone he really liked. And this applies equally be she the wife or daughter of one of the higher officials of the collieries or a member of the family of just an ordinary collier. The question of class made not the least difference to Lawrence. There was always the same scrupulous uncovering of the head, accompanied by his queer little jerky half-bow, a bright smile and a clear and well accented 'Hello, Mrs So-and-so! And how are *you* today?'

But no stopping to gossip. Just a cheery word or two, an excuse that he must be getting along, usually ending up with a promise to 'tell Mother I've seen you', and along he went, leaving a gladdened heart behind him.

'Aye! He *is* a nice lad, isn't he?' I have heard it scores and scores of times; heard it just as written there, but even more often in the big broad accent of the Nottinghamshire and Derbyshire border.

His ideals received a very rude shock, however, after he had been working at Nottingham for a little time. He was acting as foreign correspondent to a firm of surgical appliance makers, and though his duties brought him into very little direct contact with the considerable number of women and girls employed there, he naturally had to see and hear quite a lot of them. He used to tell me of the things they had said to him. They were perfect beasts; they were little devils, he said. They were filthier than anybody he had ever conceived; and they *would* persist in thrusting their filth upon him. Why should they persist in tormenting him?

I asked him if he had been shewing his resentment and he admitted that, though he had never spoken about it, he had most certainly done his best to 'kill them with looks'. He *could* do that, too; I could well imagine those 'looks'.

'That will only make 'em worse', I told him. 'The only thing to do is to take no notice, or better still, just grin and say nothing. If you can't grin, just ignore them completely and they'll soon get tired of such an unprofitable sport.'

'Grin at them! Take no notice! I could strangle them', he said savagely, and he looked as though he was ready to commence the task at once, and I knew my advice was quite useless.

The culminating point came a little time before his attack of pneumonia, and in my own mind I have always felt that the incident was directly responsible for the attack.

Lawrence usually took his lunch with him. He would eat this in the office, take a short walk out, usually somewhere towards the Castle or the Park, and then return to the office to spend the remainder of his hour with a book. He had to pass through a kind of warehouse to reach the office during the lunch-hour, and on the day referred to, as he passed through this building, a number of girls rushed upon him, seized him, threw him down, and attempted to commit upon him the Great Indignity.

I think those girls got the shock of their lives. They had the initial advantage of surprise, but I am certain that they would be utterly astonished when Lawrence got fairly started. Though only slim, he was tall and wiry, with very long arms and fingers, and in a rage he could be a very demon. I gathered that he had set about those girls with teeth, hoof and claw; that he had torn their dresses, bitten their fingers and arms, scratched their faces, kicked them, and finally driven them off, afraid of the fury they had aroused. And the outraged Lawrence, standing stiff and stark, rumpled and dishevelled in the centre of the field of battle, had tongue-lashed his tormentors in language viler than their own, until, in further alarm, they had fled, even from the sound of his voice.

For the remaining days of his service there, they tormented him no more. But the evil was done. A few days later he shewed signs of a violent cold. His mother dosed and cossetted him as she always did on the least sign. Without avail; he had to go to bed. The doctor diagnosed pneumonia in its very worst form. There was very great danger and it was doubtful if he could pull through; certainly not without the greatest possible care.

Lawrence himself has told you something of this illness, and much capital has been made out of his method of expressing himself.[2] In my own opinion he deliberately mixed up a portion of an experience he underwent in the course of a later attack with his description of this one.[3] His works are full of such transposition. But even taking his literal rendering, what happened? His dream-woman came to him; and naturally she was his mother. He had never known any other.

And now for what really happened during that illness. Practically from the time the doctor was called in, until after the crisis was passed and there was hope of recovery, Lawrence was unconscious and delirious the whole time. And his delirium took the form of turning against all the members of his own family; so much so that they left him alone as much as they dared to do, guarding him by peeps around that screen of which I have already spoken. He accused his mother of filling his pillow full of marbles – poor Little Woman! – and he had the peculiar fancy that his hands were growing bigger and bigger and would eventually fill the whole room and stifle him.

We soon discovered that I had a wonderfully soothing influence on him in this state, and I spent every evening and my half days sitting by his bedside relieving his mother and sisters the while and doing what I could to help him in his fight. And I did help him, and them. Together we saved him for his work in the world; but he was now much more badly equipped for such a task than he had been even before the illness.

Following on the decision that he should not attempt to continue his work in Nottingham, he commenced duties as a student–teacher at the Albert Street Schools, Eastwood, attached to the Congregational Church, and this was the period in which the group to which the name the 'Pagans' was afterwards given, began to be formed. From this association sprang Lawrence's earlier, important works, though there were other short and descriptive works dealing with the period prior to this. Many people consider his books of the 'Pagan' period the finest of his works. Whether these people be right or not there is no doubt in my mind that they represent Lawrence more truly than any others. They shew Lawrence before he entered the maze, and he was the true Lawrence.

There is another idol to shatter next. 'Ern' – the much beloved 'Ern' – had written home telling his mother of his engagement, sending a beautiful photograph of the lady, who, by the way, looked almost too lovely to be real – too good to be true you know! – and arranging to bring her home for the summer holidays, subject to his mother's consent and invitation. I have already mentioned how speedily we were put to preparations.

What the lady's christian name was, I don't think I ever knew. She was always referred to as 'Gypsy' – Miss D – I was naturally schooling myself to call her.[4]

I have never forgotten the first time I saw her. There was a demonstration of some kind in Eastwood Hall Park at which the whole Lawrence family attended.[5] I was not able to get there until late in the afternoon, but Bert was waiting for me inside the gate, and we went in search of the rest of the party.

'What's she like? Is she as good as her photograph?' I asked.

'Better: a thousand times better. She's just lovely – altogether!' was his enthusiastic reply.

Soon we found the group. I should like to describe 'Gypsy' to you, but it would be quite irrelevant. There was 'Ern', looking better than I had ever seen him look – the result of taking a course of physical culture, I learned later – and he hailed, 'Hello! Here's old Teufel!' and came over to grab me and make me known to 'Gypsy'. Upon my rolling out my carefully prepared 'Miss D–', she quite completed my captivation by telling me that I must call her 'Gypsy' like all the rest, because she intended to follow Ern's example and call me 'Teufel'. A wonderful week followed. Rambles, games, talks and music. We had a gorgeous picnic at Robin Hood's Well, with games on the ancient trysting-green. Then we roamed back through the woods as the purple shadows closed around, 'Teufel' acting as guide because he knew every 'ride' and by-path of the woods. There was a tour round Moorgreen Colliery, including the underground workings, visits, a trip to Nottingham and a thousand and one things organised to make their holiday an enjoyable one.

Later in the year 'Ern' took advantage of a cheap week-end trip to Nottingham to come up to see his people. I went round on the Sunday morning and in the sunshine on the yard he was telling me of his progress at the gym and that he was now including a course of boxing. We had a topping little spar, designed to shew me the progress he was making, until the Little Woman spotted what we were doing. She called 'Time and finish' I assure you, and read us a very severe lecture on the subject of the proper behaviour for Sundays. At night, we all attended the Congregational Church.

Early the next morning, he went back. Afterwards, we found out that he only just caught the London train as it was moving off and that the compartment into which he had hastily jumped was completely saturated with rain which had driven in through the open windows.

I think it was on the Thursday morning following that a letter arrived giving the particulars, and saying that he was very seriously ill. A telegram followed, and I know it was on the Thursday afternoon that Mrs Lawrence set out for London.

Poor Little Woman! 'Ern' never knew the effort she had made to help him. All that was left for her to do when at long last she reached his side was to arrange for him to come back home – dead![6]

In the depth of all our sorrow, we thought and talked of 'Gypsy', of how she had loved 'Ern', and what a frightful blow it would be to her. And then she wrote to Mrs Lawrence! A charming letter it was; but it shattered our 'Gypsy' idol into the remotest fragments, and was bitter as gall to the Little Woman. After the sweetest expressions of sympathy, sad reference to her own sorrow and love to all of us, she ended up her letter like this: 'Some day, of course, I may again think of marrying; but no man will ever possess my heart as "Ern" possessed it.'

'Woman the hunter!' That was Bert's expression. He had an early phase in that belief.

'The Cat! If she isn't thinking of another man, almost before my boy is cold!' Thus the Little Woman, and she sat down and sobbed. Nay, I think we all sobbed in unison; and quite as much for our shattered 'Gypsy' as for our remembrance of the death of 'Ern'. But I think we have none of us forgotten her, and we have long since lost our youthful intolerance.

Now I shall tell you of an incident that has always appeared to me as remarkable, of the only time that Lawrence ever beat me in a physical contest. At this period I should be in really first class physical condition. I was playing football regularly, boxing, wrestling and doing systematic training. I had won prizes on the racing track, and yet on the only occasion on which we ever had anything approaching a contest for speed, Lawrence, untrained, and without any preparation whatever, managed to beat me. And it was on an errand of mercy.

Quite near to our house lived a lady named Mrs Gibson, that same Mrs Gibson who had years before kept a little tuck-shop in Lynn Croft, and had always been so good to all of us in the matter of our ha'p'orths of sweets. Big, stout, homely and kindly she was – bonnie Mrs Gibson! At the period to which I am referring Mrs Gibson's daughter, Annie, was seriously ill, in Nottingham General Hospital, and the old lady had been visiting her daughter each cheap-ticket day – Wednesdays and Saturdays.

On this particular Wednesday morning we had attended Centre at Ilkeston, left the train at Shipley Gate in a blinding snow-storm, and set out across Newthorpe Common for home. We were Ada, Franky, Jessie, Lawrence and myself.

As we started across the fields from the top of the Common to Brookhills, we saw a big, stout figure just starting across from the allotments on the other side.

'Good Lord! There's poor old Mrs Gibson going to see her daughter, even on a day like this', said I.

'What a shame! Somebody ought to have prevented her from going. It isn't fit you know', said Lawrence, while the girls endorsed the remarks.

Suddenly, Ada clutched my arm, but I had already seen what she had seen. 'Oh, Neville! She's fallen', she fairly screamed, but Lawrence and I were already on the way.

Through the snow we raced, spurring on even more as we saw the poor lady attempt to struggle to regain her feet, and fail. And though I put in all I knew, Lawrence was slightly in front when we reached her. But the distance had been well over two hundred yards, and poor Lawrence wasn't much good when we got there.

I did what I could until he was somewhat recovered, and then, with great difficulty, we got one of her arms round each of our shoulders, our own arms locked behind her in support, and very slowly and with infinite effort, we managed to get her home.

She lived for several years after the accident, but she never walked again. My mother often told me of the kindly references she made to Lawrence and me during those long years of torture.[7]

It would be in the summer following the incident that I first persuaded Lawrence to go bathing; the same summer that he worked so much in the hayfields, and the same time[8] that, when experimenting by spending the night under a haystack instead of going home to our beds like sensible people, we had our little adventure with 'Jimmie' – the tramp. It was during this summer, too, that the family at the Haggs had a vegetarian fit. I think that they found out that George Bernard Shaw was a vegetarian. Jessie had impressed Shaw upon them very strongly. Oh yes! They got over it; and I liked the Haggs much better then.

Some attempt has been made by some of Lawrence's detractors to make capital out of his recital of that first bathing incident.[9] Largely it is Lawrence's own fault, because he only told half the story. He appeared always to decry, or entirely omit, the better side of himself, and to regard sentimentality as weakness. We *know* the latter to be so in any case.

Lawrence says: 'We bathed . . . He knew how I admired the noble, white fruitfulness of his form. As I watched him, he stood in white relief against the mass of green. He polished his arm, holding it out straight and solid; he rubbed his hair into curls, while I watched the deep muscles of his shoulders, and the bands stand out in his neck as he held it firm . . .'

'He saw I had forgotten to continue my rubbing, and, laughing he took hold of me and began to rub me briskly, as if I were a child, or rather, a woman he loved and did not fear. I left myself quite limply in his hands, and, to get a better grip of me, he put his arm round me and pressed me against him, and the sweetness of the touch of our naked bodies against each other was superb. It satisfied in some measure, the vague, indecipherable yearning of my soul, and it was the same with him. When he had rubbed me all warm, he let me go, and we looked at each other with eyes of still laughter, and our love was perfect for a moment, more perfect than any love I have known since, either for man or woman.'[10]

Very beautiful! But how much more beautiful would it have been had he told the whole story!

We bathed in Moorgreen Reservoir, undressing on the bank, beyond the remains of the landing stage, and quite near to the commencements of the 'Gullets' – the more heavily wooded portion. Lawrence, of course, had no idea of swimming. I felt like a swim. After giving him a few hints, I told him to paddle about a bit, while I swam across to see what the swans were doing on the opposite shore.

The reservoir is a bit treacherous because there is a strong central flow from the brook that comes in at the northern end, from Felley Mill, and this flow is always very cold, the water coming down from the surrounding hills too rapidly to get affected before it reaches the reservoir.

Lawrence tried to dissuade me from swimming across, but I wanted to go. I assured him that I should be alright and started off, signalling to him constantly that I was doing well. But after the stream, I made the rest of the journey on my back, and very slowly. He watched me as I got out on the farther side and stood alternately flexing and rubbing my leg. Then he shouted across the water to know what was the matter. I told him that I had got a touch of cramp in the 'brook course'. He shouted that I must not attempt to swim back, but must walk round. I replied that I would be alright and turned away to see what I could of the nesting place of the swans.

But his voice came continually over the water, and rose to a very paroxysm of fear when I returned to the edge of the water to commence the return journey. I shouted and asked him if he wanted to attract the attention of all the keepers and told him there was no need to worry as the leg was now alright. But it was of no use; he continued his yelling until he saw that it was of no use for I was well upon my way.

He stood like a statue at the water's edge as I swam towards him and spoke no word until, after entering the 'brook course' again, I turned on my back and began to proceed by means of an overhead paddle with both arms.

'What's the matter?' he fairly screamed.

'Bit o' cramp – in both legs this time!' I told him, adding, 'but I'm alright; I'll do it alright', after which I heard no more of him.

Slowly and very painfully I made the shore, dragged myself out on to the shingle and began to massage the knotted muscles of my legs, meanwhile looking around for Lawrence.

He had collapsed into a heap near the water's edge, his chin resting on his knees, his hands tight-clasped around his legs, while his eyes were starkly fixed on a point somewhere out there near that 'brook course'. I looked at him again. His eyes were fixed and staring, his face drawn with anguish, and his body was blue with cold – the frightful chill of fear!

Quite suddenly I knew what that wonderfully fertile brain of Lawrence's was seeing out there in the lake: in those few horrible moments I had died to him out there. In his imagination he had seen me swallowed by the hungry waters. He had lost me; and was frozen with the horror of it. I struggled to my feet and called sharply to him, but he paid no heed, and I seized him somewhat roughly, calling to him that I was quite alright.

Slowly, oh, so slowly, his eyes came round to mine and with the dawn of recognition his head sank to my breast and his arm went round my neck as I clasped him close to me.

And now you can proceed from where Lawrence starts: 'He took hold of me . . .' for it is all true, all true; and it is further true that, while holding and rubbing, I crooned and mumbled to him in the seemingly half-senile way I have many, many times since then crooned and mumbled to my babies when they have been in trouble, which crooning and mumbling, though seemingly half-senile it may be, seems to bring the greatest possible comfort to their souls; that, and the physical contact together, is the surest way I have discovered of making them realise that there is no further need for fear; the most certain method of assuring the fluttering heart that it is enfolded in the arms of Love. Lawrence and I realised it then as never before; and I am thankful that I was given the inestimable privilege of being the cause of so beautiful an expression of it.

One thing that has always stood out very prominently in my memory, in connection with the Lawrence household, is the fact that nearly all their troubles seemed to come in order to interfere with the due celebration of the festival of Christmas. And in telling you of this, I hope to goodness that no religious dipsomaniac will write to some paper pointing out the poetic justice of it, because there wasn't any; poetic justices don't fall on whole families and penalise a lot of other people for the fault (if any) of one of their number. Moreover Lawrence had not 'sinned' (sic) in those days.[11]

There was the long and wearisome illness and convalescence of Bert, the death of 'Ern', and then twice, when all seemed clear ahead and we were making all our plans and preparations, Arthur Lawrence met with serious accidents at the colliery[12] and the Christmas spirit was impossible. Lawrence grew very bitter on the subject, and even the Little Woman's faith sometimes appeared a little frayed. She could turn that sharp little tongue of hers to cynicism on occasion, and I remember well, at the time of Arthur Lawrence's second accident, when we were all girding at the fates for once more spoiling all our plans, I – fatuously, as I would probably agree now, but with the best of intentions, though that, being part of the pavement of the road to Hell, is no excuse! – must needs attempt to introduce a ray of cheery light by quoting the line, 'Man never is but always to be blest.'[13]

Quite fiercely the Little Woman turned upon me. 'And what do you think that means, George Neville?'

'What does it mean?' I stammered. 'Well! It means that though we're in trouble today, the troubles will pass and blessings will follow. It is the same as the silver lining to the dark clouds and a sort of a promise of a good time coming; something to look forward to.'

'Oh! Is it. Well! It isn't then!' and there was that awful little sniff and toss of the head to tell me what an idiot I must be.

'What does it mean then? Tell me that', I demanded.

'It means that you are being deceived just like so many, many thousands more besides. It is the delusive promise that keeps people going, because they deceive themselves. They read it like you do, in the method they prefer. But it really expresses one of the greatest truths of life: Man never is blessed but he always buoys himself up with the false hope that he's going to be. And he generally finds it out too late, and then starts hoping his blessings will come in the future life.'

'Nothing of the kind', I protested, and tried to argue, but nobody would take up the cudgels. The Little Woman, having said her say, had, as usual, finished. But I know that, when I raised the subject later, with Bert, he said we ought to disregard it because his mother was somewhat overwrought. She was. Never since that day have I mentioned the incident, but I have always kept a very keen recollection of it.

In a series of memoirs such as this, one ought, so far as possible, to illustrate every phase of the character of the subject. Thus I now turn, with something approaching regret, to an incident that rather alarmed me at the time and which I have never been able thoroughly to account for since. Lawrence had gone up to the farm and I had promised to go up there later, but early enough to arrive at the farm in time for a little music before we started back. I was to go the 'privileged' way, and they would probably meet me at the entrance to the wood.

As I was stepping out along the mineral line from Moorgreen Colliery towards the level crossing, I saw a tall, slim figure coming towards me round the bend.

'Looks like Bert!' I said to myself, and sure enough it was Lawrence, coming along at a great pace, head thrust forward and eyes on the ground in front of him. We were quite close before he raised his eyes and saw me, and I saw at once that something serious must have happened.

'What's up? Been falling out with somebody?' I asked using the local vernacular.

'I have', he snapped.

'Going home now?' was my next question.

'Don't care whether I do or not', he answered.

'Right, then! Let's go up Dick's Lane and have a look what's in the old quarry', I proposed, and started back, Lawrence silently agreeing by falling in step alongside.

I said no more on the subject of the quarrel, because, to tell the truth, I thought he had quarrelled with Jessie, and candidly, I was just a little 'fed up' with this apparently endless and meaningless 'farm' business. Only a little time previously, on calling at the house, his mother had said to me, 'He's up there again, George.'

'But he said he didn't think he would be going there this evening', I said.

'Well! He's gone, and I was to tell you so. I often wish he wouldn't. You know George, he may be fond of her, but he'll never marry her; he's not that sort.'

I confess I had been quite startled. 'Marry her! Of course he won't', I said. 'Whoever expected that he would?' It is absolutely true that the idea of marriage, as between those two, had never occurred to me.

'Of course not! And why of course not? Then what on earth does he want to go hanging round the girl all the time for? It isn't fair to her.'

'But he doesn't go up there to see Jessie only. He spends quite a lot of time studying the life on the farm now. I should think he is more with Alan than with Jessie in these days', I defended.

99

'Pshaw!' That was her only comment; and that, and the hated little sniff, completely silenced me. I had set out for the farm.

Lawrence and I walked along in silence for quite a distance; until we were nearly out of the quarry in fact, and then, as was quite usual, he surprised me by shewing that he knew of what I had been thinking.

'I've not been quarrelling with anybody at the farm, and so you need not be thinking I have', he said.

'Then with whom?' I asked, and added, 'and if with no-one at the farm, how is it that you're back so soon?'

'I got fed-up at the farm. Jessie had to go out somewhere, and all the rest were busy, some in one place and some in another, and there was nothing very interesting, so I came away. It was on the way back I had the quarrel.'

'But with whom?' I asked him again.

'I'm not certain', he replied, and then he fairly startled me by adding, 'but I believe it was Philip Barber.'[14]

'Philip Barber! Well of all the damn fools! Whatever were you doing to quarrel with Philip Barber?'

Lawrence went white to the lips and fairly turned to rend me. 'Aye! There you go! Damn fool! and you don't even know what the quarrel was about. You just heard the name Philip Barber, and because he is virtually the owner of all these collieries, most of this land, and, in effect, the owner of the lives and consciences of most of the folk in this neighbourhood, no matter what he did to me, I must sit down and grin and abide by it. If I defend myself I'm a "damn fool". How long have you been ready to kow-tow to Philip Barber, or anybody else?'

'Kow-tow? Me?' I asked him. 'What the devil are you talking about? Shut up, if you can't talk sense. I'll kow-tow neither to Philip Barber nor anybody else; and what's more, I don't want you to do so. And I don't believe he wants it either; I never met a decent chap yet who had any use for it. But what I can't understand even, is where you came in contact with him, and how anything approaching a quarrel could develop.'

'It wasn't really a quarrel. I did most of the quarrelling part of it. I told him just what I thought of him', he half explained.

'But why?'

'Because he was so damned snobbish, so damned rude and officious', he answered viciously.

'Tell me first, just what happened?' I pleaded.

'I was coming across the fields and had got as far as the one by the Reservoir side, when a man in a shooting suit, with a gun under his armpit, came up to me and said, "Well! Who are you? and where do you think you are going?"' Here Lawrence struck an attitude and adopted an accent in imitation of the way the question had been addressed to him. Except for the seriousness of the matter, it would have been quite humorous. 'I told him to mind his own damned business, and that he could go to hell', he concluded.

'And then what?'

'Oh! I don't know! He said something else and I got really angry and cursed him thoroughly. He told me he was a J.P. and could give me in charge for using bad language. I told him I knew nothing about him being a J.P., but that I was quite certain that he was a B.F., and that he had my full permission to use those letters as well as his J.P. if he liked, and I walked away and left him. Damned snob!'

I sat and stared at him in amazement.

'Go on! Call me a silly blighter; I know you're going to do', he said.

'I'm glad to know that you recognise that you deserve it', I told him. 'But first of all, tell me, had you no idea, at the time, who the man was?'

'Not the slightest. His manner was not nice; it irritated me . . .'

'And you were already irritated', I interjected.

'I suppose I was. But if you could have heard him, you would have been just as bad as I was.'

'Never in the world!' I denied vigorously. 'It seems so utterly senseless to me. You must have known you were on Mr Barber's land; and you were quite within your rights in being there. You were doing no wrong. On the other hand, he, seeing a stranger on his land, would consider himself perfectly justified in asking for an explanation.'

'And he would have got it, had he asked for it in a decent manner', Lawrence conceded.

'Suppose you had actually known, at the time, that it was Philip Barber; what would you have done?' I asked.

'I don't know, George. Honestly, I don't know. As a matter of fact I have asked myself the same question several times since, and I cannot satisfy myself. Probably I should have done just the same', he confessed.

'Then for God's sake never let me hear you say another word about your father and his talking. Nothing he has ever said would be likely to do him so much harm as what you have done today may do. Do you think he knew who you were?' I asked.

'Don't see how he could', was Lawrence's gloomy reply.

'Then let's hope he will not take the trouble to enquire', I remarked. 'And let's be getting along. We've been here quite a long time.'

No one ever heard any more of the incident, so far as I am aware, and if Mr Barber put down his trespasser as some poor devil escaped from Radcliffe or Mickleover, and thus dismissed it from his mind, I have to confess that there was plenty of excuse for such reasoning.[15]

It was a very long time before Lawrence used the field path again. Always he made some excuse; but I feel certain that he realised that he had stupidly put himself into a false position quite needlessly.

Just a short chapter about those holidays of ours. We had not a lot of money for holidays, or for anything else for the matter of that either, in those days, and it was of vital importance that they should be run as cheaply as possible. The arrangements were always in the hands of Lawrence, as the natural leader of the 'Pagans', and he was always indefatigable in his efforts to make them a huge success, which, I have no hesitation in saying, they always were. The usual method was to engage a cottage or small house, with attendance, for the period – usually a fortnight – and take the Little Woman, and sometimes the mother of 'Beat' also, to do the catering and generally to be in charge. When we went to the Isle of Wight, the Little Woman and Beat's mother and father too accompanied us, making the party up to nine: Lawrence and myself with Ada, Beat, Franky and Grit. They were the most delightful holidays imaginable and as the cost usually worked out at very little over a pound per week in addition to fares and personal expenses, they were very satisfactory from that point of view.

In those holidays, for weeks at a time, I lived every minute with Lawrence, heard his every word and saw his every action. I slept by his side at night, and before he slept, heard almost (if not quite) every thought that had occurred to him during the day;[16] thoughts he had not cared to discuss while all the rest were present. And never once, in all those holidays, did I ever see or hear Lawrence do or say a thing he would not just as readily have said or done had his mother or my mother been present, with the possible exception of some of those discussions we had before one or other of us turned over and said, 'Well! It's getting late. Here's one for sleep. Goodnight old man!'

The last of those holidays was in 1911,[17] when we made Prestatyn our headquarters and managed to cover the whole coast of North Wales, together with Snowdonia and a considerable portion of the hinterland. We scarcely saw a cloud for the whole of the time we were there, with the exception of the night we arrived, which was wet, and we had a holiday never to be forgotten.

Louie, the girl to whom Lawrence was engaged, formed one of the party of that year, but there was no breaking up of the holiday rule on that account; we were one party and there was no splitting up.

There was a very amusing episode at the conclusion of this holiday. On the last day of our stay, there was a regatta at Rhyl which Lawrence and I were very anxious to see. After discussing the question with the others, it was agreed that, since some members of the party wished to be back home in good time, Lawrence and I, with Ada and Louie, would stay to see the regatta, the others returning at the time previously arranged. We who remained were to catch a later special, due to arrive in Derby in time to connect with the last 'local' for home.

Unfortunately, the special was late and we arrived in Derby to find the 'local' had long since departed.

Taxi-drivers asked an exorbitant figure to drive us out so far at such a late hour and we therefore decided to stay the night in Derby. Having found a nice quiet little hotel near the Post Office, we had some supper, the girls quickly retired, and after staying for a final drink and a short chat with the host, we followed their example. The next thing we heard was 'Boots' rapping to call us in time to catch our train. Then we heard him knock on the next door, which was the room occupied by the girls, and we heard their answer.

As Lawrence and I lay chatting for a few moments, as we usually did on waking, we heard the girls open their bedroom door, and immediately Louie's joyous shriek of laughter rang out, to be followed very quickly by almost as good a burst from Ada. There was a little rustling in the corridor, and a quick closing of their door, but we could still hear their renewed laughter, practically the whole of the time they were dressing. When we came down to breakfast we enquired the reason for their early mirth, but they quite refused to satisfy our curiosity.

A few days later Lawrence said to me, 'You remember the girls being so amused at something on Sunday morning?'

'Of course! Do you know what it was all about?' I asked.

'Yes! Ada told me. When they opened their bedroom door to get their hot water, they found that "Boots" had put your shoes and Louie's outside their door, and mine and Ada's outside ours.'

'Good Lord! Silly ass! Enough to make 'em laugh!' I said, laughing heartily, Lawrence joining just as heartily, and the matter closed at that without further comment or discussion.

I remember seeing a statement that Lawrence had deep-rooted sympathy with Germany. In so far as he had sympathy with the children of learning, science and progress the world over, that was true, but only in that sense. Lawrence was British to the core, as I think the following story will probably well illustrate.

While we were down in the Isle of Wight,[18] we made a very strong point of visiting Osborne House. After the Durbar Room, with its wonderful, eastern magnificence, we proceeded with the rest of the tour. After a while Lawrence said to me, 'What do you think of it, George?'

'Not a lot', I told him.

'But what I mean is, what strikes you most about it all?' he insisted.

'German! Germany to the fore everywhere', was my verdict.

'That's it!' he said. 'That's the way it strikes me. At heart old Queen Victoria must have been absolutely and thoroughly German.'

'Looks like it; but, of course, it's just possible the Prince Consort may have had something to do with it you know', I suggested.

Lawrence waxed merry over this. 'Pshaw!' he mocked. 'I don't believe you mean a word of it. What evidence have you that she ever allowed the poor beggar to have a say in her surroundings?'

'None at all. Quite the opposite if anything; but it struck me there was just a possibility, and the sight of this makes one wish to make all possible allowances. All the same, it seems to me that, if they don't want to give people a wrong or undesirable impression, this place ought either to be shut up or have a different crowd of artistic exhibits brought in. I know where I'd rather be', I added.

'Where?'

'In the Tate Gallery.'

'I know. You'd like to be stuck on the opposite side of the gallery from Norham Castle, wondering how those Turner "washes" become, in proper focus, so wonderful a thing of beauty', he opined.

'Just that; or waiting till the light is just right, while you were prowling round after Clausen "blue-greens"', I laughed, and with that we hurried through the remainder of what was to be seen, and came away with a disappointing and unpleasant impression.[19]

Incidentally, Lawrence was not in a particularly good humour that morning. It was Regatta Week, and because of that we had deferred Cowes for the second week of our stay, thus killing two birds with one stone – Osborne and the Regatta. During the previous week we had observed posters at the stations announcing that during Regatta Week ordinary fares would be suspended and special rates would obtain; an additional inducement to us to defer our visit to Cowes, see Osborne and enjoy the Grand Fleet illuminations at night.

The day arranged for our visit arrived. We were going in full strength; the whole nine of us turning out. I was acting as cashier and walked up to the wicket.

'Nine return specials, Cowes, please', I requested.

'Nine: twenty-two and sixpence, please', said the clerk.

'How much?' I asked, thinking he had made an error.

'Half-a-crown each! Twenty-two and sixpence for nine of you', he said, very decidedly.

'But isn't ordinary fare only somewhere about eighteen-pence return?' I asked him.[20]

'That's nothing to do with it. There have been plenty of bills about telling you that there would be special rates for Regatta Week. It's half-a-crown return', he insisted.

Meanwhile, noticing that there was a hitch, Lawrence had joined me at the wicket. I explained the situation to him, meanwhile pushing forward the required amount.

'What? Don't you give it the grasping, greedy devil. Special rates! and then nearly double the ordinary fare! I never heard of anything so abominable. Don't you pay it, George. We won't go. I'm damned if I'll feed such a lot of rapacious swindlers.' He turned in fury on the poor booking-clerk, 'Ar'n't you ashamed of yourself? You certainly ought to be . . .' and he was proceeding to tell him some more, but I had noticed that there was quite a crowd round and that some of them were getting impatient, so I took hold of Lawrence's arm and gently forced him from the wicket. 'What's the good of kicking up a scene? And it's no good rowing that poor devil. I agree with you that it's an awful swindle, which certainly ought not to be allowed; but the booking-clerk can't help it anyway. He's only obeying orders', I pointed out, then turning to the clerk, I snapped, 'Punch those tickets and let's get off', and I'm sure he was very pleased to obey.

But Lawrence's expressions of anger and disgust then were as nothing compared with the anathema he called down upon the heads of the management of the little railway in the Isle of Wight during the course of the return journey.

There was a tremendous crowd for the firework and illumination display, and I suggested that it would be a good idea to sacrifice a few minutes of the display, get to the station in good time, and thus make certain of securing as comfortable seats as possible. So it was agreed – and acted upon. Having fixed ourselves up very comfortably, we proceeded to congratulate ourselves on our forethought as the crowd without commenced their frantic search for seats.

At last we got away and arrived at Newport, when, to our great surprise, the porters came along the train shouting, 'All change! All change!'

'Doesn't this train go to Shanklin?' I asked one of them.

'Not yet! All change!' he shouted.

We got out onto the cheerless platform, our little bunch, and many, many more. Soon there was a shout and a whistle, and the train backed quickly out of the station.

'What's the idea of this?' I asked a porter as soon as I found one.

'There's a whole crowd of people left behind at Cowes', he told me, 'and the train's had to be sent back to fetch 'em.'

'And have we to wait here while it does so?' I asked.

'That's it; unless you like to walk', he replied laconically as he walked away.

Lawrence got fairly wound up. He called down anathema on the heads of the people responsible in such a wonderful variety of forms that he started us all laughing; all of us, and quite a number of others who had gathered round to listen. And he waxed more amusing still when the economical souls in charge actually lowered the station lights. He raved, and we laughed, until, finally, he too saw the funny side of it and let loose his high-pitched giggle, saying, 'Aren't we a set of fools?' at which we all laughed the more.

He did not forget the incident, however, and for the remainder of our stay, he would not agree to any suggested excursions which included railway travelling, and the only other time we patronised that little railway was on our return journey homewards; and as our tourist tickets included that portion of the journey, we were no further penalised and neither did we further help to swell the profits.

The incident in itself though somewhat amusing is of course only trifling, but it serves to illustrate the manner in which Lawrence reacted to even the slightest suggestion of injustice or exploitation.

5

LAWRENCE – 'THE SON OF WOMAN'

Shortly after the appearance of my letter on 'The Early Days of Lawrence' in the *London Mercury*,[1] I received an advance notice of the forthcoming publication of the book *Son of Woman* by John Middleton Murry,[2] the book also having 'The Story of D. H. Lawrence' for a subtitle, and, of course, the subtitle was obviously intended as the main attraction.

In the notice I read that 'no conceivable biography of the late D. H. Lawrence could be as intimate as the tragic and wonderful history which Mr Middleton Murry has elicited by a patient study of his books. As Keats said of Shakespeare, so with even more truth it may be said of Lawrence, "His life was an allegory and his works are the comment on it" . . .'

'In this spirit of homage to a supremely gifted, greatly tortured human soul, Mr Murry's book has been written. Mr Murry knew Lawrence as intimately as any man living, perhaps more intimately; but he has learned in the course of writing this book, that his personal knowledge is irrelevant. Lawrence belonged to that infinitely rare order of men which cannot be known "after the flesh".'

Soon after that I saw an advertisement-extract from the first chapter of *Son of Woman*: 'In this book I shall reveal nothing which Lawrence himself did not reveal. There is nothing else to be revealed. There is, and can be, but one true life of Lawrence; and it is contained in his works. But in order to read the life therein contained, we must be endowed with imaginative sympathy, and have learned the truth of Keats' words that "A man's life of any worth is a continual allegory, and very few eyes can see the mystery of his life" . . . Lawrence himself proclaimed . . . "The proper function of the critic is to save the tale from the artist who created it." '

'To save the truth of Lawrence from "the shallow people who take everything literally"; to save it equally from the veil of self-deception in which Lawrence himself was compelled to hide it is the purpose of this book. What Lawrence was, not what he pretended to be, is of importance to mankind.'[3]

It will be readily understood that to me, who, so far as I was aware, had been admitted more closely by Lawrence to the bond of friendship than anyone else had even approached, this was all tremendously astounding, interesting and intriguing. I ordered a copy of the book, feeling that, at long last, we might be getting something of the real Lawrence, and I was aware of the tremendous and widespread interest in the subject, by reason of the number of letters on the subject which had reached me as a result of my letter to the *London Mercury*.[4]

Before the arrival of my copy of *Son of Woman*, I read a review of the book, by Max Plowman, which raised a good deal of alarm in my mind. Here is an extract:

The conflict, never merely a personal one, has been between protagonists of diametrically opposed attitudes to life, Lawrence proclaiming, with ever louder insistence, the virtues of the physical senses, Murry enunciating, in terms of modern experience, the necessity for spiritual regeneration. While Murry was writing a *Life of Jesus*, Lawrence was writing *The Plumed Serpent* . . .

Certain it is that 'the shallow people' will turn and rend Mr Murry with every imaginable epithet of abuse . . .

. . . Lawrence's tragedy lay in his mother's love. Once that fact is fully recognised the tragic story Murry tells is seen as inevitable . . .

Son of Woman is a truly great book. Its insight is marvellous; the sustained power of criticism, the ease with which heterogeneous material is formed into an organic whole, the plain honesty and finality of the statement, put it into the category of big tasks accomplished once for all. It is as brave a book as ever was written. It is a necessary book, tonic to the shifting airs and graces of Janus-headed criticism. It is desperately convincing. And yet . . . and yet . . .

True; but not the whole truth. Full of imaginative forgiving; yet not whole in its forgiveness. Why? . . .

. . . So that, actually, this is a study of the death, and not the life, of Lawrence. Another and an additional effort of the imagination is necessary to complete the picture, or rather to take the two sides of the picture and refashion it into a perfect whole. Such a work would contain all this book, and *something more.*

I am left wondering what spiritual energy could supply that 'something more', and in my imagination I conceive a quality of dynamic forgiveness which Murry does not reach. His forgiveness is perfect upon one plane, but static upon another. Were it dynamic it would give back to broken life the livingness which sustains it. It is a grace which the whole world asks to see revealed.[5]

Next, I noticed Mr Robert Lynd's comments on the book.

It is a very curious book, for in some pages we seem to be reading an almost ecstatic tribute to Lawrence, and in other pages to be reading an exposure.

There followed an extract from one of those 'ecstatic tributes' Mr Lynd refers to, and then he adds,

The astonishing thing is that nothing that is said in the later pages of the book helps to substantiate this claim. We are made to realise that, like Nietzsche, Lawrence was a great sufferer; but the egoism of much of his suffering is also made apparent . . .

Extracted from the book he gives, from Murry's address to the soul of the departed Lawrence,

'You were a man of destiny, driven to sacrifice yourself in order that men might know themselves, and the eternal laws they must obey, the laws which, even in denying them, still they obey . . . That which you sought to strangle, you are doomed to bring to birth, in men.' To a few readers the paradox will seem as clear as noonday; to the rest of us it will seem so obscure as to have no more than a fraction of meaning. We can understand praise of Lawrence as a writer of imaginative genius, but a Lawrence canonised in this misty, paradoxical fashion makes us wonder whether the sense of proportion has died in our own time.[6]

And an extract from another review:

It will be pretty certainly done again, but no book is likely to do it in just the same way that this one does – to be as complete and yet as ruthless in its sympathy. It needed, we may feel, a peculiarly assured sympathy as well as a decidedly firm conviction to write an apologia so unsparing in analysis as this . . .

. . . The language of judgement that he has had to use still lets us see that the spirit of his book is a different feeling. We need only to remind ourselves again that its concentration leaves aside the joy in life and expression which Lawrence must have also had, since it shaped itself continually into vitality and beauty.[7]

From *The Bookman*:

I was disappointed in Middleton Murry's Life of D. H. Lawrence. It is not a book, I think, which will add to Mr Murry's reputation. That it is sincere no one will doubt . . . we feel that he has called evidence which should have been inadmissable. Nor is it enough to say that Lawrence in his writings gave us the evidence. It is the construction that Mr Murry puts on some of it that made me – and will I imagine make many people – resentful . . .[8]

Other extracts:

'I implore those who read it never to forget that Lawrence belongs to the order of men who cannot be judged, but only loved . . .' Having said that, however, Mr Murry goes on to judge him. His entire book from beginning to end is a judgement and condemnation of Lawrence . . . Does not this suggest that Mr Murry had an uneasy conscience about Lawrence? Did he have to write to get something off his mind? Mr Murry seeks to use the tale to destroy the artist . . . Had it been written in hatred it would not have mattered. But to write such things in love is something that cannot be borne. I cannot help feeling that in years to come Mr Murry will wish that he had never allowed it to see the light; for it does not damage Lawrence so much as himself . . . It should not have been written.[9]

Finally, just after I had received my copy of the book, I saw in *Everyman* a letter from Lawrence's sister Ada, complaining bitterly of the misunderstanding of the true character of Lawrence likely to be caused by the widespread dissemination of this book.[10]

Owing to the fact that I had been spending a few days away from home, I had not commenced my study of the book, but when I saw this letter from Ada, I confess to being seriously alarmed. You will recollect that I have known Ada since she was a tiny little girl, with her beautiful hair in long, corkscrew ringlets, which threw out, very strongly, those chestnut highlights. (I have teased her scores of times about the long 'rags' round which those ringlets were wound at night and held in captivity during the hours of sleep.) Ada, with her ready blushes, and that deep dimple high on her cheek; with her constant cheerfulness; with her innate shyness, but everlasting will to play the game and be as good as anybody else; with her beautiful constancy in love, for, from quite a girl there was no other man for Ada but her Eddie. Lawrence has indicated that he thought Ada and I would fall in love.[11] We never needed to do that; but we had been almost as brother and sister too long ever to regard each other in any different way. Therefore I knew well that only something of tremendous importance could make her write that letter, and in consequence, it was with some amount of fear and trembling that I approached Mr John Middleton Murry's book.

You will have gathered that I am not, and never have been, anything approaching a 'Lawrence fanatic'. Always have I admired him, even in our quarrellings; but I have never failed to recognise his weaknesses. That I am not afraid to speak the truth, as I know it, where Lawrence is concerned, I hope I have already displayed, and, in spite of all those serious criticisms of, and comments on the book, I think I may justly claim that I brought a perfectly open mind to bear upon the book. But I have the enormous advantage of being able to bring my known facts into play, while Murry, for all his vaunted intimacy with Lawrence, appears to have had very few actual facts to work upon, and therefore, taking it for granted that Lawrence wrote always autobiographically, he has sought to establish his deductions as facts; to make a matter of guesswork of what ought either to be one of the most serious and exact contributions to contemporary literature, or to be left severely alone. Mr Murry himself confesses:

All the knowledge of him contained in this book was completely hidden from me . . . all through his life. When he died, something broke in my heart: but all I knew was that I had loved him, and that, at times at least, he had loved me. I knew that our relation had been a miserable and tragic failure, and I felt that the failure had been inevitable, necessary as fate. And that was all I knew when Lawrence died. Only since his death have I been driven by some inward compulsion to try to understand him.[12]

And that was written by a man, who, in the same book, says that, after a careful study of Laurentian philosophy, he was prepared, under given conditions, to jettison all his earlier beliefs and follow the living Lawrence. And it was this man's attempt to understand Lawrence, now that Lawrence was no longer able to correct any 'misunderstandings', that I had set out to study and search for my own beloved Lawrence.

I wish I could adequately describe my emotions as I forged onwards through the book, but I feel it to be quite impossible. 'What Lawrence was, not what he pretended to be, is of importance to mankind', Murry had said in his first chapter, and I had found myself most heartily in agreement, and sought forward, in joyous anticipation of finding just my own Lawrence; sought most diligently, but found him not. He is not there to be found. You cannot find him, search as you will, and therefore, since 'What Lawrence was . . .' is the important point, the book entirely fails in its object and has no significance, save that it represents the construction that John Middleton Murry puts into his own imaginary life of Lawrence. Every other man and woman is at liberty to reach his own conclusions in an identical manner, to select passages to suit his or her own construction, aye, and to use the very passages selected by Middleton Murry; but I am convinced that no other student of the works of Lawrence would give us such a needlessly nauseating and iconoclastic work as a pretence of the result of his findings, either as the result of the use of 'imaginative sympathy' or sympathy of any other kind. I reached the definite conclusion, long before I had finished the book, that Murry's sympathy was purely imaginary, though he could certainly justifiably lay claim to his 'imaginative' capacities in other directions.

But the real Lawrence is omitted, entirely omitted. Most solemnly do I make that declaration: I, who knew more of Lawrence than any man who ever lived. Not even Alan, the elder brother of Jessie, ever came within reach of my nearness to Lawrence, the nearness of an almost perfect love, which Middleton Murry recognises:

> But for the original of George and Edgar he must have felt something for which the best name is the simple one of love. In *Sons and Lovers* this friendship is but lightly touched; in *The White Peacock* the tremor of authenticity is not to be mistaken. Cyril's love for George has more of reality in it than any of the love affairs in the book . . .[13]

Murry is perfectly right; but Murry was apparently quite unaware that both of those original male lovers of Lawrence, and Lawrence-loved Males, are still alive, holding briefs on behalf of their dearly-loved memories of Lawrence; and neither, apparently, did he pause to consider the possibility of that being the case, nor of the possibility that there might be a desire, on their part, to take up arms to defend those memories from threatened besmirchings.

I sought my Lawrence of our sunny boyhood but found him not: missed my comrade of the woodland ways; sympathised with all the birds and flowers, for their friend had been most ruthlessly torn from them. The life and soul of all our parties, Lawrence the entrepreneur, was glimpsed but once, and then only for Murry's own purposes. Our 'charade' Lawrence, 'got up' in some ridiculous costume – the main constituents of which would probably be a tablecloth, a towel and an anti-macassar! – had become a sheerly impossible figure. Lawrence of our happy 'sing-songs', can never have existed. The youth I helped to re-cover the old-home sofa, while his mother and sisters shredded up stockings and all sorts of unnecessary-to-mention ladies' underwear, to make additional 'stuffing' – with Lawrence making all sorts of comical comments on their labours! – is hopelessly transmigrated. My knowledge-seeking chum had become the possessor of all the vilest knowledge of Earth, and Hell, and in between. My perfect knight has now out-Belialed Beelzebub. He, with whom I had so often sat in chapel, with his mother alongside, and his sister up there in the choir in front, has now become more blasphemous than Satan ever was. He, who, shyly and diffidently, decried his own merits on all occasions, has so increased in personal arrogance that he lightly assumes superiority to Christ, and dares dictate even to the Son of Mary. Lawrence, to whom the slightest hint of pain or cruelty to the very meanest of creatures upon earth was suffering, is made to deliberately torture civilised humanity. My frail and delicate slip of humanity, which I could so easily have broken in pieces, is portrayed as an ogre of the most fearsome conception, and the one whom I had always regarded as being the most over-flowing with the milk of love and loving-kindness – when one knew how to get behind the reserve of his shyness! – is turned into the enemy of mankind; the Devil's prototype in fact.

And the veracity of the portrayal is evidenced, in all cases, by carefully chosen extracts from the works of D. H. Lawrence. Slowly, relentlessly, the artist covers his canvas, turning into his own particular species of mud each fragment of Lawrence-pigment which he squeezes from the multitudinous and well-nigh inexhaustible tubes. It cannot be gold, even silver is too vivid, sand would be too resistant. It is, and must be, all mud; anything else is impossible.

Grotesque, leering, horrible, the finished work is thrust upon you, with the assurance that, in thus portraying him, his one-time friend, the artist is not presuming to judge Lawrence, and we are adjured, in a paragraph that, to me, savours much of irreverence, and almost of blasphemy, that we must not attempt the impossible:

> Only he can judge Lawrence who has loved as he loved. There is no such man living: of that I am convinced. I believe that once there was such a man, who loved as Lawrence loved and did not fear as Lawrence feared, or, if he did, he conquered his fear. He alone could judge Lawrence; and it was he who spoke the word 'Judge not, that ye be not judged.'[14]

'I believe . . .' says Middleton Murry, and 'He alone could judge Lawrence.' I could wish to hear him say, 'I believe that he will judge Lawrence; and I believe that, at that great bar, must stand John Middleton Murry, too.'

It is an easy matter to criticise destructively, especially when dealing with the works of an author of the Lawrence type; particularly so if one assumes that, in all cases, he must be taken literally – that in all cases, literally, he is writing auto-biographically. But it is an easier matter to be mistaken where one is dealing with so clever an artificer as Lawrence. There are cases, where Middleton Murry has not even discovered the all-too-plain reversal of sex. There are other places, passed over, or brushed aside lightly by Murry, which would have caused him to attract your attention, with a real Dervish howl, to listen to his, 'There! What did I tell you?' had he only known the underlying truth. Thank God! he did not know.

Let me not detract from the cleverness of the book. It *is* clever, cleverly written, cleverly conceived, diabolically clever, too clever. And it contains a considerable measure of truth; truth often twisted and distorted, one might almost say, with the utmost deliberation, as though to suit a definite purpose. But it is only a portion of the truth, as Max Plowman felt instinctively, and well serves to illustrate that old saying that, 'half a truth is often worse than a lie'.

It *is* clever. It is so coldly logical, so convincing and so touched with the personal element that one is inclined to say, 'This man must know the truth, and he writes of the truth as he knows it.' And therein lies its gross unfairness to Lawrence.

You will have noticed that, with the exception of one small instance, I have totally disregarded the comparisons of the life of Lawrence with the life of Christ. To me, they are so much balderdash. I know a lot of people who would call them 'tripe', without intentionally insulting a probably much-appreciated and useful variation in their dietary. I am not, never have been, and so far as I know, have never pretended to be, any angel myself – I always treat supposed or rumoured men-angels with the very gravest suspicion! – and I never heard of Lawrence feeling any little knobbly excrescences where wings were sprouting, but I do like fair play; and this book left me with the impression that it was not 'cricket'.

What shall we say when we come to needless, vicious and perverted innuendo? 'Let us be clear, as Lawrence himself tried to be clear in the *Fantasia*. Lawrence was not, so far as we can tell, sexually precocious; he was spiritually precocious.'[15] Read it again. 'So far as we can tell.' Though Lawrence himself has specifically pointed out that it was not so, well! we know Lawrence was a bit of a liar when it suited his purpose, and it still may have been so. If it were so, it might explain points which are left somewhat hazy. Middleton Murry knows, now, definitely, that it was not so; I have put the evidence on record.

But why bring in such an innuendo? What lies behind such a deliberate attempt to suggest a morally perverted youngster? That question: 'What lies behind?' has come to me many times while studying this book.

In dealing with the 'Autobiographical Sketch' to which I have already made reference, Murry says:

> By this time, we know more about Lawrence than Lawrence knew. He is a disintegrated man; he has fled from, and denied, the spirit which makes vital human contact possible for such a man as him – 'the love that seeketh not its own'. And now, as ever, it is not he that is at fault. The something that is wrong is wrong with the world, not him.[16]

Lawrence actually wrote:

> Something is wrong, either with me or with the world, or with both of us. I have gone far and met many people, of all sorts and all conditions, and many whom I have genuinely liked and esteemed.
>
> People, *personally*, have nearly always been friendly. Of critics we will not speak, they are different fauna from people. And I have *wanted* to feel truly friendly with some, at least, of my fellow-men.
>
> Yet I have never quite succeeded. Whether I get on *in* the world is a question; but I certainly don't get on very well *with* the world. And whether I am a worldly success or not I really don't know. But I feel, somehow, not much of a human success.[17]

That is the disintegrated man. That is the man, who, by this time, has developed a hatred towards all mankind, and that is the man of whom Murry says, 'And now, as ever, it is not he that is at fault. The something that is wrong is wrong with the world, not him.' You may use your own judgement upon such palpably, deliberately designed extractions. To what end? What lies behind?

Let us turn to what he has to tell us of the earlier days of his quondam friend. He is quoting from *Lady Chatterley's Lover*, and he says:

Not an imaginary Lady Crystabel is the figure of woman now –
'all vanity, screech and defilement' – but the very women
whom Lawrence knew. The sexual youth of Mellors is
Lawrence's own youth: there is barely an effort at disguise.[18]

And then the quotation:

The first girl I had, I began with when I was sixteen. She was
a schoolmaster's daughter over at Ollerton, pretty, beautiful
really. I was supposed to be a clever sort of young fellow
from Sheffield Grammar School, with a bit of French and
German, very much up aloft. She was the romantic sort that
hated commonness. She egged me on to poetry and reading:
in a way, she made a man of me. I read and I thought like a
house on fire, for her. And I was a clerk in Butterley Offices,
a thin, white-faced fellow fuming with all the things I read.
And about *everything* I talked to her: but everything. We
talked ourselves into Persepolis and Timbuctoo. We were the
most literary-cultured people in ten counties. I held forth with
rapture to her, positively with rapture. I simply went up in
smoke. And she adored me. The serpent in the grass was sex.
She somehow didn't have any; at least, not where it is supposed
to be. I got thinner and crazier. Then I said we'd got to be
lovers. I talked her into it, as usual. So she let me. I was
excited, and she never wanted it. She just didn't want it. She
adored me, she loved me to talk to her and kiss her: in that way
she had a passion for me. But the other she just didn't want.
And there are lots of women like her. And it was just the other
that I *did* want. So there we split. I was cruel and left her.
Then I took on with another girl, a teacher, who had made a
scandal by carrying on with a married man and driving him
nearly out of his mind. She was a soft, white-skinned, soft sort
of a woman, older than me, and played the fiddle. And she
was a demon. She loved everything about love, except the sex.
Clinging, caressing, creeping into you in every way: but if you
forced her to the sex itself, she just ground her teeth and sent
out hate. I forced her to it, and she could simply numb me
with hate because of it. So I was balked again. I loathed all
that. I wanted a woman who wanted me, and wanted *it*.[19]

Then John Middleton Murry comments:

That is the most veracious account of Lawrence's early sex
life that he has given. The two women are Miriam and Helen;
and the true origin of *The Trespasser* is plain to see. Lawrence

is now nearing the end of his mortal career, and he comes nearer to acknowledging the truth about his relation with Miriam than ever before. We had guessed it long ago: it is no revelation now. His entry into sexual life was self-imposed, willed, mental: everything that Lawrence condemned. It was a violation of himself, and of Miriam . . . It was a willed and personal purpose they had to fulfil.[20]

Wonderful! 'We had guessed it long ago: it is no revelation now.' This is on page 363. But 'long ago', back on page 57 in fact, whcn, for the *second* time he uses part of the extended quotation he achieves at the *third* attempt, he has a very striking comment to make, after this quotation from Lawrence, 'I was cruel and left her (Miriam) . . . So I was balked again.' This is his comment: 'The account is not to be trusted, any more than the account of Bertha Coutts which follows,' while back on page 34, commenting on the same thing from *Sons and Lovers*, he (Murry) says:

Miriam did not want him, but she wanted to give him *it*, because he wanted it. The indulgence of their 'passion' was disastrous, because it was not passion at all. On both sides it was deliberate, and not passionate. Miriam's charity was passionate, but she had no sexual desire for Paul; Paul's need for the release and rest of sexual communion was passionate, but not his desire for Miriam.

And now, wonder of wonders! on page 363, 'we had guessed it long ago'. There was no guesswork about it. Lawrence told the story quite plainly and honestly, but Middleton Murry's 'veracious account', which, according to him is 'not to be trusted', is very much on a par with a considerable amount of his 'detail' – possessing a smattering of truth and tendered in its very worst light. But 'detail' does not appear to matter very considerably so long as the main purpose is served.

'The account is not to be trusted.' Murry knows, by some means, that the account is very doubtful by comparison with other facts within his knowledge, and so 'the account is not to be trusted'. Then why, in the name of friendship, does his 'imaginative sympathy' allow him to bring it in, so long afterwards, as part of 'the most veracious account'?

He misses out an all-important factor; and he misses it out because he knows nothing at all about it. He confuses other chapters and his interpretations of other characters and stories by reason of his ignorance on the subject, and that same lack of knowledge causes him to describe one of the books merely as 'a monument of Lawrence's disintegration',[21] when, had the real truth been open to him, he would have been able to give vent to a very orgy of triumphant, strutting, 'I told you so's.' And apparently he would have had reason; and again he would have been wrong.

Lawrence himself has told us that he was virgin until he was twenty-three; and Murry knows that. Judging by the time when Lawrence apprised me of his intention of trying sexual experiences and his telling me of the accomplished fact, there is no reason at all to doubt Lawrence. Previous to that time, what his attitude on the point had been is aptly described in *Sons and Lovers*.

> A good many of the nicest men he knew were like himself, bound in by their own virginity, which they could not break out of. They were so sensitive to their women that they would go without them for ever rather than do them a hurt, an injustice. Being the sons of mothers whose husbands had blundered rather brutally through their feminine sanctities, they were themselves too diffident and shy. They could easier deny themselves than incur any reproach from a woman; for a woman was like their mother, and they were full of the sense of their mother.[22]

And that is the real, the absolutely true Lawrence, as I knew him.

In spite of all this, however, Murry chooses the 'veracious' extract and says in effect, 'Behold Lawrence! The most veracious portrait in existence! I, John Middleton Murry, the artist, who was Lawrence's most intimate friend, declare it', and he shews us a Lawrence, apparently depraved in his very tenderest years, messing about with girls at sixteen years of age, whining to, and worrying after, his lass, even as Lawrence must have seen the bulls whining, worrying and irritating at the farm, until, at last, he got his own way – as usual. When? That doesn't matter, except that the inference is that it was quite early in life and that the whole thing shall give a *nasty* impression.

But in this, as in many other instances, Middleton Murry,

by his very lack of knowledge, does but advertise the fact that really he knew very little of Lawrence, and that though there may have been at some time some shew of friendliness between him and Lawrence, there was no confidence in the friendship, from Lawrence's side at any rate. Possibly another instance of Lawrence's 'prophetic instinct'.

Lawrence, at sixteen, wouldn't have known what to do with himself had he been left alone with a girl. He liked to be with a bunch of nice girls, his sister and some chums of hers, but there was never any question of any 'sweetheart', to use the local phrase.[23] And this was the time when the girls at the factory were annoying him so dreadfully. It was not until many years after he was sixteen that Lawrence had any friends over Ollerton way, and there were certainly no love passages between Lawrence and the daughter of that family.[24] He never worked either in Butterley Offices or in any capacity for the Butterley Co., and so on, and so on . . . but it is all comparative with a considerable number of the analytical deductions. He doesn't even know that the Strelley Farm described was not really the home of Miriam at all. He says that the influence of the Little Woman was too strong for Miriam ever to have any chance of holding Lawrence,[25] but Lawrence, to my certain knowledge, was visiting the farm systematically for over six years, and the Little Woman's influence never affected it, while Lawrence quite definitely says they split on the rock of sex.

Murry says that Lawrence and his eldest brother were the clever ones of the family, but that, when the eldest died, all his mother's thoughts went to the Lawrence we know.[26] The eldest brother is alive today, living in Nottingham, and is not to be taken for anybody's fool by any means. And in spite of all the Little Woman's thoughts going to Bert, I beg to state that Ada was never neglected – far from it in fact.

It apparently suits Murry's purpose to cast doubt on the veracity of Lawrence's account of his sisters. He admits to having no knowledge on the point and so is content just to say that it could not be so.[27]

He states that Lawrence first met, in May 1912, the woman who was to be his wife, who immediately enters the very substance of his work and remains in it to the end. Lawrence knew the woman who was afterwards his wife long before that time, the events referred to by Murry as having happened on their honeymoon[28] were not relative at all and they never had a honeymoon in the accepted sense of the term. The facts are that the full circumstances are, again, evidently not known to Middleton Murry and he puts his own construction on his deductions, while his statement that Lawrence's wife immediately became the very substance of his works is demonstrably absurd.

Further than that, the statement is a gross insult to a lady who is more or less forced to allow such remarks to be thrust upon her without any hope of adequate defence, a position which applies equally to several other living persons to whom this effort of Mr Murry's must have come as a terrible shock.

With regard to the story of *The Trespasser*, I know of no reason why the whole of the story should not be told. Lawrence is not Siegfried of *The Trespasser*, and Siegfried is not a composite figure.[29] Naturally he is padded, because Lawrence had to give him an existence prior to the main story, but the true story of Lawrence and Nell C–,[30] the original of the girl Helena, has not yet been told: and it is not to be found in *The Trespasser*.

Lawrence and Nell had got into the habit of running down to the vicinity of Rottingdean for week-ends, and it was while they were lying in the bracken on the hills behind the pretty little town that Nell told Lawrence the story upon which *The Trespasser* is founded. The man was the leader of an orchestra at a well-known place of entertainment and a very successful teacher of the violin. Unhappy at home, he sought consolation with Nell, who had gone to him for tuition. She apparently misunderstood her feelings for him, for she failed him at the crucial moment; failed him and drove him to utter despair. Finally, the poor devil committed suicide. The real story of Lawrence and Nell is a vastly different one.[31]

The horrible probing into the condition of affairs between Lawrence and his wife (as Murry sees them!); the way he makes Lawrence shriek to be 'fulfilled', and shriek again because he is 'fulfilled'; the stress given to the point that Lawrence was, physically, a sexual failure, but yet absolutely dependent upon his woman; the manner in which he shews us how what love Lawrence ever had for his wife turns into bitterest hatred, particularly because of her past motherhood, since there is no possibility of fatherhood for Lawrence; these, all these, are things upon which I refuse to comment. Let Middleton Murry keep unspotted, if he can or may, whatever honour he may have gained by such efforts.

One thing he overlooked here, a tiny thing, but of the utmost importance. And it is a sentence of his own, used only just a little while before he commences 'probing' – 'Lawrence', he says, 'was a man capable of anticipating experience.'[32] Why, then, assume that everything must have been actual experience? To what end? And why not try to deal with a pleasant thought occasionally for a change? There were plenty of them, and they are just as much part of the story of D. H. Lawrence as those portions having either a sordid undercurrent, or being capable of a somewhat sordid interpretation.

In commencing to deal with *The Rainbow*, Mr Murry is determined to continue his probing. He is also very, very certain that he is right. He says:

> In *The Rainbow* is a still more intimate record of the experience confessed in *Look, we have come through!* The correspondence is exact and unmistakable. The story of Anna Lensky and Will Brangwen is, in essentials, the same story as the story of the poems; but the story is told more richly, and more fearfully . . . It describes their 'honeymoon'; the rebirth of the shy and shamefaced man in a long world-forgetful ecstasy of passion with a carefree, beautiful, passionate, unashamedly physical woman.[33]

Lawrence must have been, indeed, a prophet. Lawrence was most truly 'a man capable of anticipating experience'. Lawrence Murry tells us, did not meet the lady who became his wife until May 1912. *The Rainbow* was, to all intents and purposes, completed while Lawrence was staying with me in March of that year.[34]

As soon as it suits his purpose, Mr Murry tells us, 'Then the story of *The Rainbow* departs from the naked facts of Lawrence's experience.'[35] Exactly! Lawrence was again anticipating experience, because, here, Mr Murry cannot possibly defend his contention. But back we go to Murry's real Lawrence

and we have a whole series of more or less nauseating extracts
from portions that suit the little of Lawrence he is trying to see.
We transfer the soul of Lawrence, in a somewhat coarsened
form, miraculously, into the body of his daughter's lover and
we shiver as we read of the terrible consummation on the sands
in the full light of the moon.

> This is the end. Anton has failed at the proof. Ursula lies in a
> cold agony of un-satisfaction, and he creeps away a broken
> man . . . *The Rainbow* is, radically, the history of Lawrence's
> final sexual failure . . . One shrinks from the necessity of thus
> laying bare the physical secrets of a dead man; but in the
> case of Lawrence we have no choice.[36]

Fancy that now! Actually, when *The Rainbow* was written,
Lawrence, sexually, was very, very much alive, as I know
living witnesses to prove.

Towards the end of the section we are told that, in order to
discover what underlies this fearful consummation, we have
to see Mellors' account of his sexual experience with Bertha
Coutts in *Lady Chatterley's Lover*, but that, in the present state of
affairs is unquotable. Later in the book we are informed that
the reason for this is that the language is so vile.[37]

Just for a moment let us try to see something of the psychology
of this psychologist who tells us that he knows more about
Lawrence than Lawrence knew about himself. Dealing with a
very fine Lawrence paragraph from *Twilight in Italy*, he says,

> Now this, if it were possible, would deceive the very elect; for
> it is divided only by a hair's breadth from the enunciation of a
> great truth. Instead, it is a great falsehood. To explain why it
> is a great falsehood may be hard, because the great truth which
> it simulates, and from which it must be distinguished, is known
> to few. We must follow the simplest clue to unravel the decep-
> tion.

And then, this self-elected member of the very distinguished
'few' who have found the bottom of the well, proceeds:

> We begin by an absolute assertion.
> Sexuality is right; sensuality is wrong. This assertion is
> absolutely true, for the simple reason that sensuality *is* sexuality
> which is conscious of guilt. It is the consciousness of guilt that

makes sensuality of sexuality. Take the consciousness of guilt away from sensuality, and it becomes sexuality once more – completely innocent . . . Therefore, he had sinned; for sin *is*, where there is a sense of sin.[38]

Is it an argument set up merely to condemn Lawrence? Or have we discovered part of what we sought? To me, it sounds more like the weak argument of one who seeks to defend himself. We have heard it many a time. It is made an excuse for all sorts of things. And Lawrence is to be made a liar by one who puts forward such an argument! But I think we have made our discovery – 'Qui s'excuse, s'accuse.'

'Sex is a state of grace', says Lawrence in *Pansies*, 'and you'll have to wait.'[39]

'It is true', says Murry. 'Sex *is* a state of grace; but there is a natural way of attaining that state of grace, which Lawrence, by destiny, had forfeited . . . He was a fallen angel . . . and the darkness of sex into which he had fallen was an evil darkness . . . He embarked irrevocably on a course which led him to complete disintegration.'[40]

Lawrence's 'state of grace' is an evil 'state of grace' entirely opposed to the real 'state of grace', which only the few elect, among whom is numbered Mr Murry, can know. There is no possibility of Lawrence being in real earnest when he makes that statement. It emanates from Lawrence, and there must be evil in it. And Murry makes another 'find'.

When dealing with some of the poems, it comes almost as a delight to hear Mr Murry say frankly, 'I do not pretend to understand that.' And again, 'Once more I do not claim to understand this wholly.'[41] But the respite is all too short and he returns to his quest. 'But, even though one may not understand the experience which is recorded, one may reach certain conclusions.'[42]

He sets forth his analysis and his conclusions. We are back to autobiography. The psychological position is unchanged. The physical situation is more mysterious. Then he trots out our old friend Will Brangwen to set forth the position again.

Why could he not leave her? He could not, he could not. A woman, he must have a woman. And having a woman he must be free of her. It would be the same position. For he could not be free of her.[43]

Admittedly the poems are beautiful (*vide* Murry),[44] but the poet must keep his cloak of horror. It must be so, even if one does not really understand.

Thus we proceed to the final exposure:

> At this crucial moment, Lawrence turns desperately upon the accusing figure of Jesus. He will justify himself against Jesus, prove that the Son of Man and not the Son of Woman has betrayed mankind . . . Lawrence has identified himself with Jesus; that Jesus is become for him, Lawrence (only with the mighty and agonising difference, that he is Lawrence who chose another way) the Lawrence who might have been. And this Jesus – the Lawrence who might have been – is wrong, and the Lawrence who is, is right . . .
>
> . . . On the Cross, the man who kept his spirit whole, and let his flesh be crucified; standing beneath, the man who would keep whole his flesh, and let his spirit be crucified. On the Cross, the man who severed his bodily love from Woman, that he might give it to all women and to all men for evermore; standing beneath, the man who would not sever his bodily love from Woman, so that it turned into hate of all women and of all men. On the Cross, the man who himself took and preached the eternal way of resurrection in the spirit; beneath it, the man who refused it, or could not take it, crying in anguish for the resurrection of the body. 'The abominable trinity on Calvary!'[45]

Poor old Lawrence! On the Cross, the One who said, 'Come unto me all ye that labour and are heavy laden and I will give you rest.' Beneath it, Lawrence, for whom, by the stern decree of judgement of John Middleton Murry, there was no possibility of rest. There might be a promise of Paradise for the thieves; for Lawrence there is nothing but eternal damnation; there is no hope of Redemption. Christ died that Lawrence might not live.

Luckily, Lawrence had proclaimed his redemption; but Murry refused, or did not wish to see it, though even Murry admits that 'Lawrence, without knowing what is happening to him, falls finally into the creed of the superstitious "Christian", with his "happy land, far far away".'[46]

To what end? To the end that the lovers of Lawrence may be multiplied? I think not; for there is little in the book to cause mankind to love. On the contrary, the Lawrence of this book is well-nigh an ogre, a betrayer of mankind, a hopeless derelict, a horrible example, a lost soul howling in the wilderness of the unredeemed against the Christ.

To what end? Was it truly necessary that each tiny weakness of Lawrence must receive the light of full exposure? Must the tortured soul and body of Lawrence be laid utterly bare, nay, even the poor body be torn open, that we might know his message? If so, we must not dare call ourselves lovers of Lawrence any more.

To what end? 'The evil that you did, is done; and it *is* evil. You muddied the spring of living water that flowed in you more richly than in any man of your time. In the world of good and evil, wherein men must struggle for ever while they live, you quenched the light more often than you kindled it. You bewildered men who might have learned from you, betrayed men who would have followed you. We needed a leader and a prophet, you were marked by destiny to be the man; and you failed us.'[47] Thus does Murry address the soul of the now-departed Lawrence, and in doing so, betrays, not Lawrence, but the personal feeling still rankling in his mind beneath the assiduously applied, but thin veneer of 'love and imaginative sympathy'.

What kind of a Lawrence was John Middleton Murry prepared to follow, according to his own admission? The Lawrence which was not Lawrence. When Middleton Murry went to a party and saw there the real, beloved Lawrence, the magnetic Lawrence drawing the attention of all, the sparkling, bubbling Lawrence, effervescing joy and human delight, the sympathetic Lawrence whom everyone knowing must love, he sat there, with a dark cloud of anger brooding o'er his soul, brooding, brooding, until the psychic Lawrence felt the *dark* influence, the fountain of the bubble and sparkle was stilled, the joys and delights were over, and Lawrence left it all to go to Murry and ask what he had done to arouse such an evil spirit in Murry's breast.

'Why can't you always be yourself?' asked Murry.[48]

Which self? There was only one Lawrence known to Murry; and it was not the real Lawrence.

'Do not betray me!' Lawrence asked of Murry. Murry may rest assured that he has carried out that behest. He says he has not: that he *has* betrayed Lawrence. 'This "betrayal" was the one thing you lacked, the one thing I had to give, that you might shine forth among men as the thing of wonder that you were.'[49]

But it is no betrayal. It is merely a recital of the things Lawrence himself has told us, with such 'interpretations' put into them as it pleased John Middleton Murry to give. And because there were many essentials that Murry could not know, and because his sympathies were more 'imaginary' than 'imaginative', his 'interpretations' suffered accordingly.

I am afraid that the real betrayal must come from me, but since Murry has carried the matter, to such an extent, it is essential that the real truth of Lawrence should be saved to mankind. And Lawrence will know that the 'betrayal' is made in all that bond of love which we forged between us in the long ago and which he, in his earlier writings, so fervently confessed, while the constant longing for a similar love-bond with a man is so constantly apparent, but never realised.

6

LAWRENCE – THE SON OF MAN

The greatness of Lawrence lies, not in the facts of his experiences, of his knowledge, of his power of expression, of his love and sympathy for mankind, or of his sufferings, but in the fact that he was the only man who ever had the courage to tell the world quite frankly of his own experiences – and the other experiences he was able to glean – in the particular line of research he had deliberately adopted, i.e. the relationships of the sexes from all aspects. I believe that many men have suffered more, much more, than Lawrence suffered by reason of his sexual adventures, which were not numerous, measured by certain comparisons available today. But those others have suffered in silence. We have all long known of it, but, with regard to such matters, as with others of importance but a little inclined to be – well! shall we say? – 'awkward' to deal with, we prefer, or have preferred, to pursue a policy of 'Hush! Hush!' and, one might almost add, 'Here comes the Bogey Man.' That has been a natural result of our foolish self-consciousness in respect of questions of sex and sexual matters generally. Lawrence has done more to eradicate that evil, that very great evil, than any man who ever lived; but there is still a tremendous amount of work to be done in that field.

Lawrence avowed to me his desire to go much more deeply into his chosen subject than any man hitherto had done: he had no wish to be a 'surface-skimmer', and he knew the dangers awaiting him, both publicly and privately. But he felt within him the urge to handle this matter of sex, and the intercourse of the sexes, in a manner which should cause men to consider the question from every possible aspect, and, unless he shall achieve this, his work is vain. Happily, there is plenty of proof of the ever-rising tide of the influence of the work of

Lawrence, and of the fact that, largely through his influence, the sex question is now receiving more solid and deliberate attention than at any other period of the world's history. And the present state of things in the world demands that it shall be so. If Lawrence had done no more than draw such vivid attention to the haphazard bringing of souls into the world, and the even more haphazard handling of them when they have arrived, he would not have lived in vain.

There is an enormous field for educational work on the subject of sex-knowledge. In my immediate area there are tremendous numbers of young men and maidens who have never heard a lecture or had a lesson on sex-relationships in their lives, and, so far as I have been able to observe, have had no opportunities.

Many years ago, I got into the habit of gathering the elder young men round the fireplace after evening school, and giving them an hour on varying aspects of the question – aspects suggested by them at the previous meeting – and I dealt with them with the most perfect frankness, often quite deliberately 'calling a spade a spade'. Those evening-school classes were held in a Church of England school building, and when some local busybody made a point of acquainting the parson of this extra work I was doing, the rector came to see me and asked me if I did not think it would be better to have the subject dealt with by a clergyman or a doctor.

I told him I was heartily of the same opinion, an expression of opinion which he said he was very pleased to hear, upon which I pointed out that, as he was Rector of the Parish, doubtless he would be delighted to seize the opportunity thus offered of dropping in, two nights per week, from nine p.m. till ten p.m. to ensure this all-important information being handed out to the fellows in a proper manner. But he raised his hands in pious horror at the mere idea. 'Oh, No, No!' he said, 'I couldn't do it. I really couldn't do it.'

'Well! The Doctor will come to do it if some arrangement can be made to pay him', I informed the old man. He had plenty of money – was a wealthy man in fact! – and was always ready to 'get his hand down' for a children's treat, an old folk's tea or the Parochial Mission – to the Jews and similar organisations – and I hoped my suggestion might be met by an offer to arrange for the Doctor to give us a short series of talks. But it didn't come off.

'There isn't any money available for the purpose, I'm afraid', he replied.

'So we're back again at where we started', I stated. 'It's a certain fact that these fellows are not going to be allowed to remain in such an appalling state of ignorance as they are at present, and if you can't undertake the work, and we are unable to get a doctor, what are we to do?'

'Really. I'm sure I don't know, but I still think that my suggestion is the better one', said the Rector.

You will have gathered that I am not in the habit of mincing matters when I am convinced of the correctness of the attitude I have adopted, and perhaps my regard for the feelings of my opponents is not always as fine as it might be. Lawrence used to twit me on this subject, although I know he envied me my capacity for doing it. In the case of the Rector, I said, 'But you haven't made any suggestion. You have merely expressed an opinion. Actually you have criticised, destructively, what I thought was a good job of work I was doing gratis, and with no wish for recognition, payment, or even thanks. I have said I am in hearty agreement with your opinion; but, since you have no suggestions for the work to be continued under the better conditions on which we are both agreed, I refuse to allow such an important work to be postponed or delayed in any way, so I shall just carry on until something better is arranged. I'm giving my time, trouble, knowledge and services, and, so far as I can see, it's nothing to do with anybody else.'

Rough? Yes, if you like; but not so rough as the suggestion that I should cease to instruct those fellows in the subject which was, in my opinion, of even more vital necessity than the subjects in the set curriculum for the evening-school proper. I'm afraid the Rector didn't love me very much after that, but I had my reward. In due course came the outbreak of the Great War and over seventy fellows who had attended at that little evening-school joined the Forces. On their 'leaves', and after the war, a very considerable number of them made a point of informing me that, many a time in their wartime experiences, they had found cause to be thankful for the memory of those little talks round the fire after evening-school. I remember very vividly the expression used by one collier lad who was lucky enough to come through. 'You know, Sir', he said to me, 'we used to think sometimes that you were pulling our legs, but by God, Sir, we know now you never told us half of it.'

Parents, too, appear to treat the matter lightly. Men appear to adopt the attitude that sex adventures are voyages of discovery on which everyone, arrived at men's estate, must set out, unaided and alone, to make his own discoveries, or to be wrecked by any careless or unskilled navigation. If one points out to them that it is their duty, as parents, to educate their children in matters of sex, more often than not one gets the answer, 'I know it ought to be done; but it's no use, I *couldn't* do it. I simply couldn't do it.' In one or two cases men have said to me, during such discussions, 'As a matter of fact, I *have* wondered whether you would mind giving him an hour or two sometime.' I resigned from the teaching profession during the war and, since I have never re-entered it, I have not had the opportunity of extending the little talks round the fire.

But there is something radically wrong with our sex-consciousness where such a state of affairs obtains. It is against such consciousness that Lawrence has had to fight. The modern novel deals more and more with the question, in an infinite variety of ways varying, as the Cockney said, 'from the sublime to the Gorblimey', but only a very, very small proportion of the population of this country reads such works. I know that fact positively from library figures, and it should be remembered that, as the freedom of the world stands today, each member of the population, unless by some mischance physically incapacitated, is a potential parent.

Lawrence, properly studied in the spirit in which he intended his works to be studied, will do much to assist towards remedying the existing sex-evils, but only if Lawrence himself can be presented in a true light. Unfortunately, at present one only has to mention his name in many cases to be aware immediately that there is no place for Lawrence or his works in that home, and to find oneself regarded almost with suspicion, though in the majority of cases it will be admitted quite frankly that they have no personal knowledge of the man or his works; but they have 'heard enough of him'.

It is with the declared intention then of attempting to eradicate these many misconceptions of Lawrence that this section is designed, and further, to try to prove that Lawrence instead of being something to fear is something to be loved greatly; a gift for which we should be profoundly thankful.

By birth, early training and inclination, Lawrence was a deeply religious man. His feelings and thoughts on matters of religion were always very profound and utterly sincere. His knowledge of God was very real and his knowledge of the Word of God was very wide as will at once be realised by the student of his works. That he 'wandered away from God' admits of no discussion – and which of us has not done so? – but he was always aware of this, always aware that he was sinning against his own Holy Ghost, always fighting, fighting in spirit, fighting obstinately to force himself to continue along the path he had deliberately marked out for himself; fighting to his own hurt; and fighting until he was of the opinion that he had finished the work he had set out to do, when he just 'let go', ceased to fight longer, and allowed his spirit to wander back to the Truth of his early convictions.

Even in the midst of his wildest 'thought-adventures',[1] the Spirit of those early convictions was with him, and constantly forces for itself a place in his works. *Fantasia of the Unconscious* itself, that 'pseudo-philosophy'[2] (there is great significance in Lawrence's own names for it!) cannot shut out that spirit, and we find this wonderful sentence creeping in: 'We must live by all three, ideal, impulse, and tradition, each in its hour. But the real guide is pure conscience, the voice of the self in its wholeness, the Holy Ghost.'[3]

I am aware that it may be contended that Lawrence had a special Holy Ghost of his own creation; that he even fitted every living person with a separate Holy Ghost, and to a very large extent he was right, because, just as no two persons can hold an identical conception of God, it follows that the effect of the Holy Ghost cannot be exactly the same in any two individuals. Again, in the only recorded visible appearance of the Holy Ghost in multiple, each individual had his own 'cloven tongue of fire'. Lawrence meant the Holy Ghost in its truest sense – the completion of the Trinity.

Let us pass on to *Twilight in Italy*.

> The consummation of man is twofold, in the Self and in Selflessness. By great retrogression back to the source of darkness in me, the Self, deep in the senses, I arrive at the Original, Creative Infinite. By projection forth from myself, by the elimination of my absolute sensual self, I arrive at the Ultimate Infinite, Oneness in the Spirit. They are two Infinites, twofold approach to God. And man must know both.
>
> But he must never confuse them. They are eternally separate. The lion shall never lie down with the lamb. The lion eternally shall devour the lamb, the lamb eternally shall be devoured. Man knows the great consummation in the flesh, the sexual ecstasy, and that is eternal. Also the spiritual ecstasy of un-animity, that is eternal. But the two are separate and never to be confused. To neutralise the one with the other is unthinkable, an abomination. [4]

Perfectly true, as to the first part, provided the consummation in the flesh is sanctified by love. Lawrence had tried to reach his consummation without such sanctification, with deliberate disregard of its necessity in fact, and he confesses the result – an abomination. Later, we find him making a direct admission of his transgression:

> This is the Holy Ghost of the Christian Trinity. And it is this, the relation which is established between the two Infinites, the two natures of God, which we have transgressed, forgotten, sinned against. The Father is the Father, and the Son is the Son. I may know the Son and deny the Father, or know the Father and deny the Son. But that which I may never deny, *and which I have denied* (the italics are mine!), is the Holy Ghost, which relates the dual Infinites into One Whole, which relates and keeps distinct the dual natures of God. [5]

Then compare the following:

> This individuality which each of us has got and which makes him a wayward, wilful, dangerous, untrustworthy quantity to every other individual, because every individuality is bound to react at some time against every other individuality, without exception – or else lose its own integrity; because of the inevitable necessity of each individual to react away from every

other individual, at certain times, human love is truly a relative thing, not an absolute. It *cannot* be absolute.

Yet the human heart must have an absolute. It is one of the conditions of being human. The only thing is the God who is the source of all passion. Once go down before the God-passion and human passions take their right and rhythm. But human passion, without the God-passion always kills the thing it loves . . . Any more love is a hopeless thing, till we have found again, each for himself, the great dark God who will sustain us in our loving one another. Till then, best not play with more fire. [6]

That is from *Kangaroo* which I have heard described as being so chaotic as to be beyond understanding.[7] Yet there appears to be not the least equivocation about the statement quoted. Lawrence is back to his God of his earlier convictions, and he is giving us the truth as he himself has experienced it, and in his love for us he advises that we shall not play with the fire by which he has already been so fearfully scarred.

It is possible to twist and turn the statement in many ways – there are people who will say that, being Lawrence, it certainly must not be accepted as read! – it may be criticised strongly by comparison with other parts of *Kangaroo*, but I still claim it as part of my chain of proof of the purity of the convictions of the inward and true Lawrence, as opposed to the Lawrence who spent so many, many weary years 'kicking against the pricks', without even the excuse of St Paul who had not received the Light at the time of his 'kicking'.

But even when, at first sight, he would appear to have decided to accept one of those dark, unspeakable Gods he sought so diligently – only to prove to himself and to us the hopelessness of seeking salvation through them – his true inward convictions revolted from them at the last stage. His honest soul rejected them in their entirety:

The call and the answer without intermediary. Non-human gods, non-human human being.[8]

The Holy Ghost speaks individually inside each individual, always, for ever a ghost . . . Each isolate individual listening in isolation to the Holy Ghost within him . . . (listening to) the thing which prompts us to be real, and not to push our cravings too far.[9]

Eternal truth, though, in his writings, sadly mingled with worrying 'thought-adventures', seeking, seeking always a way of escape, and finding none.

> There is only one thing that a man really wants to do, all his life; and that is, to find his way to his God, his Morning Star, and be alone there. Then, afterwards, in the Morning Star, salute his fellow-men, and enjoy the woman who has come the long way with him.[10]

God first, then the God-passion, and then the full realisation of the Woman who has come the long way – the long way to God and the God-passion – with him. The fulfilment, in God, of the purpose of God. The dream-realisation of Lawrence because of the knowledge that, by his own act, he had made the true and actual realisation of fulfilment for ever impossible for him, unless he surrendered his self-imposed task.

> I always believed that people could be born again if they would only let themselves.[11]
>
> It's awfully important to be flesh and blood. Think how ghastly for Jesus, when he was risen and wasn't touchable. Oh God, I'm glad I've realised in time.[12]

In time! In time for what? For the greater confessions and expressions of his real beliefs which were to follow. Lawrence accepts the belief that Jesus is risen again in every human being who accepts the Christian Entity; that each man's life is a test of the power of the Spirit, the Jesus, that is within him. He confesses that he has refused to allow his Jesus to display His power; that he might have been born again if only he would have let himself; that every act of his has affected others:

> It occurred to me that in this crucifixion business the crucified does not put himself alone on the cross. The woman is nailed even more inexorably up, and crucified in the body even more cruelly.
>
> It is a monstrous thought. But the deed is even more monstrous. Oh, Jesus, didn't you know that you couldn't be crucified alone? – that the two thieves crucified along with you were the two women, your wife and your mother! You called them two thieves. But what would they call you, who had their women's bodies on the cross? The abominable trinity on Calvary![13]

Notice particularly that he says, 'The crucified does not put himself alone on the cross.' 'Put himself'. And then, 'You called them thieves, but what would they call you . . .'

Confession and belief, at last, at long, long, last. What was it I had told him many years before? 'It's a damned lie; you haven't done anything of the sort. What you've done is to insult yourself and every woman on earth. If you wanted a woman, because, being a healthy, red-blooded sort of chap, you had begun to feel an urge towards woman, I would say nothing at all about it . . . but . . . you wanted a woman merely as an experience . . . something to write about . . . insulting your chosen woman and desecrating your own manhood.'

'The abominable trinity on Calvary!' To each man his own Calvary, and with his own 'thieves' with him, if he has not 'let' Jesus take the Calvary in his stead. Lawrence has not the least suggestion of a blasphemy here; it is his cry of sorrow to the women he has wronged, his cry of sorrow, because of that wrong, uttered for all the world to hear and heed, and it is Lawrence's confession and acceptance of the Jesus – his own Holy Ghost – that is in him.

> The heart of man cannot wander among the years like a wild ass in the wilderness, running hither and thither. The heart at last stands still, crying: 'Whither? Whither?' Like a lost foal whinnying for his dam, the heart cries and nickers for God, and will not be comforted.[14]

Instead of being divided, disintegrated, Lawrence is becoming 'whole' again, and that miracle, that miracle which he must 'let' happen, is occurring: Lawrence is being 'born again'.

> My triumph is that I am not dead. I have outlived my mission and know no more of it . . . I have survived the day and the death of my interference, and am still a man . . . The teacher and the saviour are dead in me; now I can go about my own business, into my own single life. . . . Now I can wait on life and say nothing, and have no one betray me . . . I wanted to be greater than the limits of my hands and feet, so I brought betrayal on myself. Now I can live without trying to sway others any more. For my reach ends in my finger-tips and my stride

is no longer than the ends of my toes. Yet I would embrace multitudes, I who have never truly embraced even one.[15]

It is wrong to attempt to say that 'The Man who had died' is Jesus: he is Lawrence: Lawrence born again because he has 'let' himself be 'born again to a new birth unto righteousness'; because he has realised in time. It is Lawrence who has turned again to the God he had never truly left, and who had never left him, but from whom he has attempted to flee; a hopeless task because 'in the uttermost parts of the earth, I am there'.[16]

And the risen Lawrence pursues his allegorical 'thought-adventure' still further, consistently going back to his own ideal, 'Back to God, his Morning Star . . . and enjoy the woman who has come the long way with him.' And in a wonderful way we realise again that Lawrence, as a man capable of anticipating experience, was absolutely supreme.

To assume that by 'The Man who had died' Lawrence means Jesus, a most horrible picture is presented; too horrible. But it is wrong. It is not Jesus who recants. It is not Jesus who admits that he set out on an impossible task; it is Lawrence who confesses to his years of hopeless seeking, seeking for that which his own Holy Ghost was constantly telling him was, for him, unattainable: Lawrence, the while obstinately refusing to hear or heed.

He visualises now, for us all, the fulness of a perfect love, perfectly achieved, perfectly realised and perfectly fulfilled. He adds a pledge of fulfilment, with that wonderful throb of joy that he always produces when his mind goes forward to that pledge for which he always longed – his child within her womb.

> The virgin birth, the baptism, the temptation, the teaching, Gethsemane, the betrayal, the crucifixion, the burial and the resurrection, these are all true according to our inward experience. They are what men and women go through in their different ways . . . Jesus was risen flesh-and-blood. He rose a man to live on earth. The greatest test was still before Him: His life as a man on earth. Hitherto He had been a sacred child, a teacher, a messiah, but never a full man. Now, risen from the dead, He rises to be a man on earth, and live His life of the flesh, the great life among other men. This is the image of our inward state to-day.[17]

'This is the image of our inward state today.' Lawrence!

'That we may dwell in Him, and He in us.' You all remember that don't you? If that means anything at all it means that Jesus may live again, in the flesh, this life on earth, in the case of every human who will 'let' Him, and that Lawrence is right once his allegory is rightly accepted. It means more than that; it means that Lawrence is making full confession of his faith and belief. It means that Lawrence, instead of standing over against Jesus, had ranged himself alongside. It means that the soul of Lawrence had come safely to harbour.

We had an old jingle, when we were youths, which we used to put, under floral sprays, in autograph albums. It ran:

> 'Pansies are for thoughts', they say;
> Thoughts sincere and true.
> That is why I plant them here –
> Ever near to you.

I have often wondered if that old jingle had returned to the mind of Lawrence when he named his poems *Pansies*[18] I think perhaps it did. I love to think it did. Have you read *Pansies*? If not, I wish you would. And in fairness to Lawrence you *must* do so. Read it and see if you can discover anything to indicate that it was written by a man who did not know what he was doing. Study it to find the man whose soul had been taken from him. Try to discover there the one whose intense love had turned to hatred of all men; and in all those quests you will fail. But read it to discover the man who has been through the fire and come out purified; who has sinned, suffered, confessed and at last found peace; whose greatest anxiety is to give to the world a message of love, before he leaves that world; whose thoughts are solely to direct his fellow men to a happier, fuller and more complete enjoyment of their life on earth, and he is with you at once, and the pure flame of him will help you to see much of that which now is wrapped in darkness.

It has become quite the usual thing to see reference made to Lawrence as a 'man of destiny', and then, immediately, to read a moan that he was not other than he was. If there is anything at all in the 'man of destiny' idea, then surely we know the Lawrence of that destiny; he had to 'dree his weird'.[19]

I am free to confess that, probably without exception, the friends of his youth would all join in the wish that he could have been other than he was – for his own sake. Lawrence, craving the love of all men, took the most certain road to lead to a denial of that love, in spite of warnings and advice. It is exceptionally hard to obtain even companions, when kicking against the pricks, and the risk of public opinion is still the greatest deterrent from the giving of our hearts in friendship.

Lawrence, then, pursued his way; and the way became more and more lonesome as his life proceeded. I have said before that Lawrence was 'intense'. Having made up his mind as to the course he would pursue, I can visualise him following up his investigations on every conceivable occasion, in every possible circumstance and under any and every condition. Quite obviously he experimented in every grade of society, and it is easy to conceive that, as he made mistakes in judgement, misread the psychology of some of his 'subjects', or misunderstood the enthusiasm of a number of those who were wont to enthuse over him, it was not long before detrimental whispers were circulated. The remarkable thing about it, to my mind, is that he did not find very serious trouble. I know that he ought to have expected it.

With the inherent obstinacy to which I have already referred, too, he continued on his way, in spite of those inward promptings which would, at times, assail him, and which, occasionally, he allowed to run riot to such an extent that, within a comparatively short distance of each other, in quite a number of his works, apparently contradictory theories or maxims may be discovered. But, instead of being upbraided for these, he should be given credit for his very honesty in giving us so wonderful an account of the opposing forces at work in his mind. He gives us a kind of psychological vivisection the like of which has never before appeared.

And with it all, from a sexual point of view, what does he tell us? If we are honest with ourselves, we shall admit that he tells us nothing more than we have already known. There is no new idea in Lawrence. The only newness is in the finding of a man who had the courage to set forth all those things that past and present generations have known but largely have not dared to utter. It *is* true that the world is being damned and deadened by the question of the relationship of the sexes. It *is* true that what we chiefly see of so-called love is evil, because it is a prostituted love just formed and fashioned by and for the service of mankind. It *is* true that love can only be learned through years of trial, and that the salvation of the world lies only through the study and application of love applied in all things. It *is* true that, under the cloak of what we know as love, the world is becoming more and more evil every day. It *is* true that, under our present arrangements for the intercourse of the sexes, and for the propagation of the races of mankind, death and damnation of the spirit – the pure spirit – is inevitable in the majority of cases, and that the children grow up under the shadow of a doom that was cast over them even before they appeared upon the earth. It *is* true that, under present conditions, innumerable men and women degenerate, lose their pure spirit, lose their native control and their personal integrity, until their be-all and end-all of existence is just that licensed intercourse which is given to them under that state in which they exist. It *is* true that thousands and thousands of otherwise good and useful men are slaves, bound by the sex-call, from which they cannot free themselves. It *is* true that thousands and thousands of otherwise good women must prostitute themselves, become embittered, fail in their duties both family and personal, and lose their real selves to answer that sex-call, from which the way of escape is all too difficult. It *is* true that these facts are more fully realised today than ever before, and that they explain the constant seeking, seeking of ever-increasing numbers of men and women for a something, a substitute, a way of escape; anything; they will try anything that hangs out even the flimsiest hope of escape from the bondage of sex.

It *is* nothing new for men to crave to get away, to be alone, to be themselves again, to regain once more that pure part of them they well know they have lost; only to find the way of escape too hard, too difficult, and finally to allow themselves to slip down into the great abyss, and there be lost in all its utter darkness.

Some there are, however, who fight on: and to them, also,

life becomes an utter weariness of the spirit, which often gladly makes its own escape.

It *is* nothing new for a man to seek throughout the world for a peace he cannot find, or for the similitude of a friendship he has lost. It *is* nothing new to be told that it ought not to be possible for every man or woman capable of producing children to be able to do so at will, or even willy-nilly. It *is* nothing new to be told that the physical act of intercourse may be the most beautiful and wonderful thing on earth, and that equally it may become a most disgustingly bestial performance. It *is* nothing new to be told that the great purposes of God must be interpreted through the body as well as through the mind or spirit, and it is no new thing to hear the vilest and filthiest words of the language applied in connection with that which should command only the purest. Lawrence uses such language to demonstrate the fact that he had pursued his studies and enquiries right down to the very dregs, and not in any joyful spirit, as I have seen supposed. Lawrence knew that he was soiling himself in the very act, though to those who chance to have seen an original Burns, for example, there will be nothing new in the words of Lawrence's description in *Lady Chatterley's Lover*. And finally, there is nothing new in the fact that a man may bring to bear every possible argument to justify the actions of his life, and, at the last, find that he has fought the truth in vain. But that in no way need detract from the ultimate value of the works of such a man. The failures of certain men have been of greater value to mankind than the combined successes of many thousands of other men. The man who never makes a mistake never does anything, and, if Lawrence made mistakes, they are fully confessed before the world, and, in several cases, there is the only possible attempt at atonement.

We bemoan, I bemoan, Lawrence as a lost leader of men. I believe that, could his undoubted gifts have been applied in other directions, he would have become the leader of a new world movement. I know that he could have become such a leader, but I sometimes feel that, even now, he has completed his real work, and that, ultimately, when a right conception of our Lawrence has been spread throughout the world, that dreamed-of leadership will yet be his. At the present time I am aware that in almost every one of the great countries of the world, savants are busily seeking the truth of the inner teachings of Lawrence. I, myself, have been in touch with some of them, and I know that, though the prophet has, as yet, very little honour in his own country – in a comparative sense – the students of the world of men, away from home, are making preparations to give to all of us their own conceptions of the life and works of Lawrence.

The belief is very widely held today that the fact that women have been allowed to usurp, have been given, or have been allowed to win for themselves, their present position of dominance in the affairs of today, is largely responsible for the troubles of the civilised world, and it is certain that there are very few aspects of national and individual life that are not considerably affected by it.

Towards the end of the Great War, I recollect giving a lecture – by special request – which included something in the way of a forecast of after-the-war conditions – this part also by request! In that lecture, after pointing out the special and unwonted lines upon which feminine independence had perforce developed, I asked the question: 'And, with the end of the war, what will you do with all these women you have drawn from their quiet humdrum lives, taken from what has hitherto been a quiet preparation of their real work in the world, and placed in a position of independence, self-reliance, and, above all, realisation of their own freedom and independence? So far as I can see at present, you are anticipating that you will be able to give them a dear little pat on the shoulder, tell them that they have been very good girls, give them a medal, or possibly a certificate of service, and then request that they will now be good enough to go back to the monotony of their pre-war existence. All I can say is, that if such be your ideas on the subject, you are utterly deceiving yourselves. Women, having won anything for themselves, do not readily or lightly relinquish their gains, and you may take it from me that women realise quite fully that this represents the very greatest gain of theirs all through the generations.' And the fact that I had struck the nail on the head was testified by the fact that I was interrupted, at that point, by quite a storm of applause.

It goes without saying, of course, that I am by no means attempting to ascribe the advance towards the final predominance of women entirely to the Great War; but the movement did undoubtedly make an advancement during that period – a very phenomenal advancement! – which probably would not have been possible in a century under normal conditions.

The introduction of women to the predominant position in all the essentials of a hitherto man-ruled world – and a world still attempting to progress on the old, chivalrous-gentlemanly lines! – can spell nothing but disaster, because temperamentally, mentally, psychologically, and in every possible way, those man-ruled lines are not of the slightest use to her; she recognises neither the lines nor the rulings. I was severely criticised for stating publicly, early in the war, that the conduct of the war, so far as the methods to be employed to ensure ultimate victory were concerned, ought to be taken out of the hands of the men who, at the moment, decided it, and women should be given charge of that department. In spite of that criticism, I have yet to see any reason for altering my opinion.

Lawrence points out the danger in a particular direction – though he very obviously indicated the danger in a general way also – and this is the probable explanation of the fact that he is often accused of having come to hate all women in his later years. The idea is utterly erroneous: hatred of women was quite impossible to the gentle soul of Lawrence. But he most certainly did hate the effect that the changed position of woman was producing on the soul of man. Lawrence looked back longingly to those days when man, tired and aweary from following his own part in the work of the world, went back to his woman to find refreshment, solace (if he needed it!) and, above all, rest. He knew that, here and there, men still are able to find the same conditions; but he also knew that the instances are very rare, and that the women who are content to act such a part are, today, mightily few, and that, where they do exist, they are, more often than not, of the class that our prudish, conventional civilisation affects to treat with the greatest contempt – they are not married to their men. But Lawrence knew that, by those men, they are valued as jewels beyond price, and that, to those men, they are the most beautiful thing the world can hold. And they represent full value for that estimation.

Lawrence is by no means alone in his seeking for a way out. I remember the very vivid impression made upon him by Tolstoi's *Anna Karenina* while he was still quite a youth.[20] H. G. Wells' fantastic vision made nothing like as deep an impression on either of us. Balzac, Daudet and even Flaubert were of the 'surface-skimmers' to Lawrence – and that after carefully studying *Salammbô* from the original text.[21]

But Lawrence took his own way, and, in doing so, carried out the work he had set out to do. He was no 'surface-skimmer'. Lawrence went right to the dregs, but no one will deny that in doing so, at some stages of his journeying he lighted up for us, as they were never before lighted, many of the glories of the high places.

It has been hinted that Lawrence, sexually, had no personal control. That is entirely wrong, as I could prove by many instances. As an example I will tell you of quite an exciting time we had one year when we had decided to spend the last portion of our summer holiday together at Blackpool.[22] Actually the holiday worked out as a whole series of incidents, some interesting, some amusing, some, to me, merely annoying. We had arranged to stay with a relative of mine who had a boarding-house not far from North Pier.

'We have quite a nice company already', our hostess told us on our arrival. 'Several musicians, including a professional violinist, so you will be pleased, George; and tonight, we are expecting two young ladies from somewhere near Wolverhampton, schoolmistresses I think, quite up-to-date and stylish ladies I hear and so you will have something in common. Miss J– and Miss W–. You may possibly know them, George?' I remarked that I had not that pleasure but should certainly look forward to it.

After a rush round the town on the Saturday night, including a little promiscuous dancing on Central Pier, where Lawrence had an experience which filled him with chuckles – he asked a lassie for a dance; she was a real Lancashire mill lass from Oldham and Lawrence could scarcely tell what she said, but he grasped her meaning when, after a few turns round the enclosure she said, 'Lead me aht, ah'm ma-a-zy!' – we returned to the house, Lawrence saying several times as we went along, 'Lead me aht, ah'm ma-a-zy!' and chuckling with glee, and enquired after the new arrivals, but we were informed that they were fatigued with the journey and had gone to bed, but Mr P–, the violinist, had just promised to give a little music in the drawing room and we were lucky to be in time.

When we walked into the drawing-room, the professional, instead of getting on with the job, invited me to give a selection. We were highly amused at that. I told him at once that, while I certainly played the fiddle, I was only very much an amateur. In spite of that, however, he made an excuse for calling me out of the room and then asked if I minded allowing him to examine the tips of the fingers of my left hand. Discovering that such callouses as were there were only very tiny ones, he declared himself satisfied that I did not play very much, went back into the drawing-room and gave us a really beautiful rendering of Raff's 'Cavatina'[23] (I remember it so well because I so eagerly awaited the double-stopping movement, but it presented not the slightest difficulty to P–) and for quite a long time he delighted us with his wonderful technique in addition to sweetly sympathetic renderings of simple ballads. At Lawrence's request he gave us some Brahms Folk Songs of the Baltic and we sang them quietly in German as P– played.

P– was a very great addition to that holiday, in spite of his very queer beginning. But, after all, I suppose it was only natural, though it would not have occurred to me to take the same line of action. Lawrence lay on the bed and howled with laughter when I told him the reason P– had asked me out of the drawing-room.

On the following morning, Sunday, punctually on time, all the visitors, with the exception of the two latest arrivals, were assembled at breakfast. Directly opposite to Lawrence and me places were laid for two, and I noticed that, by the side of one of the plates, there was a pink-coloured newspaper which had arrived by post and which appeared to be familiar.

'They're evidently something by way of being sports at any rate', I remarked to Lawrence.

'How do you know!' he asked

'If I'm not very much mistaken that's a copy of our local

"Football Special". I'll be able to see how our crowd went on yesterday', I told him.

At this moment the door opened and our hostess walked in followed by two wonderful figures, and announced, 'Ladies and gentlemen Miss J– and Miss W–.'

She made the round of the table making individual introductions while we rose to make our separate bows to the magnificent though incongruous figures to whom we were presented. Miss J–, tall and stately, was wrapped in a dressing-gown of heavy brocade of a wonderful old-gold shade, which caught the brilliance of the atmosphere and seemed to light up her hair and complexion in a charming manner. Miss W–, shorter, dark, and 'fluffy', was an ideal foil for the magnificence of Miss J–. The dressing-gown in her case was of clinging, delicate silk, and the rose-du-barri shade gave to Miss W– an even sweeter complexion than that with which Nature had endowed her.

After making his bow and passing some ordinary remark, Lawrence bent his head downwards towards his plate, only raising it to take quick sidelong glances up and down the table, but never looking directly at the ladies opposite, and I knew from long experience that Lawrence was simply tickled to death over something – I fancied it was probably the visible effect of those dressing-gowns on some of the other ladies! – and I expected, every moment, to hear that peculiar high-pitched giggle of his come bursting out, causing something in the way of consternation round the table. I hastened to make conversation and found the football edition a very useful medium for that end. When I asked about my own team, Miss J– said, 'Do you know that district then? I thought you came from Nottingham?' at which Lawrence bent over still further and indulged in a little ankle-tapping under the table to draw my attention to the fact that the ladies had quite obviously been making careful enquiries as to the rest of the visitors in the house. I acknowledged the hint in the same manner, but with interest, and that cured him.

'Ask them if their names are "Old Gold" and "Rosie",' he suggested, *sotto voce*, under cover of his serviette, and down went his head again, while I struggled hard for composure and explained that Lawrence had suggested that possibly their 'boys' were footballers and they were therefore interested in the football news. Up went their heads in disdain. They didn't bother about 'boys' and as for footballers – horribly brutal people playing a horribly brutal game. They merely had the paper sent on to keep in touch with the latest home news.

Lawrence had by this time recovered from the effects of his inward mirth and commenced pretending to 'pull my leg' – as he loved to do! – for the benefit of the two ladies in particular and the table in general.

'There you are old man! I've never been able to understand why you will put in so much time at your games or in preparation for them. You see the opinion people get of you: "Horribly brutal people playing horribly brutal games." Now what about it?'

I laughed as I said, 'Just fancy that now! All the same I should have been playing yesterday had I been down there I know. For the rest, the ladies will pardon me, but, like you, they are not really entitled to pass an opinion.'

There was quite a bit of interest round the table now.

'Indeed!' said 'Old Gold' (incidentally, we always referred to her, privately, as 'Old Gold' during the whole of our stay – and afterwards), lifting her head in a haughty manner. 'And how do you make that out, Sir?'

'Well! I know Lawrence has never played football in his life, and I am assuming that, up to the present, you two have never donned jerseys and shorts, and that being so, I cannot see that you are competent . . .'

But before I could finish, Lawrence was off in that silly squealy laughter he would sometimes produce when highly tickled, and so many other people joined in his mirth that I began to wonder what I had done. But when I looked at the two ladies across the table and saw the dismay in their eyes and the blushes spreading right to their hair and necks, I understood that they fully realised the humour of my suggestion, knew why all those people were bubbling with laughter and did not like it much. Jerseys and shorts, after those dressing-gowns and with those carefully manipulated coiffures! I was well-nigh as dismayed as the ladies.

Lawrence came to the rescue in his wonderful way. Carefully he led the conversation into more general lines, and all went swimmingly under his direction until, breakfast ended, we were all enjoying cigarettes and admiring the view of the fast-filling front in the early morning sunshine.

Somebody had remarked on the lovely weather and on what a delightful place Blackpool was under such conditions, when I said to 'Old Gold', quite casually, 'I expect that, like us, you find it infinitely preferable to kid-walloping, which we shall all too soon be back at. What?'

I was aghast at the effect of that innocent remark. 'Old Gold' jumped up as though electric wires had suddenly 'shorted' under her. 'I don't know what you mean, Sir, and I think you're just trying to be disagreeable. We will not stay to be insulted by you any longer. Come along J–', and, seizing her companion, she hurried her off from the room, quite obviously in high dudgeon.

'What the devil have I done *this* time?' I asked Lawrence, breaking the dead silence which followed their departure.

'I dunno', Lawrence managed to gasp through his chuckles, and it was left to our violinist to solve the problem. 'I think you have committed the deadliest sin of all, young man', he hazarded.

'But I've done nothing at all', I protested.

'I know; but from their point of view, you've probably spoilt their holiday', he persisted.

'Good God!' broke in Lawrence. 'Are you suggesting that all the fuss is because George happened to let it out that they are schoolteachers?'

'You can bet that's it. Did you ever see schoolteachers "got-up" in that fashion for breakfast? You may depend upon it that they are usually great ladies when away on holiday.'

And our violinist was perfectly correct in his surmise, for our hostess waylaid us in the hall, asked us into her room, said that Miss J– and Miss W– were highly offended, were crying up in their room, talked of leaving the house, and then asked us to give her our version of what had occurred. Lawrence did so rather heatedly and I'm afraid I was lacking in sympathy. 'If they're crying, its their own faults. I'm not ashamed of my profession, if they are, and I certainly don't feel that I've done anything wrong.'

'They say that you have quite spoilt their holiday and that

they have never had to come down to being schoolteachers on any previous holiday', she said.

'Well! Tell 'em from me that the sooner they consider it a "going up" to be teachers, instead of a "coming down" the better it will be for the profession and for the kiddies they have charge of,' I said, and walked out of the room and upstairs.

Lawrence stayed down, and I knew that he had been attempting to pour oil on troubled waters, for when I came downstairs, he was chatting gaily with the two ladies in the entrance lobby.

'Ready Billy?' I called, using that affectionate diminutive I kept for very rare occasions. He excused himself, the ladies went off towards the promenade and we set off for a ramble out to Poulton-le-Fylde where I had promised to shew Lawrence the old cross, the stocks and other ancient objects in the queer, cobblestone-paved market square. Lawrence told me that, while I was upstairs, those ladies had suggested that he might like to accompany them to church and, if so, a message could be left explaining to me where he had gone. Of course, he had explained that we had a definite arrangement to visit Poulton.

Then followed a most amusing couple of days. Those ladies tried every possible wile to draw Lawrence away from me, while I just loved defeating their plans, and, with the exception of the requirements of good manners, otherwise completely ignored them. I was entirely relieved from my task, however, by the arrival of two more visitors. We knew that they were expected and had learned that they were a young widow who kept a hotel somewhere in the neighbourhood of Keighley, Yorkshire, and her elderly companion filling the role of duenna.

Just before dinner I rushed down from our room where I had been writing letters, to go out to post before dinner, when I remembered that Lawrence had written some postcards during the day and that they had not been posted. Throwing open the door of the drawing-room, I called, 'Billy, what about those postcards?' and then stopped just where I was the better to study the scene before me. In the centre of the room, with his back towards the door, Lawrence was down on his knees before one of the most charming little female humans it has ever been my pleasure to see. All round the room were faces full of laughing enjoyment, save over on the farther side of the room, where 'Old Gold' and 'Rosie' were sitting with faces as black as a thunder-cloud.

'An' who's Billy?' came a broad demand from the little beauty.

'I should think you ought to know', I laughed. 'You seem to have got him alright. What on earth is he doing?'

'Oh! Is this him?' (she was never very hot on grammar at any rate!) she asked leaning forward to pull that rebellious forelock playfully. 'Aye! Ah've got him raight enuff. What's he doing? Why, ah asked him to fasten me sho-lace, but I think he'll be having to fasten me garter as well while he's at it.' She made another pass at the forelock as a voice from a dark, elderly lady sitting near said, 'Clara!' in tones of shocked remonstrance.

Lawrence turned his laughing eyes over his shoulder to me and said, 'George, come and meet Clara.'

The introductions over, Clara resumed her seat, placed her foot on a footstool, showed quite an expanse of the most shapely leg imaginable and said, 'Come on, Billy! Tha c'n get on wi' thi job.' I delayed him long enough to get the postcards, promised to be back in a few minutes, and left them. When I returned they were still fooling around and it was obvious that Lawrence was delighted with this lovely little wild Yorkshire rose, who just said and did whatever came first to her mind, and who was just as obviously charmed with the grace and courtly manner of Lawrence.

'Ah'll tek yer round a bit after dinner, Billy', she said. 'Yer look ter me as if yer want motherin' a bit', at which Lawrence rose and making her a deep bow, said, 'Many thanks fair lady! Thy slave appreciates thy kindness and consideration.'

'Ha, ha', she exclaimed, and, jumping up, she imitated his bow in the most ludicrous fashion and then addressed us all, 'Me lord duke in disguise, ain't he now? Ha, ha,' and after another deep bow she flicked her leg behind her in a most comical manner, sending us all into shrieks of laughter. There was not the least doubt about it; she had just simply 'adopted' Lawrence, and I was highly amused at the efforts of 'Old Gold' and 'Rosie' to get somewhere near to him. They just had no chance with Clara. She was much too elemental for that and the 'niceties' meant simply nothing to her.

'Old Gold' called Lawrence over to her after dinner and began saying something to him, but she had scarcely commenced when Clara joined them and said, 'Nah Billy! Don't be wastin' a lot o' time. Tha looks as if a bottle o' stout or two would do thee good and we'll get off aht an' have 'em. Then we'll have a bit of a run round the town – all four of us. Come on, Billy!' and she grabbed his arm, brought him round to where I sat talking with her companion, and issued orders that we were all to be ready within five minutes.

'What is it?' I asked of Lawrence up in our room, but Lawrence was just hugging himself. 'Isn't she just lovely? What a lucky find! I've always wanted to meet somebody of that type but I never thought I should find anybody as real as Clara. Let's give 'em a good time, George.' He was as happy as any child with the toy of its dreams.

'Seems to me it's likely to be the lady who'll be giving us a good time if I'm any judge. But I must say I like her and I'm game for anything', I answered him.

'Knew you would be – as usual', he said, placing his hand on my shoulder and we went downstairs like that.

'Look out for "Old Gold" and "Rosie"', I warned, but Lawrence merely sniffed and said, 'Give me the natural before the artificial every time. Clara is so refreshing because she is just Clara all the time. You're a watch-dog no longer old man', and he chuckled to himself as he thus told me that he had been fully aware of all my efforts to defeat the plans of the lady schemers in the last few days.

She was a lovely little sport, that Yorkshire lass, full of fun and *joie de vivre*, and she just loved that period of playing up to the grace and bubbling sparkle of Lawrence. Those two simply kept the house uproarious with laughter by their fun and 'love-making foolery', but there was one object that Clara was never able to achieve. On the second night she invited us along to their room 'to help to lower the level of the whiskey bottle' as she put it. We excused ourselves, and we excused ourselves from the same invitation each other night of our stay.

On the Thursday of this week, by the way, we went across to Barrow-in-Furness to visit the Stewarts, whose two daughters had been at college with Lawrence.[24] I think they were the most 'advanced' people I had met up to that time. International or world socialism was apparently their ideal. They were strictly vegetarian, and the girls wore the shortest of dresses and heavy shoes, had their hair 'eton-cropped' even in those remote days, and smoked whenever they felt like it. They were a remarkably well-read and up-to-date family and it was perfectly clear that the girls and their little coterie had gone in for something approaching 'Lawrence-worship' – they appeared almost to have idolised him. All his life I had known girls like that.

They came to see us off by the boat and I think we might have had a very interesting discussion, but a couple of foolish people in a rowing-boat had disregarded the danger notices and gone too far down Walney Channel, and in the excitement of watching to see what would happen to them when the 'wash' of the steamer struck them, the Stewarts were forgotten. The two people? They were capsized; but when it was observed that they had both managed to scramble ashore to the nasty mud of Walney, our captain blew a siren-signal of some sort and we resumed our journey back to Blackpool, and to the anxiously waiting Clara. I had no further trouble in keeping 'Old Gold' and 'Rosie' at a distance. Lawrence and Clara kept up their love-making buffoonery, but there was no foolery about the tears which Clara shed when the time came for us to leave. She made us promise that, at some time, we would visit her in her Yorkshire home, but, though we often spoke of it, we never went there. I think I vastly prefer to remember Clara as I knew her, and possibly a sight of her in her home surroundings would have spoilt that memory; and I know that Lawrence had the same idea.

Shortly after I got married, Lawrence came to stay with me,[25] and it was then that I realised my own great 'betrayal' of Lawrence, though I still fail to see how, under the circumstances, I could have acted differently. On the last evening of his stay, as we were walking over the moors, he asked, quite suddenly, 'What about Easter?'

'I've promised to go down to the wife's people', I told him.

'And midsummer?'

'We shall be at Eastwood for some part of the holiday: I

don't know which part yet, and I'm afraid I cannot say what we shall be doing during the other portion.'

'But what about our usual holiday with the crowd?'

'I'm afraid you will have to make your arrangements without including me, this year, old man.' I told him. There was quite a long pause before I added, 'I'm very sorry, Billy, but I'm sure you see that I can't very well do otherwise.'

'But what am I to do? Where shall I be? Just stranded by myself with all the crew. I can't do it. You *must* come. Can't your wife go down to her people for a fortnight or stay up at Eastwood? Why not bring her with us? I simply can't fix it up without you. Say you will arrange it somehow', he pleaded.

'I think it's just quite impossible, Bert', I told him. 'My wife knows none of the crowd. She wouldn't understand them in the very least. She would be just like a fish out of water. And to suggest leaving her either at her home or mine would only lead to trouble. I'm afraid that, for this year at any rate, you must count me out of it.'

We argued on those lines for a very long time, Lawrence alternately pleading and cursing, neither of which made any impression on me, for I was convinced that the position I had taken up was the correct one under the circumstances.

Finally, Lawrence appeared to realise that he was spending his energies in vain. We walked along without speaking for a considerable distance, until Lawrence stopped suddenly and turned to me with blazing, searching eyes, 'And so all the past goes for nothing when this strange woman has to be considered?' he demanded.

'Not so very strange, old man', I assured him, 'I have known her for over five years you know.'

'But she is strange to our crowd; and now you propose to let consideration for her outweigh all thought for the old crowd, to say nothing of any feeling for me, personally', he said.

'You know very well that there is no truth in that', I replied with some heat. 'Since we were tiny boys together we have always thought of and for each other. I think we have thought more of each other than we have of anyone else except our mothers, and nothing in the world will ever take that thought away. There is no reason why it should. In the natural order of things we shall all get married eventually. You will do so – and

all the rest.' He shook his head sadly at this.[26] 'You must see
that the fact that I happen to be the first to get married is more
or less accidental. It might have been any of us.'

'I wouldn't have cared a damn about any of the rest. It's
you I'm talking about, and you I look like losing', replied
Lawrence.

'But you will not lose me. I don't want to lose you and I've
certainly no wish to be lost to you. It's only that I think it
better to count me out of this year's arrangements. I don't quite
understand all this. You didn't make a fuss when Alan and
Alvina were married.[27] You did all you could to push it along;
almost engineered it in fact', I told him.

'That was a different thing altogether. You can't compare
Alan's case with yours; and Alvina was never in the crowd.
Look at the years we've been together every holiday, Christmas,
Easter, Whitsun and, above all, midsummer. Was Alan in all
those arrangements? He wasn't in any of them except in so
far as visits to the Haggs or to our place were concerned.
Don't you see that you are leaving me stranded?' he asked
fiercely.

'No: it's not fair to say that', I insisted. 'Having got married
I feel that there are certain duties I have to perform and,
possibly certain sacrifices to make. And, damn it all, man,
don't *you* see that I shall be missing everything that you have
mentioned? Do you imagine that, this Easter, I shall not miss
my day in Derbyshire? Do you think I shall be forgetting the
way round Felley Mill, the silver of the willow catkins, the
sheeny haze over the newly-awakened trees, the little path by
the old kennels to Newstead, Misk Hills and Watnall Woods?
I shall be missing them all as much as you will – if you don't
go there as usual. Look at my side of it as well as yours, and
look forward, as I shall do, to midsummer when we shall again
be at Eastwood, and able to arrange some rambles, some of the
old parties and some of the good old times again.'

'If that's your decision, finally, I'm afraid I shall not be at
Eastwood', he said slowly and softly.

'Not at Eastwood! Why not?' I asked, quickly.

'It seems to me, George', he said slowly and very deliberately,
'It seems to me that the old days have gone; gone altogether;
gone beyond recall. I've had an offer to go abroad and do some

descriptive pieces – Austrian Tirol and so on. I've put it off and put it off, but now I shall accept, and God knows when I shall be back.'[28]

I scarcely knew what to say. I know I was filled with a great sadness. It seemed as though he thought that I was deliberately driving him to exile. I turned from him and commenced to walk along. He fell in by my side in silence and thus we walked until Lawrence gritted fiercely, through his tightly clenched teeth, 'Blast women! They are nothing but destroyers. They destroy everything they touch as soon as their sex is concerned.'

'Nothing of the kind; they don't destroy anything unless we let 'em', I defended.

'Not for you; I know. You never would let them either spoil or destroy anything for you – up till now. But what about it now?' he suddenly demanded.

'Nothing is destroyed. Nothing will be destroyed even now unless you allow the destruction to come. We have not altered: only our conditions are changed. But we are surely adaptable and I hope we shall all be able to grow accustomed to the changes as they come and still keep our old and very dear footing with each other.'

I shall never forget the sweet sadness of his smile as he slowly shook his head and said, 'You are asking for what I know to be impossible.' Suddenly he raised his head and said very resolutely, 'I shall go abroad.'

'And you will take all our love with you as always', I assured him. 'We shall be watching and waiting for the beauties you will find and will shew to us.'

When we visited Eastwood during the following midsummer holidays, Lawrence had acted upon his resolve. He was seeing new wonders in the Tirol and Northern Italy. While I made the round of the old, beloved spots with no company save my own thoughts which proved somewhat dreary companions.

I have never been able to understand quite clearly why Lawrence, of whose wonderfully fertile and vivid imagination we have such abundant proof, should so constantly refuse to put his imagination into action when seeking names for his characters. Practically all the names of his more important characters are the actual names of people he knew in his youth or are so flimsily disguised as to represent no real attempt at disguise. Sometimes the fact is material, but these cases are very few. In the majority of cases he appears to have taken a name at random and utilised it entirely without reference to the original holder or holders of the name. I have mentioned previously that this indiscriminate use of familiar names for by no means familiar characters has given rise to considerable resentment in the home district and I feel that a few words on the subject may serve a good purpose.

'Leivers' is quite a common name in the Eastwood district, but I do not think that Lawrence came into direct contact with any of them in the true sense of the word.[29] There was one family of the name living at Gilt Brook, of which the daughter, Helen, was a schoolteacher – much older than we were – and the other two children, twin boys, Hanford and Sam, Hanford a butcher at the Co-op, and Sam a schoolteacher, would be known to Lawrence, Hanford the better of the two, for Lawrence often did little shopping errands for his mother, and I remember we had a standing joke about Hanford and his sausages: 'Thick or thin, missis?' I seem to remember another daughter, older than these others, married to a man in the Civil Service and living in London, but by no stretch of the imagination could Lawrence be described as ever being on intimate terms with this family. In my own opinion, the real reason this name came first to his mind was that the name was directly connected with the outstanding events of his life and with all those things that made the deepest impression on Lawrence. Mr Leivers was the proprietor of the local livery stables, and without hesitation I say that William Leivers was the best known man in the district, for it was from him that carriages were obtained for all ceremonial occasions – weddings or funerals chiefly, so far as the working classes were concerned.

'Edgar' and 'Miriam', 'Cyril' and 'Paul'[30] – just borrowed christian names of friends or acquaintances of his youth.

'Annable'[31] was the name of an old man, quite a character and not by any means of the most amiable, who lived at the old mill in Beggarlee Lane, where the open-air baths have since been constructed. Though Lawrence uses the name, there is hardly a trace of the real 'Annable' in the character as drawn by Lawrence; the real prototype lived about four miles away, and, as a character study, Lawrence's portraiture is very wonderful.

'Alice' and 'Beatrice'[32] are taken from our own 'Alice Beatrice' of the Pagans; 'Beat' – a real John Blunt; 'Beat' – the oft-times giddy and gay; 'Beat' – who loved nothing better than a romp and who seemed to love to hear the Little Woman tell her, after a 'scuffle' that she looked as though she had been pulled through a hedge backwards; 'Beat' – the constant sufferer, but with the strength of mind to rise over her sufferings; 'Beat' – of the great heart and beautiful disposition; 'Beat' – whose memory is as full of sweet savours today as it always was.

'Carlotta'[33] is merely a derivative from 'Lottie Carlin', a girl for whose beauty Lawrence always had a great admiration, though except for the fact that she attended at the same chapel, he can scarcely be said to have known her. He was even more charmed by the lovely voice of her friend Emmeline Smith (whose brother she married) who still charms audiences occasionally in the south Staffordshire district where she lives and looks after that family of which she is so very properly proud. I met her in Lichfield only a short time ago; and her smile is as charming as ever.

'Coutts'[34] is probably a misspelling of the 'Cutts' family who lived in the 'Breach'. Lawrence might have told many a good story of these girls and boys, but any of the stories would necessarily have differed greatly from that of 'Bertha Coutts'.

An exactly similar statement will cover the 'Roddy' family, from which I have no doubt that 'Roddice'[35] is derived.

I think Mr George Chatterley was chief cashier – he was certainly a departmental head – at the Barber, Walker and Co.'s Collieries. They lived in a very nice house at the corner of Wellington Street and Nottingham Road. The family consisted of two very lovely daughters, of whom Connie[36] was the elder, and Lawrence was a great admirer of the beauty of those girls, though they were neither of them of that type which always seemed to appeal most to him.

The members of the 'Crich'[37] family were all known to Lawrence, though never intimately. He took an interest in the love affairs of Bert Crich – though Crich was older than we were – because of the beauty of the girl he afterwards married – a governess or companion in the Lindley family.

'Emily'[38] – there were quite a number of 'Emilys' well enough known to Lawrence, but the obvious source in this case, is his elder sister, Emily of the fiery mop – Lawrence's 'Injun Topknot'.

'Helen' – 'Helena'[39] – the name of a favourite relative – not quite first cousin if my recollection serves correctly – 'Nell' Hallam; Nell, the schoolteacher and representative; Nell of the quiet mind and calm disposition; Nell of the constant love, and whose 'boy and girl' affair with J. Edward Watson always promised to develop on the real, old-fashioned lines: and did.

'Houghton'[40] – the name of an elderly miner who lived a little further along Walker Street than the Lawrence home. Beyond passing the time of day with the old man, I only remember Lawrence coming into really intimate contact with him on one occasion, and that was a painful one, because the old man laid his stick heartily across both our backs.

We were preparing for some children's theatrical performances and had been experimenting in 'getting up' as Indian fakirs and practising the steps of the dance and the peculiar ditty that was to be sung:

> Yurra, yurra, yurra, yurra, moodkee, yah!
> Travancore-i-paniput rhino!
> Yurra, yurra, yurra, yurra, moodkee, ya-ah!
> Travancore-i-paniput rhino, rhino, rhi-i-i-no-o-o!

when somebody suggested that we ought to try the effect of it on people who were not expecting it. In the pale moonlight we stole along to old man Houghton's house, up the entry, on to the back yard where we commenced our idiotic song, and weird, unearthly dance.

I've never known exactly whether the old man thought we were deliberately and with great insolence calling him names – you will notice how that first line sounds remarkably like 'You're, you're a — monkey, y'are' – but be that as it may, we had not proceeded far with our row before he dashed out of the house without warning and belaboured us soundly with his stick. And I, at any rate, never bore any grudge because of it, for it served us right. Lawrence howled with laughter till the tears ran down his face as he told his mother and the others what had happened, when we returned to the house. Why Lawrence should couple 'Alvina' with 'Houghton' is quite beyond me. 'Alvina' or 'Tim' as she was usually called by the Pagans, was another cousin of Lawrence, a widow, young, fair and 'fluffy', with a little trouble that caused her to limp. She had a house near the back entrance (Barber Street entrance) to my father's place on Lynn Croft. This was the 'Tim' who married Alan, the elder brother of Jessie.

'Lettie'[41] was Lettice Ada, Lawrence's youngest sister of whom I have written in an earlier chapter.

'Rawdon Lilly'[42] is something of a puzzle, for among the early friends of Lawrence there is only Lilly Rawson, the daughter of a family living on Dovecote Lane, whose name approaches it, though there were several branches of the 'Lilley' family in the neighbourhood. 'Luke Lilley' was one of them – a well known local character. 'Tanny' is easy to find, but is quite without significance.

'Lou' and 'Lewis' in *St Mawr* each have their own significance to those who are acquainted with Lawrence's personal history, but Lawrence's mother, save one perhaps, was the only person who was ever qualified to comment adequately on *St Mawr*.[43]

'George H. Saxton'[44] was the son of the proprietor of Saxton's Stores, grocers and wine and spirit merchants, a very widely respected family, and members also of the Congregational Chapel. George was considerably older than Lawrence, and I question if he very much more than knew him. He married the statuesque Miss Bircumshaw and I can give no reason as to why Lawrence should use his name for a character of which, without doubt, I happen to be the prototype.

'Aaron Sisson'[45] was a member of a family who lived near the 'Three Tuns', on the Hill Top side. Aaron was something connected with the building trade – a carpenter, I think – a sound and serious type of man, musically inclined, but there was no intimate connection with the Lawrence family, and the real Aaron Sisson is as far from Lawrence's creation as the poles are asunder, except for the fact that both are men.

I have mentioned the 'Mellors'[46] – neighbours of the Lawrences at the Walker Street house. There was also the Lynn Croft family of Mellors – in fact there were three Mellors families in Lynn Croft – living at the Pottery House. The younger daughter, Mabel, attended Nottingham High School for Girls at the time we were travelling to school and we often walked up together from the station. The elder daughter, Maud, married George Hodgkinson, who, some considerable time after Maud's death, took as his second wife 'Floss' who might be called almost a Pagan.

'Dawes' and 'Pynegar'[47] were names of families very well known to us in our youth, families still represented in the district. The youthful pranks of Walt and Bill Pynegar might have found Lawrence much material for stories – but they were not of the type he sought, being chiefly merely mischief in much of which my brothers and I had a fair share.

'David' was Lawrence's own name of course, while of the 'Birkins',[48] I think the only member of that family in whom Lawrence was really interested, was Joe, of whose violin-playing neither Lawrence nor any of us ever wearied.

There are people who affect to bemoan Lawrence as a great loss to the 'working-class movement' – whatever that may be supposed to mean exactly! They may cease their moanings; Lawrence never belonged to the working class in spirit and certainly never had the slightest interest in any of their 'movements', except possibly academic interest. He was always quite out of sympathy with anything of that description. I do not mean to say that Lawrence was ever of the opinion that the working classes were getting fair treatment: he held a deep-rooted conviction that such was not the case; but he knew that, apparently, like the poor they must ever be with us and he treated with derision their efforts towards obtaining emancipation through political channels or organisations.

Politics he dismissed in his airy way: 'A dirty game for very dirty players', and later, when he knew that I was doing a good deal of political 'spade-work', he would add with his sly twinkle, or perhaps a quick wink to the Little Woman if she were present, 'And don't forget, Teufel, you can't touch pitch and not be defiled.' Sometimes this kind of thing would cause me to begin on an attempt to arouse him politically but he would say, 'For goodness sake don't talk *politics* to me. I can think of no greater infliction. Tell me, if you will, why my father is a

Liberal, or why your own father is a Liberal and I'll be interested; I should like to know the thought-processes by which they arrive at that blessed state. But you can't do it.'

I never attempted to explain why our fathers were Liberals – I never understood it myself – but I often attempted to make him see why I was not following in their footsteps. He would always agree with my point that we must be a nation of fools to be buying so many things we could make ourselves, and at the same time have great numbers of men walking about without jobs, and many others on short time; but even then he would pull down his brows, screw up his face in that peculiar way he had, wave his left hand very furiously about six inches from his left ear and say laughingly: 'I know; and I know you are very much in earnest, George. Forgive me laughing won't you? But I also know that you are only wasting your time with your political work and your platform 'spouting'. There are too many interests – financial, shipping and general commercial interests! – up against you. And what the devil do you think it matters to those interests that a few working men are out of jobs? or on short time? or that their families are suffering? or that their children will never even get a chance in life? Nothing. There's the root of the trouble. One half of the world cares nothing about what happens to the other half, and the men who are supposed to be looking after the general welfare are chiefly concerned in looking after just their own, or, at the very most, each other's welfare. But as for the idea of so organising the working classes that they shall run the country – the idea is absurd. You would lose your working men. They would lose the desire for work through lack of incentive. It would be the utter ruin of your country.'[49]

Thus the youthful Lawrence; and you will note that he maintained that attitude right to the end, In 'Myself Revealed', he stated:

> Yet I find, here in Italy, for example, that I live in a certain silent contact with the peasants who work the land of this villa. I am not intimate with them, hardly speak to them save to say good-day. And they are not working for me; I am not their 'padrone'.
> Yet it is they, really, who form my 'ambiente', and it is from them that the human flow comes to me. I don't want to

live with them in their cottages: that would be a sort of prison. But I want them to be there, about the place, their lives going on along with mine and in relation to mine.

I don't idealise them. Enough of that folly! It is worse than setting school-children to express themselves in selfconscious twaddle. I don't expect them to make any millennium here on earth, neither now nor in the future. But I want to live near them, because their life still flows.

There is no ambiguity about that statement; but it is not going back to his own class, and Lawrence himself knew it quite well, for, after a tirade against both the middle class and the working classes, he says, 'One can belong absolutely to no class.'

Then why don't I live with my working people? Because their vibration is limited in another direction. They are narrow, but still fairly deep and passionate, whereas the middle class is broad and shallow and passionless. Quite passionless. At the best they substitute affection which is the great middle-class positive emotion.[50]

And you will not require anything further than that to agree that, in spirit he never had been, and never could be, of the working classes.

Towards the end of his life he appears to have become quite convinced that money, wealth or riches is the cause of all the troubles of the world. Indirectly he may be in the right, but there is nothing new in the doctrine, for even in our 'copy-book days' we wrote, 'Money is the root of all evil.' And I fear that all the good that exercise ever did most of us was to make us pray that we might have more of the 'root' and resolve to risk the 'evil' which might follow.

What then was the vision of Lawrence? for surely such a man, in his 'thought-adventures', had visions of the world as he would have it. He had. His vision was that of a world which had adopted Love as the only sacred thing, a world in which nothing but Love as the one essential, was taught from the cradle. Love – in all things and for all things. The peoples of the world going along the broad highway together, each in his place and loving his place, obeying the behests of a beloved leader, chosen in Love and in Love leading his world onward.

My soul takes the open road. She meets the souls that are passing, she goes along with the souls that are going her way. And for one and all she has sympathy. The sympathy of love, the sympathy of hate, the sympathy of simple proximity; all the subtle sympathisings of the incalculable soul, from the bitterest hate to passionate love. . .

The love of man and woman: a recognition of souls and a communion of worship. The love of comrades: a recognition of souls and a communion of worship. Democracy: a recognition of souls, all down the open road, and a great soul seen in its greatness as it travels on foot among the rest, down the common way of the living. A glad recognition of souls, and a gladder worship of great and greater souls, because they are the only riches.[51]

Lawrence, in his 'thought-adventures', explored all the terrible possibilities for us and to save us, and future generations of men, misery, pain and humiliation. But with Lawrence himself was always present that true kingdom of heaven which had its being in his inmost consciousness and which peeps out in the most unexpected ways – often most incongruously – throughout all his works. It is the very incongruity of the fleeting glimpses that is responsible for our tardiness in belief, but, even though we be unwilling to believe, we must admit the fact of their existence, and, finally see and recognise the kingdom that was within him and know that, for Lawrence, in his heart of hearts, the love he sought for himself and for all men, was the one true Love based on the Love of the Source of Love. 'Communion of worship', and again, 'Communion of worship'. Let us believe, and join him in that communion of worship 'all down the open road'.

CONCLUSION

For the present my task is done. I cannot express the feeling that is within me that I have not been able to do full justice to a subject of such great importance, but at the very least I have given to you much more knowledge of the real Lawrence than you could ever have had without this work.

Together, we have seen our fragile boy living his heavily handicapped youthful days. We have seen something of their loneliness, the loneliness which, in sensitive children, usually results in a highly developed imagination and a highly-strung nervous system. We have taken a peep into the sanctity of his home at this and other times. We have tried to get a better, truer and fairer knowledge of his parents than has before been possible and we have met his brothers and sisters once again. Through his adolescent days we have watched his slow development and seen some of the influences affecting that development. We have caught fleeting glimpses of a few of the places of his early stories but there is nothing to add to Lawrence's descriptions of them. We have sometimes cast more than a passing glance at some of the people of his early stories. Here and there we have attempted some small correction of the delineation by Lawrence. We have exposed at times something of that sentimental side of himself that Lawrence always so carefully hid. We have watched his rapt admiration for strength and beauty, realised his secret longing for the attainment of strength and beauty in himself, longing for the impossible. We have sat by him in his sufferings. We have noted the course that he laid for himself and have marked his stead-fast holding of that course. We know something of his 'baptism into sex' and of his passing through the fires. Carefully we have avoided the Scylla and Charybdis of his wedded life; his life with that German lady he could only marry after the other man had released her. His sufferings because of his physical defects have drawn nothing from us but the genuine sympathy we would accord to any other cripple, and along the intricate mazes of his 'thought-adventures' we have followed him, as best we might and always, as I believe, in love, the very love he wished. And always have we sought for glimpses of the good that we knew was in him and which he never was able entirely to deny. Right to the very end we have sought those traces, and always found them, and at the last we have rejoiced, because then, and only then, have we found the most complete and perfect expressions of his love for all the world. And there, with you, I leave my Lawrence.

There is a short poem of mine, written many years ago, which always calls up Lawrence to my memory. I give it to you in the hope that, for all of you, it may perform a similar service. I call it 'Mem'ry's Garden'.

> I've been in Mem'ry's Garden,
> Dreaming dreams:
> The roses are all blooming;
> Beauty teems.
> Pearls are for dewdrops,
> Wings are of gold,
> Scents are enchanting,
> Skies never cold:
> Breezes, that chant of Love
> Make scarce a petal move:
> Sweet is the calm above
> My Mem'ry's Garden.
>
> But now, the Present calls me
> Back again,
> And I, from sweetly dreaming,
> Wake to Pain.
> Dewdrops are frozen.
> Wings, black and grim,
> Crush me, and press me
> To Hell's dark rim.
> Love, crush'd, disfigur'd lies
> Staring with sightless eyes:
> God! Can she only rise
> In Mem'ry's Garden?

APPENDIX A: THE RAINBOW

Discussion of Neville's five perplexing paragraphs on *The Rainbow* in section 1 of his Memoir must be highly conjectural. It may be helpful to begin by itemising the substance of his account.

1 Lawrence was bringing *The Rainbow* into 'final shape' in March 1912.
2 Neville knew that the 'bedroom scene' was true; predicted trouble; suggested a method of rewriting it. Lawrence refused.
3 Later (presumably during publication) Lawrence was asked to rewrite the chapter to avoid the trouble, but he refused.
4 *The Rainbow* 'fell'.
5 Today (i.e. 1930 or 1931) only American copies of *The Rainbow* are available. (In fact it had been re-issued in England in 1926.)[1]

Unless we are to dismiss the first two assertions as fabricated or confused, we should attempt to consider whether there might be any kernel of fact in them. Part of the difficulty is that we do not know whether Neville and Lawrence met again or exchanged letters, but it seems unlikely, for surely Neville would have mentioned it if they had. If they did not, what is Neville's evidence for connecting his conversations with Lawrence about a 'bedroom scene' in March 1912 with the 'fall' of *The Rainbow*? Another difficulty is that we do not know how closely Neville read Lawrence's works after their parting in 1912, and in particular whether he ever read *The Rainbow*. But if we are to give serious consideration to Neville's story, we must suppose he had at least sufficient acquaintance with *The Rainbow* as published to make the identification. Therefore: either he read the book himself, or someone who had read it made a sufficiently specific reference to a 'bedroom scene' contained therein (either verbally, or in a report of the trial, for example) for Neville to recognise it.

When Nehls published these five paragraphs he correctly noted that no second authority agreed that Lawrence was working on the novel that was to become *The Rainbow* and *Women in Love* so early as Neville recollected – the first months of 1912.[2] On the one hand all

167

the evidence in Lawrence's letters of this period points to 'Paul Morel' (not retitled *Sons and Lovers* until October 1912) as the novel Lawrence was working hard to complete before leaving for Germany in May 1912. On the other hand conventional wisdom dates the origins of the novel, 'The Sisters', which was to develop into *The Rainbow* and *Women in Love*, to the early months of 1913. Lawrence told Edward Garnett on [2] May 1913 that he had written 180 pages of the first draft of his newest novel 'The Sisters', which he expected to be about 300 pages long.[3] But it is worth considering the possibility that some at least of the material was drafted earlier. Lawrence wrote to J. B. Pinker his literary agent on 23 April 1915: 'I hope you are willing to fight for this novel. It is nearly three years of hard work, and I am proud of it, and it must be stood up for.'[4] When Lawrence said 'nearly three years' in April 1915 it is un-likely that he was merely exaggerating or that he would lightly confuse three years with two, for April 1912 had been the crucial period of his departure from England. The three years should not, however, be counted back from April, but from the date at which Lawrence had completed the novel. The certain date there is 2 March 1915, when Lawrence wrote to his friend Viola Meynell: 'I have finished my Rainbow, bended it and set it firm.'[5] Moreover, Lawrence had written to Pinker on 24 February 1915: 'I am very, very near the end of the novel.'[6]

Is it possible, therefore, that when Lawrence called 'The Sisters' in early 1913 'only first draft'[7] and 'the first crude fermenting',[8] he was in fact reworking something he had written out once by March 1912? (He had called his third version of *Sons and Lovers* 'the first draft'.)[9] Lawrence was, certainly, an exceptionally rapid writer who could complete a draft of a novel in a matter of weeks; and there is still some scope for studying what pieces of work he started, drafted and abandoned during the course of 1912.[10]

However, even supposing there was some such early document, *that* is not the same as Neville's 'final bringing into shape of *The Rainbow*'. The evidence of Lawrence's letters tells us that the 'Sisters' material, whenever it was begun, was rewritten many times and radically altered between its first mention in April 1913 and the publication of *The Rainbow*. Surely Neville cannot have read the published work and thought it so much the same as whatever he read or discussed with Lawrence in Bradnop that he could find the words 'final bringing into shape' appropriate?

The title *The Rainbow* was not thought of until May 1914; the novel was published in September 1915, banned and destroyed in November 1915; and reissued in 1926 and 1929. Neville, writing in 1930 or 1931, is clearly unaware that it has been republished in England, and this casts some doubt on his acquaintance with the finished work.

Certainly Neville was not the close student of Lawrence's writings that Jessie Chambers was, and he might well pass over changes of tone and even some changes of substance produced by Lawrence's revisions. The detailed interest he had so far manifested in the early novels is largely confined to incidents that strikingly concern himself. But however inattentive and selective a reader, had he read *The Rainbow* in its final published form, he would surely have found the developments in it too radical to warrant his insistence that it 'was to all intents and purposes completed' in March 1912?[11]

However, Neville seems so exceptionally clear about the 'bedroom' incident he is referring to (and even gives the impression that it had happened to himself rather than to Lawrence); he is so emphatic about the title of the novel and the book's 'fall'; and he is so confidently sarcastic at Murry's account of *The Rainbow*'s autobiographical basis, as to suggest that his assertions were grounded in some genuine knowledge of the work.

Nehls offered the conjectural identification of the bedroom scene in the 'Anna Victrix' chapter of *The Rainbow*. This may be the best candidate in *The Rainbow* as published. But if we wish to conjecture what Neville was referring to, we must take into consideration the qualifications outlined above. Either Neville had his mind set so exclusively on a certain incident that when he found it in the published novel, or learned by some other means that it was there, he ignored all questions of the novel's evolution, and simply assumed that it must have been complete back in 1912. Or he did not read, or hear any detailed account of, *The Rainbow* but when it 'fell' he jumped to the conclusion that this was the trouble he had predicted, and it must result from the very incident he had failed to dissuade Lawrence from using in his fiction. (He may have been encouraged in this conclusion by newspaper reports of the trial of *The Rainbow*[12] in which it was claimed that Lawrence had, after some co-operation, refused to change the novel further.)

But the effect of Neville's confidence about the scene in question, is to convey that it was not merely an incident but a piece of writing that he and Lawrence quarrelled over in March 1912. Neville says he 'suggested a certain method of rewriting the chapter' containing the 'bedroom scene'; his account implies that the scene in question was written out at the time, and indeed that he himself read it.

It is difficult to suppose that Neville had mistaken merely the title and was referring to a scene in 'Paul Morel', as it was still called, a novel that Lawrence *was* bringing into final shape at the time – he repeatedly declared he was finishing the novel,[13] though he revised it twice after this. It certainly could not have been a scene that was retained through the revisions and published in *Sons and Lovers*, for not only does Neville show in his Memoir that he was well acquainted with *Sons and Lovers*, but that novel certainly did not 'fall'. Therefore a tempting resolution of the puzzle in the identification of, for example, the scene in chapter XI 'The test on Miriam' or that in Clara's mother's home in chapter XII 'Passion', seems to be ruled out.

Is it possible, however, that the scene Neville saw in manuscript was contained in that, current, version of *Sons and Lovers*, but was removed during the two subsequent rewritings of the novel, and later put into *The Rainbow*? The final manuscript of *Sons and Lovers* is now published in photographic form.[14] Many pages are heavily revised and contain earlier stages of composition. But much of the end of the novel was written out afresh during the last stage of writing – presumably, either copied out neatly from much-corrected pages, or completely redrafted. It is not impossible, therefore, that Lawrence had written the scene in question into the latter part of this draft of *Sons and Lovers*, and later redeployed it. Were this the case, it would follow that Neville later found, or learned, that the scene was in the published *Rainbow* and thus jumped to the conclusion that the novel Lawrence was finishing in 1912 must have been *The Rainbow*.

In conclusion: if Neville saw a bedroom scene written out as part of a novel in March 1912 which was later published in *The Rainbow*, what did he see? Either 1. There was an earlier draft of some 'Sisters' material, done by about March 1912, containing a bedroom scene which survived into *The Rainbow*. (N.b. Lawrence called *The Rainbow* nearly three years' work.) Or 2. The antepenultimate version of *Sons and Lovers*, a draft Lawrence was finishing in March 1912, contained the scene (which Neville read in a manuscript he did not realise was 'Paul Morel'), but Lawrence later removed it and re-used it in *The Rainbow*.

On the other hand, if Neville did not actually read anything in manuscript, but only argued with Lawrence about including the incident in a novel, whether or not into his current, nearly finished novel, what happened? Perhaps 3. Their argument must have been about an incident that did later find its way into *The Rainbow*, but it need not have been written down by Lawrence until later.

These three conjectures seem to be the only possible logical conclusions from Neville's story if one accepts the claim made at the outset of this discussion: that he must have had sufficient, direct or indirect, knowledge of the published *Rainbow* to make the connection between the novel and the incident. If such knowledge is called into question, one final solution, perhaps a rather severely sceptical one in view of Neville's confident tones, remains. Possibly 4. Neville simply guessed that the incident he had tried to dissuade Lawrence from recounting in fiction must have been what caused the *Rainbow* scandal. (He may have thought his hunch confirmed by newspaper reports of the trial.)

APPENDIX B: LAWRENCE, NEVILLE AND GREIFFENHAGEN'S 'IDYLL'

Lawrence is known to have made at least three copies of Greiffen-hagen's *Idyll* as presents in 1911: one for Louie Burrows, one for his sister Ada, and one for Agnes Holt.

Maurice Greiffenhagen (1862–1931) first exhibited his oil painting *An Idyll* at a Royal Academy Exhibition in 1891. An article in *The Art Journal* of August 1894 by 'A.G.T.', tells us that *An Idyll* was not hung to great advantage at that exhibition and consequently no sale was made. It was displayed later in the year at the Liverpool Autumn Exhibition and was then acquired by the Walker Art Gallery, Liverpool, for £150. The picture began to be well known in 1892 when it was lent by the Liverpool Corporation for the Guildhall Loan Exhibition, where it occupied a prominent place.

From this time onwards it was very popular, and was reproduced in various forms. It accompanied the article referred to above in *The Art Journal*; it was reproduced in the *Magazine of Art*, January 1892, and in *The Studio*, vol. III, 1894. It also appeared in calendars and as a Christmas card continuously from 1892.

Lawrence, who knew *The Studio*, may have first become acquainted with the painting in one of the black-and-white magazine reproductions (he seems to have known it before December 1908). But he must have made his copies in 1910–11 from a colour reproduction.

On 31 December 1908, Lawrence wrote to Blanche Jennings (*Letters*, i. 103): 'As for Greiffenhagen's *Idyll*, it moves me almost as much as if I were fallen in love myself . . . it is largely the effect of your *Idyll* that has made me kiss a certain girl till she hid her head in my shoulder.' An explanation for the phrase 'your *Idyll*' may be found in Lawrence's letter to Blanche Jennings of 15 December 1908 (*Letters*, i. 99) where he discussed the kiss in Balzac's novel *Eugénie Grandet*, a book he had sent her as a gift a few weeks before. His discussion may have led her to think that *An Idyll* would be an appropriate calendar or Christmas card (she sent him *A Shropshire Lad* as his main Christmas present). Why she might have thought it appropriate becomes more obvious if we refer to the article in *The Art Journal*, where we read that 'seldom, if ever [before] had the passionate embrace been pictorially attempted'. And fourteen years later, in 1908, the painting still seemed striking enough for J. E. Phythian to write in *Fifty Years of Modern Painting: Corot to Sargent*: 'Mr Greiffenhagen's . . . *Idyll* in the Liverpool Art Gallery, strong in colour and fine in draughtsmanship, is as elemental – is an as simply profound interpretation of the passionate love of youth and maiden – as Madox Brown's *Romeo and Juliet.*'

It is possible, then, that in whatever form Blanche Jennings sent this picture to Lawrence, he retained it and made his copies from it. Another possible source may be a colour reproduction in *100 Popular Pictures*, a series edited by Spielmann and published by Cassell, which appeared fortnightly at 7/6d per issue throughout 1910. An excellent colour reproduction of *An Idyll*, of the kind that could be detached and hung, appeared in the issue for the latter half of May.

Lawrence began a copy for Louie on 3 March 1911 (*Letters*, i. 234) and had finished it by 27 March (*Letters*, i. 242). The copy for Ada was also finished by 27 March (*Letters*, i. 243): 'I've painted you a little *Idyll* – about 14″ x 7″. Do you remember I began to draw it the night mother died? – and I said I should never finish it. Now I've done a big one for Louie, and a little one for you. It looks nice.'

(His mother had died on 9 December 1910. In chapter XV, 'Derelict', of *Sons and Lovers* Lawrence wrote: 'He could not paint. The picture he finished on the day of his mother's death – one that satisfied him – was the last thing he did.' The picture that Lawrence finished on the day of his mother's death was a copy of Frank Brangwyn's 'The Orange Market'; but in contrast to what he said of Paul Morel, he himself then started an *Idyll* copy.)

The third copy, for Agnes Holt, was begun by 7 July 1911 (*Letters*, i. 282): 'Now I've begun a little *Idyll* for Agnes Holt. She marries in early August, and has asked me for this picture. I must race and get her a couple done.' On 22 December 1911 Lawrence wrote to his Croydon schoolmaster friend, Arthur McLeod (*Letters*, i. 341): 'I sketched the *Idyll* for you in the week – I wanted to do the painting for you – but the lumbering drawing-board was too much for me, damn it. I will try if I can get the thing done before I go away [i.e. to convalesce].' Lawrence was still offering to paint a copy for McLeod a year later (*Letters*, i. 488, 498). But by 9 July 1916 he had concluded, in a letter to Catherine Carswell from Cornwall (*Letters*, Moore 461): 'Greiffenhagen seems to be slipping back and back. I suppose it has to be. Let the dead bury their dead. Let the past smoulder out.' The *Idyll*, then, challenged Lawrence to interpretative attention for at least four years and Grieffenhagen was in his thoughts for a further four.

Neville's comments in his Memoir not only confirm Lawrence's repeated effort to paint copies of the picture but suggest that he started with a series of abortive attempts because he found the figures too difficult. Neville claims that only after he had posed for Lawrence was Lawrence able to draw the figures and so begin to complete a copy of the painting. Neville's other main claim is that his posing distracted Lawrence from the immediate practical need to make sketches. If the full significance of the material to which Neville's anecdote leads could be teased out, it would carry us deep into the youthful Lawrence's psychology. The first step is to note how differently Lawrence wrote about Greiffenhagen's *Idyll* in life, where he simply assumed the man's rôle, and in fiction. In the letter to Blanche Jennings of 31 December 1908 (*Letters*, i. 103) he wrote:

As for Greiffenhagen's *Idyll*, it moves me almost as much as if I were fallen in love myself. Under its intoxication, I have flirted madly this christmas; I have flirted myself half in love; I have flirted somebody else further, till two solicitous persons have begun to take me to task; it is largely the effect of your *Idyll* that has made me kiss a certain girl till she hid her head in my shoulder; but what a beautiful soft throat, and a round smooth chin, she has; and what bright eyes, looking up! Mon Dieu, I am really half in love! But not with the splendid uninterrupted passion of the *Idyll*. I am too conscious, and vaguely troubled. I think it is a good thing I must go back to Croydon. Where there is no 'abandon' in a love, it is dangerous, I conclude; mother declares the reverse. By the way, in love, or at least in love-making, do you think the woman is always passive, like the girl in the *Idyll* – enjoying the man's demonstration, a wee bit frit [frightened] – not active? I prefer a little devil – a Carmen – I like not things passive. The girls I have known are mostly so; men always declare them so, and like them so; I do not.

However, fiction gave him the opportunity to respond to the painting simultaneously from a woman's point of view also, in the conversation between Lettie and George in part I, chapter III of *The White Peacock*. For it is evident, as Jessie Chambers noted (E.T. 118), that in that novel, 'Cyril and Letty are each aspects of Lawrence.'

They turned on, chatting casually, till George suddenly exclaimed, 'There!'
It was Maurice Greiffenhagen's 'Idyll'.

'What of it?' she asked, gradually flushing. She remembered her own enthusiasm over the picture.

'Wouldn't it be fine?' he exclaimed, looking at her with glowing eyes, his teeth showing white in a smile that was not amusement.

'What?' she asked, dropping her head in confusion.

'That – a girl like that – half afraid – and passion!' He lit up curiously.

'She may well be half afraid, when the barbarian comes out in his glory, skins and all.'

'But don't you like it?' he asked.

She shrugged her shoulders, saying, 'Make love to the next girl you meet, and by the time the poppies redden the field, she'll hang in your arms. She'll need to be more than half afraid, won't she?'

She played with the leaves of the book, and did not look at him.

'But', he faltered, his eyes glowing, 'it would be – rather – '

'Don't, sweet lad, don't!' she cried laughing.

'But I shouldn't – ' he insisted, 'I don't know whether I should like any girl I know to – '

'Precious Sir Galahad', she said in a mock caressing voice, and stroking his cheek with her finger, 'You ought to have been a monk – a martyr, a Carthusian.'

He laughed, taking no notice. He was breathlessly quivering under the new sensation of heavy, unappeased fire in his breast and in the muscles of his arms. He glanced at her bosom and shivered.

'Are you studying just how to play the part?' she asked.

'No – but – ' he tried to look at her, but failed. He shrank, laughing, and dropped his head.

'What?' she asked with vibrant curiosity.

Having become a few degrees calmer, he looked up at her now, his eyes wide and vivid with a declaration that made her shrink back as if flame had leaped towards her face. She bent down her head, and picked at her dress.

'Didn't you know the picture before?' she said, in a low toneless voice.

He shut his eyes and shrank with shame.

'No, I've never seen it before', he said.

'I'm surprised,' she said. 'It is a very common one.'

'Is it?' he answered, and this make-belief conversation fell. She looked up, and found his eyes. They gazed at each other for a moment before they hid their faces again. It was a torture to each of them to look thus nakedly at the other, a dazzled, shrinking pain that they forced themselves to undergo for a moment, that they might the moment after tremble with a fierce sensation that filled their veins with fluid, fiery electricity. She sought almost in panic, for something to say.

'I believe it's in Liverpool, the picture,' she contrived to say.

He dared not kill this conversation, he was too self-conscious. He forced himself to reply, 'I didn't know there was a gallery in Liverpool.'

175

'Oh, yes, a very good one', she said.

Their eyes met in the briefest flash of a glance, then both turned their faces aside.

Once Lawrence had had Neville pose for him and had seen how different from his own was a well-developed male physique he was edged crucially towards assimilating himself to the woman in the painting. Neville's account, as a glance at the reproduction will show, is not quite straightforward, because the man in the picture does not have his back displayed, nor could it be thought necessary for Neville to strip completely to give Lawrence the model he needed. Neville, in effect, was creating for himself an opportunity to pose for Lawrence.

Part of the value of Neville's anecdote, is that it calls attention to the importance *An Idyll* had for Lawrence by describing this notable piece of his behaviour. In addition it contains small but crucial linguistic likenesses to a passage in *The White Peacock* (part II chapter II) – but only in the form in which that passage stood before it was censored for publication in England. (It is highly unlikely that Neville acquired the uncensored American edition of the novel, and all but impossible that he could have carried in his mind the manuscript reading.) The censored version of the passage which appeared in all English editions, reads:

> We got married. She gave me a living she had in her patronage, and we went to live at her Hall. She wouldn't let me out of her sight. Lord! – we were an infatuated couple – and she would choose to view me in an aesthetic light. I was Greek statues for her, bless you: Croton, Hercules, I don't know what! She had her own way too much – I let her do as she liked with me.
>
> Then gradually she got tired – it took her three years to be really glutted with me. I had a physique then – for that matter I have now.

The uncensored version, which appeared in American editions only and is restored by Andrew Robertson in the new Cambridge edition of *The White Peacock*, reads:

> We got married. She gave me a living she had in her patronage, and we went to live at her Hall. She wouldn't let me out of her sight. God! – we were a passionate couple – and she would have me in her bedroom while she drew Greek statues of me – her Croton, her Hercules! I never saw her drawings. She had her own way too much – I let her do as she liked with me.
>
> Then gradually she got tired – it took her three years to have a real bellyful of me. I had a physique then – for that matter I have now.

Lawrence like other writers of the period strongly associates the word 'passion' with the *Idyll* and that is how the Greiffenhagen picture is feeding into this apparently different passage from *The White Peacock*; 'passion', at any rate in the charged phrase 'passionate couple' in this context, clearly meant sexual passion, and for that reason needed toning down to 'infatuated'. But the direct connections between Neville's anecdote and the uncensored passage, apart from the fact of posing which has itself been censored, lie in the words 'Hercules', 'statues', and the sentence 'I never saw her drawings'. Neville, it will be recalled, recollected Lawrence calling him a pocket Hercules and commented that he never saw Lawrence's sketches. (Readers might well wonder what artistic coherence 'I never saw her drawings' has in the novel.)

Neville's belief that Lawrence was momentarily overwhelmed by the spectacle of human beauty may be well founded with respect to life; but in the novel, apart from the phrase 'a passionate couple', nothing is conveyed in the account of the Lady Crystabel's behaviour of the rapt admiration of Lawrence in life. In the fictional representation of the episode more complicating factors are evident.

The unusual and mistaken name 'Croton' provides the clue to the hinterland of associations which constitute the first element of complication: the contrast between a strong, impressive physique and a slender one. Lawrence had not been to Greece and therefore his notion of Greek sculpture relates either to what he had seen in England or to reproductions. The name Croton appears to have come from an extract called 'The Olympic Games' by Georg Ebers contained in the *International Library of Famous Literature* (edited by Richard Garnett, 20 vols. 1899). These volumes were described by Jessie Chambers as 'one of the most treasured possessions of the Lawrence household' (E.T. 92), and were a seed-bed of Lawrence's thought. The article, in volume 2, is accompanied by an illustration of a statue of a nude male discus thrower. The relevant passage (pages 509–10) reads:

> The Sybarites sent messengers to the festival, whose appearance was simply dazzling, the Spartans simple men, with the beauty of Achilles and the stature of Hercules; the Athenians distinguished themselves by supple limbs and graceful movements; the Crotonians were led by Milo, the strongest man of human origin . . .
>
> The youth and the man stood opposite each other in their nude beauty, glistening with golden oil, like a panther and a lion preparing for combat. Young Lysander raised his hands before the first attack, adjured the gods, and cried, 'For my father, my honor, and Sparta's fame!' The Crotonian gave the youth a condescending smile . . .
>
> Now the wrestling began. For a long while neither could take hold of the other. The Crotonian tried with his powerful, almost irresistible, arms to seize his adversary, who eluded the terrible grasp of the athlete's claw-like hands. The struggle for the embrace lasted long,

and the immense audience looked on, silent and breathless. Not a sound was heard, save the panting of the combatants . . . At last – at last, with the most beautiful movement I ever saw, the youth was able to clasp his adversary. For a long while Milo exerted himself in vain to free himself from the firm hold of the youth . . .

. . . At last the youth's strength gave way . . . he collected his strength with a superhuman effort, and tried to throw himself again on his adversary, but the Crotonian had noticed his momentary exhaustion, and pressed the youth in an irresistible embrace. A stream of black blood gushed from the beautiful lips of the youth, who sank lifeless to the earth from the wearied arms of the giant . . .

Milo was obliged to resign the wreath, and the fame of the youth will resound through all Greece.

Readers of *Women in Love* will feel that this account prefigures the wrestling match between Gerald Crich and Rupert Birkin in the chapter with its title significantly taken from the ancient world, 'Gladiatorial'. A small piece of evidence that Lawrence's mind was partly fixed upon images from the classical Greek world is provided by Eldon S. Branda when he records (*Texas Studies in Literature and Language*, Autumn 1964): 'in the typescript [of *Women in Love*, Lawrence] deleted a passage which seemed to expose his own fears about the acceptance of such a relationship: "To them the relation-ship of Achilles and Patroclos was moving, but womanly and suspect."' (The encounter in *Women in Love* also draws upon another extract from *The International Library of Famous Literature*, 'Jiujutsu' by Lafcadio Hearn, vol. 18, pages 8512–14).

The contrast between Lawrence's physique and that of a strong well-developed contemporary (setting on one side the question of how much George Saxton in *The White Peacock* owes to George Neville and/or Alan Chambers) is brought out most clearly in the chapter entitled 'A Poem of Friendship'. There once again Lawrence reverts to art to provide him with key images for his description, and in particular, the notion of classic grace to characterise his own slender figure:

We stood and looked at each other as we rubbed ourselves dry. He was well-proportioned, and naturally of handsome physique, heavily limbed. He laughed at me, telling me I was like one of Aubrey Beardsley's long, lean ugly fellows. I referred him to many classic examples of slenderness, declaring myself more exquisite than his grossness, which amused him.

When Lawrence is handling this material fictionally in an all-male context there is no complicating factor of social inequality present; whereas when George and Lettie are looking through the art book, and when the Lady Crystabel is drawing her husband's poses, social difference is a key factor. What sexual associations, in addition to social ones, accompanied for Lawrence the distinction between the words 'woman' and 'lady'?

Jessie Chambers touched on this in her account of *The White Peacock* (E.T. 116):

> I had not a high opinion of the first version of *The White Peacock*, in which George married Letty . . . The novel, apart from its setting, seemed to me story-bookish and unreal. The upright young farmer, hopelessly in love with the superior young lady (very conscious of her social superiority) who had been served shabbily by a still more socially superior young man, married her after a puritanical exposition of the circumstances by her mother, and a highly dubious conjugal life began in the melancholy farmhouse, with, one imagined, Letty always in the parlour and George in the kitchen.

This plot-structure was not, I conjecture, accidental but was shaped by life-pressures rooted in Lawrence's mother's own history. In the opening pages of *Sons and Lovers* there is yet another version of this plot-structure in the miniature story of Gertrude Coppard and John Field, which is as intruded there as the history of Annable's marital relationship is intruded into *The White Peacock*:

> She used to walk home from chapel with John Field when she was nineteen. He was the son of a well-to-do tradesman, had been to college in London, and was to devote himself to business . . .
> 'But you say you don't like business', she pursued.
> 'I don't. I hate it!' he cried hotly.
> 'And you would like to go into the ministry', she half implored.
> 'I should. I should love it, if I thought I could make a first-rate preacher.'
> 'Then why don't you – why *don't* you?' Her voice rang with defiance. 'If *I* were a man, nothing would stop me.'
> She held her head erect. He was rather timid before her.
> 'But my father's so stiff-necked. He means to put me into the business, and I know he'll do it.'
> 'But if you're a *man*?' she had cried.
> 'Being a man isn't everything', he replied, frowning with puzzled helplessness.
> Now, as she moved about her work at the Bottoms, with some experience of what being a man meant, she knew that it was *not* everything.
> At twenty, owing to her health, she had left Sheerness. Her father had retired home to Nottingham. John Field's father had been ruined; the son had gone as a teacher in Norwood. She did not hear of him until, two years later, she made determined inquiry. He had married his landlady, a woman of forty, a widow with property.

When we add to this the sentence (a page later): '[Gertrude

Coppard] was to the miner that thing of mystery and fascination, a lady', and recollect that Lawrence himself later met and married an aristocrat (a marriage with Frieda 'always in the parlour' and Lawrence 'in the kitchen'), we see how the various versions of a similar social-sexual narrative cited above belong to Lawrence's deepest conditioning. It becomes clear how Annable's intruded and baffling marital history could have incorporated aspects of Lawrence's response to the 'passion' of the Greiffenhagen *Idyll* and to his experience of Neville's posing for him: that 'history' was a concentrated revelation of the ambivalent basic disposition of Lawrence's personality.

NOTES

Editor's introduction

1 'E.T.' [Jessie Wood], *D. H. Lawrence: A Personal Record*, (Jonathan Cape, 1935; reprinted Cambridge University Press, 1980) (hereafter E.T.).

2 *Renaissance and Modern Studies*, 16 (1972), pp. 5–17, esp. p. 13.

3 *The Letters of D. H. Lawrence*. vol. 1, ed. James T. Boulton (Cambridge University Press, 1979) (hereafter *Letters*, i.) pp. 65, 67.

4 See p. 94.

5 See pp. 104–7.

6 *Sons and Lovers* (Duckworth, 1913), chapter XIII, 'Baxter Dawes'.

7 See pp. 151–3.

8 Privately communicated by Ernest Wilson's son, Mr Roy Wilson, in a letter to the editor, 22 Oct. 1975.

9 *Letters*, i. 294.

10 Emile Delavenay, *D. H. Lawrence: L'Homme et la Genèse de son Œuvre* (2 vols., Librairie C. Klincksieck, Paris, 1969) (hereafter Delavenay), p. 706.

11 'Sex Locked Out' appeared in the *Sunday Dispatch* for 25 Nov. 1928. It was collected into *Assorted Articles* (Secker, 1930) as 'Sex versus Loveliness'. *Assorted Articles* is reprinted in *Phoenix II: uncollected, unpublished and other prose works by D. H. Lawrence*, ed. Warren Roberts and Harry T. Moore (Heinemann, 1968) (hereafter *Phoenix II*).

12 John Middleton Murry, *Son of Woman: the story of D. H. Lawrence* (Jonathan Cape, 1931) (hereafter *Son of Woman*). His sense of rivalry with Murry led him to take up Murry's description of *Son of Woman* as a 'betrayal' and subtitle his Memoir with the same word. His own betrayal consisted in the corrective disclosures about Lawrence's private life.

13 'Myself Revealed' appeared in the *Sunday Dispatch* for 17 Feb. 1929. It was collected into *Assorted Articles* as 'Autobiographical Sketch'; see *Phoenix II* 592–6.

14 Edward Nehls, *D. H. Lawrence: a composite biography* (3 vols. University of Wisconsin Press, 1957–8) (hereafter Nehls), i. 25–7, 33–4, 41, 46, 153–5.

15 Harry T. Moore: *The Priest of Love* (Heinemann, 1974) (first published as *The Intelligent Heart*, New York: Farrar, Strauss and Young, 1954) p. 112.

16 E.T.; for May Chambers's Memoir see Nehls, iii. 552–620.

17 *The Letters of D. H. Lawrence*, ed. Aldous Huxley (Heinemann, 1932) pp. 28–9; *The Collected Letters of D. H. Lawrence*, ed. Harry T. Moore (2 vols., Heinemann, 1962) (hereafter *Letters*, Moore) i. 102–3. Both print this letter with Neville's surname omitted. Moore also published Lawrence's letter to May Holbrook of 27 March 1912 in which Neville's identity is established (p. 104).

18 *Letters*, i. 373–4.

19 E.T. 125–6.

20 *Letters*, i. 283.

21 *Ibid.* 51.

22 *Ibid.* 141.

23 *Ibid.* 403.

24 E.T. 151.

25 Delavenay 692.

26 Ms. at The Bancroft Library, University of California, Berkeley.

27 For 'crisp hair of the "ginger" class' see *The White Peacock* (Heinemann, 1911), part I, chapter II, 'Dangling the Apple'; for 'had that fine, lithe physique' etc. see chapter V, 'The Scent of Blood'.

28 *The White Peacock*, part I, chapter II, and above, section 3, 'The effect of the farm'.

29 Mark Kinkead-Weekes, 'The Marble and the Statue: The Exploratory Imagination of D. H. Lawrence', *Imagined Worlds, Essays on some English Novels and Novelists in Honour of John Butt*, ed. Maynard Mack and Ian Gregor (Methuen, 1968) p. 375.

30 For *Mr Noon* see *A Modern Lover* (Secker, 1934), pp. 168–312; see also *Phoenix II* 109–91. For *The Married Man* see *Virginia Quarterly Review* 16 (Autumn 1940) pp. 523–47; see also *The Complete Plays of D. H. Lawrence* (Heinemann, 1965) (hereafter *Complete Plays*).

31 For the 'Burns novel' see Nehls, i. 184–95; for the passage referred to see pp. 192–3.

32 *Phoenix II* 127.

33 *The Rainbow*, chapter VIII, 'The Child'.

34 *Letters*, i. 386.

35 *Ibid.* 369.

36 *Complete Plays* 182–3.
37 *Letters*, i. 377.
38 *Ibid.* 379.
39 E.T. 206–8.
40 Nehls, i. 162–3.

Introduction

1 Neville may have felt uneasy because of his position as a teacher; though he was a teacher only up to the end of March 1918, and the earliest journalism I have found by him is dated 25 January 1919. For further details, see editor's introduction; his *nom de plume* was Neville Wood (i.e. Neville of Eastwood). Much later, in 1931 – the period of the composition of this Memoir – he received a note from the editor of the *Staffordshire Advertiser*: 'Your market articles appear to have given offence in some quarters and we have decided, therefore, to discontinue them.' By modern standards his articles are only moderately opinionated or argumentative.
2 Staffordshire.
3 No other memoirist of the early years records such intimacy as this expression lays claim to; see also editor's introduction, pp. 8, 22.
4 See section 1, note 1.

1. Early days

1 Although Neville writes 'we have been called "Pagans"', he is the only memoirist to adopt the term. It has been taken up subsequently from him by Lawrence scholars. If Lawrence's group of friends had at all regularly called themselves the 'Pagans', it is surely likely that one of them would have used the name somewhere. The term's origin is now impossible to determine, but Neville may have created it from someone's saying, for example: 'You're nothing but a bunch of pagans', just as he appears to have created the nickname 'Princess' for Jessie Chambers (see note 24 below).

Neville began writing his Memoir in 1931. It seems likely that the group he had principally in mind by his term 'Pagans' comprised: Lawrence, his sister Ada, Francis ('Franky') and Gertrude ('Grit') Cooper, Alice Beatrice ('Beat') Hall, Louie Burrows, Jessie Chambers, and perhaps Alan Chambers and Florence ('Floss') Cullen ('almost a Pagan', p. 161). Some of these did write Memoirs.

Ada Lawrence, working together with a Nottingham journalist, G. Stuart Gelder, produced *The Early Life of D. H. Lawrence* (first issued in Italy under the title *Young Lorenzo*) which was published in 1932; and later on in his Memoir, Neville refers to this book. Alice Hall wrote to the *Nottingham Journal* in 1932 about Lawrence's early years (see below, section 2, note 24). In 1935 Jessie Chambers published *D. H. Lawrence: A Personal Record* (E.T.), some chapters of which appeared as magazine articles in 1934.

Franky and Grit Cooper (Franky died in 1918 and is the 'Pagan' Neville had in mind in saying 'the majority of us . . . are still living') did not write about Lawrence; but a few of his letters to Gertrude Cooper have survived. Louie Burrows did not write about Lawrence, but preserved all, or nearly all, his letters to her, which were published in 1968 under the title *Lawrence in Love*, edited by James T. Boulton. They are reproduced in *Letters*, i. *passim*.

Jessie Chambers's elder sister May, not considered by Neville as part of this group, also at some point wrote down her reminiscences, which were later discovered and published by Edward Nehls in *D. H. Lawrence: a composite biography*. Harry T. Moore, for his biography of Lawrence, *The Priest of Love*, and Nehls also elicited and recorded reminiscences from other Eastwood contemporaries of Lawrence.

Neville, then, responding to the obituary press and Middleton Murry's *Son of Woman* was, together with Ada Lawrence, in the van of writers correcting Lawrence's lurid reputation by an appeal to biographical facts. His repeated use of the word 'story' alludes to the subtitle of Murry's book, 'The story of D. H. Lawrence'. In his first draft Neville cited another example of what he was seeking to combat, 'Early days' ms. 1:

> I am aware that it is true that, not so very long ago, an article was printed in the local paper published in the town of Lawrence's birth, in the vicinity of which town most of the remaining 'Pagans' still reside, pointing out that the Lawrences of the past, in that district, had been a credit to the district and the name, one had even been canonised apparently, while on the contrary the present David Herbert of that name (this was before the death of Lawrence) was a disgrace to the name and a discredit to the town.

The article in question appears to be 'Saint and sinner. Local great men. The two Lawrences' (unsigned), *Eastwood and Kimberley Advertiser*, Friday 26 July 1929. A comparison is made between Robert Lawrence, prior of Beauvale who was hanged in 1535 for resisting the royal supremacy, and 'Then in this twentieth century the parish has produced a novelist, poet, and painter who is certainly celebrated, even if his fellow-parishioners are ashamed of him.' Neville has perhaps mistaken the purport of the article. It is certainly about honouring Robert Lawrence, but obliquely invites readers to consider whether D. H. Lawrence is not being martyred for standing up for his principles.

2 J. D. Chambers's recollections, published in *Renaissance and Modern Studies*, include (pp. 7–8): 'When she asked him what he did for a living he said he was a contractor. Now that was strictly true. He contracted to get coal from an area called a stall; he employed and paid his own workmen and sold the coal to the Barber and Walker Company . . . But of course he worked down the pit and came home black.' See also this Memoir p. 51. On the marriage certificate Arthur Lawrence's profession is given as 'mining contractor'.

There is no innuendo in Neville's expression: the date of the marriage was 27 December 1875 and the first son, George Arthur, was born 26 September 1876.

3 Ernest's death was 11 October 1901.

4 Lawrence was a clerk with J. H. Haywood Ltd, Nottingham, for three months in late 1901. Pictures of the factory girls at work and of sections of Haywood's catalogue of 1902 (showing their surgical appliances and one of their brand trademarks, a phoenix) can be found in *Young Bert, an exhibition of the early years of D. H. Lawrence*, Castle Museum, Nottingham, 1972.

5 'D.H.L. of Eastwood, Notts. – early days', typescript:

> The father of Lawrence was born at Brinsley in a little cottage near the Mansfield Road mineral line level crossing, where his father carried on a business as a tailor, the major part of the business being the making of cord and fustian garments for the use of the local colliers.
>
> There were other sons besides Arthur and you may read of the passing of one of them in 'The Odour of White Chrysanthemums' [*sic*].

6 It is not clear why Neville is so dogmatic on this point; presumably he heard it from Mrs Lawrence herself. It is perhaps worth noting that there is no hint of such opposition in *Sons and Lovers*, and that the two witnesses who signed the wedding certificate both came from the bride's family. The marriage of 27 December 1875 was witnessed by Lydia Beardsall's father, George Beardsall, and her younger sister Ellen Beardsall. The date of Lydia Beardsall's mother's death is not known. Whether the absence of her signature on the marriage certificate is a sign of family opposition cannot at present be determined.

7 This sniff must have been very characteristic. Alice Hall

comments on it (see section 2, note 24), and Lawrence makes the Little Woman in *The White Peacock* and Mrs Morel in *Sons and Lovers* regularly sniff in disapproval.

8   'D.H.L. of Eastwood, Notts. – early days', ts.:

> The eldest son, George, who had been 'rescued' from the Army, and his buxom wife Ada, were living in Nottingham where George, bluff, hail-fellow-well-met and more like his father than any of the others, worked as an engineer.
>
> [Emily] was 'out in service' and later married Sam King . . . who drove his steam wagon from his father's bottom of Church Street yard to places all round the district. You will have read of their courtship and the good-nights in the entry, from Lawrence's own description.

9   Number 43 Lynn Croft. Neville was seven in 1893.

10   'D.H.L. of Eastwood, Notts. – early days', ts.:

> a rippling, rising trill when he laughed, which . . . was indeed very often, and a trill to which it was a joy to listen.
>
> I see him now coming along with that forelock of light hair shaking down his forehead almost to his eyes, to be thrown back again by a hasty toss of that forward-carried head. The left shoulder was always higher than the right, mainly because he was seldom seen without a book – or several books – held tightly in the left arm-pit, while his right arm swung loosely, ready for that quick little dab at the peak of his cap which always accompanied the upward glance and shy smile with which he greeted some lady of his acquaintance and note that I mean *any* lady. Constant politeness was one of his most striking features.

11   'Middle lane' refers to the row of outside lavatories; see e.g. 'Nottingham and the Mining Countryside', *New Adelphi*, June–August 1930; reprinted in *Phoenix*, ed. E. D. McDonald (Heinemann, 1936) (hereafter *Phoenix*), pp. 133–40.

12   'D.H.L. of Eastwood, Notts. – early days', ts.: 'worked in the office at Turners at Langley Mill.'

13   See section 4, note 6.

14   Lawrence was taught at Beauvale Board School by Messrs Bamber and Lane, Harry Lindley, Charlie Rowley, 'Nocker' Bradley, J. George Rowley and in the final form by the headmaster, William Whitehead. In 1932 Mr Lindley gave his impression of Lawrence to a *Nottingham Journal* reporter: 'Lawrence was a brilliant boy when he was here. He was taught in this school between the ages of five and twelve. He struck me, though, as being rather effeminate, compared with his brother. He was fortunate in being a member of a very clever class.' Mr C. P. Taylor has recorded that 'five of the teachers were sons of miners'. (See his series of articles in the

Eastwood and Kimberley Advertiser beginning 30 Dec. 1960, 'Boys of the Beauvale Breed'.) A factor possibly contributing to William Whitehead's joy at Lawrence's success was that he was himself on the point of retirement. G. H. Neville was the only other success, in his last year at Beauvale in 1899.

15 See editor's introduction, p. 5.

16 The Lawrences lived in Walker Street from 1891 to 1902.

17 See D. J. Peters: 'Young Bert Lawrence as pupil of city High School', *Nottingham Guardian Journal*, 22 March 1972.

18 Cf. E.T. 110: 'He was enthusiastic about a nature magazine that came out in fortnightly parts. He came up with the first part one Sunday afternoon and stood by the field gate looking with intense appreciation at the frontispiece, a photograph of a sedge-warbler feeding a young cuckoo. Lawrence's intimacy with nature was a constant revelation.' This magazine has now been identified as *The Nature Book*, which was later published in a set of six volumes by Cassell and Co., 1908. Neville's niece, Mrs Jean Temple, possesses a copy of *Our Country's Flowers: and how to know them* by W. T. Gordon, Day and Son, signed: 'D. H. Lawrence 28 July 1900'.

19 Midsummer 1901.

20 See also note 4, above. Neville is wrong here: in his 'Auto-biographical Sketch' (*Phoenix II* 593) Lawrence wrote, 'After leaving school I was a clerk for three months, then had a very serious pneumonia illness, in my seventeenth year, that damaged my health for life.'

21 Lawrence was a pupil–teacher at the British School, Albert Street, from October 1902 to July 1905, and an uncertificated teacher there from August 1905 to September 1906. George Holderness was headmaster of the school throughout these years; by 1912 he had moved some miles north to Eakring (the 'Eakrast' of *Mr Noon*) near Ollerton, as headmaster of the Public Elementary School. His daughter, Edith ('Kitty') Holderness, was a friend of Lawrence's, see below, p. 121.

22 The date of the Education Act was in fact 1902. The Act reorganised the elementary and secondary school structure of the country, and provided channels for funding an expansion of secondary education.

23 Lawrence attended part-time at the Pupil–Teacher Centre, Ilkeston, Derbyshire, from March 1904 to July 1905.

24 See note 1 for the names of the 'Pagans'. On the 'Princess' see 'Autobiographical Sketch', *Phoenix II* 593:

> It was while I was at Croydon, when I was twenty three, that the girl who had been the chief friend of my youth, and who was

herself a school-teacher in a mining village at home, copied out some of my poems, and without telling me, sent them to the *English Review*, which had just had a glorious re-birth under Ford Madox Hueffer.

Hueffer was most kind. He printed the poems, and asked me to come and see him. The girl had launched me, so easily, on my literary career, like a princess cutting a thread, launching a ship.

This illustrates how Neville transmutes fact into saga material (see editor's introduction, pp. 13-14). In *Sons and Lovers* Miriam thinks of herself as a princess (chapter VII) and this, together with Lawrence's phrase here 'like a princess' has become the basis for Neville's nickname the 'Princess'. This penchant for transmutation is shown also, I believe, by Helen Corke, who entitled one of her reminiscences of Lawrence, 'D. H. Lawrence's "Princess"' (The Merle Press, 1951, gathered into *D. H. Lawrence: The Croydon Years*, University of Texas Press, Austin, 1965).

25 The Lawrences moved in 1902 to 97 Lynn Croft Road, Eastwood.

26 From September 1906 to June 1908 Lawrence was a student at University College, Nottingham.

27 Cf. the play based on Neville, *The Married Man* (*Complete Plays* 173): 'Brentnall opens the door for her and whistles quickly a private call – repeats it. Grainger's whistle is heard in answer.'

28 'Early days' ms. 1:

> But, in 'launching' Lawrence thus, Jess defeated the efforts of all the rest of the 'Pagans'. We all saw the danger of a literary career for Lawrence. The Little Woman had sniffed, Ada had 'pshawed and rubbished' times without number, 'Injun Topknot' [his sister, Emily] had talked of prospective disappointments, 'Beat' had angered him, as usual, by ruffling his hair and clinging on to him while she said, 'Why David lad, tha' knows it's nobbut rubbish.' (Beat could be very annoying when she dropped into our local dialect.) Franky and Grit had asked him what was the good of bothering, serious Alan had looked upon the prospect with alarm and I, in secret agreement with the 'Little Woman', had adopted an attitude of sheer contempt and often refused even to look at his manuscripts and advised him to do something useful. Incidentally, I ought to confess that the 'Little Woman' and I generally found a speedy method of obtaining a private perusal of those manuscripts and, though she characterised the action of Jess in submitting the manuscripts to Hueffer without permission as 'a piece of cheek', yet I, who knew her so well, knew that the 'Little Woman' realising, as I think we all had

done, that it was inevitable, was well-nigh bursting with pride in 'that Bert'. But, as some of us had foreseen it must be, the 'Pagans' knew, from that day, that their 'Billy', 'Bert', 'David' was lost to the 'Pagans' as a group, he was quite swallowed by London and the literary group to which he had become attached.

In his 'Autobiographical Sketch', quoted in note 24, Lawrence had said that Jessie 'copied out some of my poems, and without telling me, sent them to the *English Review*'. Jessie Chambers herself gives a full and scrupulous account in which she claims that she did have to prevail on Lawrence to send something, but that she acted with his permission (E.T. 157):

> 'How do you know unless you try?' I persisted, and he suddenly said:
> '*You* send something. Send some of the poems, if you like.'
> 'Very well, which shall I send?'
> 'Send whatever you like. Do what you like with them,' he answered.

Neville's account suggests that it may have been the hostility in Lawrence's home circle that compelled him to have it both ways by giving Jessie permission but disclaiming responsibility.

29 Neville writes, as always, from memory. Lawrence taught at Davidson Road School, Croydon, from October 1908 until a serious illness in November 1911; he resigned his post in February 1912. He lived during these years in Colworth Road, Addiscombe, Croydon.

30 Neville appears to be mistaken. Lawrence had no serious illness between October 1908 and his mother's death in December 1910. The illness which caused him to give up teaching was that of November and December 1911.

31 *The Trespasser* was published on 23 May 1912. Lawrence was with Neville at Bradnop, Leek, Staffordshire, from 25–31 March 1912.

32 Lawrence wrote to Edward Garnett on 1 April 1912 reporting this search for a title: 'I was away in Staffs when your letter came. I can't think of another title. Would: A Game of Forfeits or The Forfeit or The Man and the Dreaming Woman or anything like that do? I try to get something that would catch. Even *The Trespasser* has been used before, I believe by Gilbert Parker.' *Letters*, i. 378–9. The publisher was Duckworth.

33 'Early days' ms. 1:

> I remember discussing this point with Lawrence quite in the early days of his career. The basis of the argument was as to whether or not that chapter in *The Rainbow* to which objection

was taken, should be cut out. Subject to the deletion or rewriting of that chapter, the English publication of *The Rainbow* would go forward.

See appendix A.

34 'Early days' ms. 1:

[after 'contributions'] 'The world would have been so much wiser today had this been truly done.' I objected that the capacity was not given to all. There was a flash of the old, impatient Lawrence as he answered that it was always possible to relate one's own experiences to someone who could perpetuate them and hand them on to posterity.

2. Lawrence and his parents

1 See *Phoenix II* 592–6. *Diana of the Crossways* (1885) by George Meredith (1828–1909); *East Lynne* (1861) by Mrs Henry Wood (1814–87).

2 'The Dead Mother', reproduced in the English edition of Ada Lawrence and G. Stuart Gelder's *The Early Life of D. H. Lawrence* p. 161. (This book appeared while Neville was writing his Memoir.)

3 'D.H.L. of Eastwood, Notts. – Early days' ts.:

drunkard.] It was not so – and I told Lawrence what I thought of him for giving that impression. I know. Four or five days out of every seven I was at the Walker Street house for some part of the day, and later, at the Lynn Croft house and thus I am able to speak of what I know.

'D.H.L. and his parents' ts.:

drunkard.] He certainly went out at the week-end for a drink with his cronies, but three parts of the population of the district did that and were no worse thought of in consequence. And he certainly went out most other evenings for a single drink before going to bed – when he could afford it – but that was because there was a family objection to having drink in the house; a foolish business which Arthur Lawrence should have crushed most rigidly many years before or gone altogether teetotal.

There is no firm evidence that Neville had any contact with Lawrence after March 1912; it may be therefore that he reproached Lawrence on the occasion of his depiction of his father as a drunkard not in 'Myself Revealed' or in the published *Sons and Lovers*, but in an early draft of *Sons and Lovers*.

4 This backwashing scene entered Lawrence's imagination deeply and is directly presented in the early works: 'Daughters of the Vicar' and *Sons and Lovers*, and obliquely handled in Connie's 'vision' of Mellors washing in *Lady Chatterley's Lover*.

5 Presumably Neville refers to Mr and Mrs J. W. Jones, Lawrence's Croydon landlord and landlady. Cf. Moore, *The Priest of Love* 112; cf. also, in Delavenay 656, J. W. Jones's letter of February 1936:

> I believe Mrs Jones will interest the gentleman concerned more than I can. She is an ex-schoolmistress and she mothered DHL during his stay in Croydon for 4 years . . . Lawrence made 4 female friendships. One was platonic (genuinely). One gave him up because she was morally frightened of him. One derided him and led him up the garden and showed him the back gate. It would be mean for me to describe the other one.
>
> Probably Lawrence would have remained in Croydon (not as a teacher) had I not told him to clear off.

The four women are perhaps Agnes Mason, Agnes Holt, Helen Corke, and Mrs Jones. Cf. further Lawrence's letter to Louie Burrows of 29 August 1911: 'I find Colworth queer after a month of absence. Mr and Mrs Jones are very quiet – not on the very best of terms . . . I've been reading William Morris' "Defence of Guinivere etc" . . . And then Mrs Jones has been telling me things – very un-Morris-like: marital and faintly horrifying' (*Letters*, i. 298).

6 Neville is continuing to comment on Lawrence's 'Autobiographical Sketch', as at the beginning of section 2. The 'Sketch' continues (*Phoenix II* 592):

> He practically never had a good stall all the time he was a butty, because he was always saying tiresome and foolish things about the men just above him in control at the mine. He offended them all, almost on purpose, so how could he expect them to favour him? Yet he grumbled when they didn't.

'Stall' means a specified stretch of coal-seam for working; 'butty' means a mining subcontractor (see section 1, note 2).

7 *Sons and Lovers* was not published until 29 May 1913, so Neville cannot here be being strictly accurate. There had certainly been complaints in Eastwood about Lawrence's use of identifiable persons in *The White Peacock*, and it is possible that friends who read the first version of *Sons and Lovers*, called 'Paul Morel', in manuscript, had expressed misgivings at some aspects of the biographical immediacy of the work.

8 Another extract from 'Myself Revealed', slightly misquoted; see *Phoenix II* 594.

9 'Winders' are angled steps used to turn a corner in a staircase.

10 A set-pot is a fixed cauldron or boiler used for heating water for domestic purposes.

11 May Chambers remembered one such rug being made:

he looked like a captive as he sat by the window, his elder sister beside him, a big rug in the making, like a barricade over their knees. He was snipping lengths of cloth while his sister pegged them into the rug. (Nehls, iii. 556).

12 'D.H.L. and his parents' ms.: 'The red and blue quarries of the floor were bare and were always scrubbed to a most scrupulous cleanliness.'

13 If Neville is right about the date, he must mean the Lynn Croft house; or, the incident was pre-1902.

14 There are comparable confrontations between Walter Morel and his son William in chapter IV, and Morel and his son Paul at the end of chapter VIII of *Sons and Lovers*.

15 Neville has stated that this incident took place during the period when Lawrence attended University College, Nottingham, that is, between September 1906 and June 1908 when Lawrence was aged twenty-one to twenty-three. It is an irony of which Neville was no doubt very conscious, and of which he must have presumed that his readers could have no inkling, that he had already, in the spring of 1906, been in disgrace for begetting an illegitimate child. This being so, one must wonder whether any conversation much like the one Neville 'reports' here could ever have taken place. He presents himself as arguing the responsibilities of fatherhood, and Lawrence sceptical as to how many local fathers took their responsibilities seriously. Neville may well be accurately reflecting Lawrence's position whilst concealing his own. Nevertheless in the last sentence of the episode where he fails to seal his part of the pledge, he obliquely hints at his own irresponsibility. Equally probably Neville is blending together the impression of a number of perhaps pre-1906 exchanges when Lawrence expressed rage at his father's behaviour, and unifying his impressions in this form of an account of a single incident.

16 Arthur Lawrence's love for his son at the time of Lawrence's illness of late 1901, set out fully here by Neville, is reflected by a single sentence in *Sons and Lovers* (end of chapter VI): 'Paul was in bed for seven weeks. He got up white and fragile. His father had bought him a pot of scarlet and gold tulips. They used to flame in the window in the March sunshine as he sat on the sofa chattering to his mother.'

17 This may be a reference to Ada Lawrence's letter to *Everyman* 14 May 1931, for which see note 10, section 5. Neville gives an example of Lawrence's generosity to his sister in 'D.H.L. of Eastwood, Notts. – Early days', ts.: 'Ada learnt to play the piano very successfully and I am happy to remember that, as

soon as D.H.L. could afford it, he sent his sister into transports of delight by presenting her with a full copy of "Finlandia" which she had long desired. How we all loved it!'

18 Neville clearly had in mind a paragraph in Murry's Preface 'To the reader', *Son of Woman*:

> This is the story of one of the greatest lovers the world has known: of a hero of love, of a man whose capacity for love was so great that he was afraid of it. We little lovers do not know and cannot dream what it is to be afraid of love as he was. Love grows slowly in us little men, if it grows at all. But in him it was a devouring flame while yet a boy: a love that consumed his soul, and threatened his very life. It was not love of his mother only, but love of all men and all women and all things created: a devouring flame of universal love.

19 Neville is referring to p. 29 of *Son of Woman*:

> *Sons and Lovers* is the story of Paul Morel's desperate attempts to break away from the tie that was strangling him. All unconsciously, his mother had roused in him the stirrings of sexual desire; she had, by the sheer intensity of her diverted affection made him a man before his time. He felt for his mother what he should have felt for the girl of his choice. Let us be clear, as Lawrence himself tried to be clear in the *Fantasia*. Lawrence was not, so far as we can tell, sexually precocious; he was spiritually precocious. We are told that Paul Morel remained virgin till twenty three. But his spiritual love for his mother was fully developed long before. What could be more poignant, or in implication more fearful, than the story he tells of the illness which fell upon him at sixteen? (He had told the same story before, in *The Trespasser;* it was a crucial happening in his boyhood.)
>
> 'Paul was very ill. His mother lay in bed at nights with him; they could not afford a nurse. He grew worse, and the crisis approached. One night he tossed into consciousness in the ghastly, sickly feeling of dissolution, when all the cells in the body seem in intense irritability to be breaking down, and consciousness makes a last flare of struggle, like madness.
>
> "I s'll die, mother!" he cried, heaving for breath on the pillow.
>
> She lifted him up, crying in a small voice:
>
> "Oh, my son – my son!"
>
> That brought him to. He realised her. His whole will rose up and arrested him. He put his head on her breast, and took ease of her for love.'
>
> It is terribly poignant, and terribly wrong. Almost better that a boy should die than have such an effort forced upon him by such means. He is called upon to feel in full consciousness for his mother all that a full-grown man might feel for the wife of his bosom.

The passage in *The Trespasser* to which Murry refers is in chapter XII.

> 'It certainly feels rather deathly,' said Siegmund to himself. He remembered distinctly, when he was a child and had diphtheria, he had stretched himself in the horrible sickness, which he felt was – and here he chose the French word – *'l'agonie'*. But his mother had seen and had cried aloud, which suddenly caused him to struggle with all his soul to spare her her suffering.

20 He became engaged to Louie Burrows on 3 December 1910, in the last week of his mother's life. In a letter to Louie of 6 December 1910 Lawrence wrote:

> I said – but you know, my mother has been passionately fond of me, and fiercely jealous. She hated J[essie] – and would have risen from the grave to prevent my marrying her. So I said, carefully, about a month or six weeks ago 'Mother, do you think it would be all right for me to marry Louie – later?'
>
> Immediately she said 'No – I don't' – and then, after half a minute 'Well – if you think you'd be happy with her – yes.'
>
> So you see, I know she approves, and she always liked you. (*Letters*, i. 197).

Lawrence broke off the engagement on 4 February 1912.

21 No letters from Ada Lawrence to Neville appear to have survived. The photograph mentioned is reproduced in Moore, *The Priest of Love.*

22 September 1899.

23 Eddie was William Edwin Clarke whom Ada married in 1913.

24 On 23 June 1931, Alice Beatrice Hall Holditch, here referred to as 'Beat', wrote to the *Nottingham Journal* giving her impression of Lawrence's early days. The points she made were largely in response to matters raised, but differently interpreted, in the article to which she refers.

> It was with great pleasure that I read the article by Lewis Richmond in last Thursday's issue of your paper. I was surprised to find that no mention was made of the house in Lynn Croft, for I think it was here that the 'White Peacock' was written and where Mrs Lawrence had her illness, nursed by D.H.L. and his sister, and passed away.
>
> I remember sitting on the sofa there and Mrs Lawrence telling me that Bert had written a book and I was mentioned in it. The house in Walker-street, and afterwards the above mentioned was the rendezvous of quite a little group of young teachers. There we spent many happy hours. Mrs Lawrence, a demure little figure, was generally seated in her chair by the fire, quietly enjoying the fun, and occasionally giving her characteristic little sniff of disapproval if she thought we had overstepped the mark.

Naturally Bert was the organiser of most of our games and expeditions and it was our delight to get him to impersonate anyone we knew. The local clergymen were the ones we liked best, or the different folks that attended the Christian Endeavour [interdenominational organisation, founded in 1881, formed for the purpose of promoting spiritual life among young people] meeting including his sisters and some of their friends. On one occasion Mrs Lawrence was very cross and said we were a stumbling block to them and had better have a millstone round our necks.

Mr Lawrence was generally in bed about 7.30 during the early part of the week, partly owing to the fact that he had to rise so early and also that he had no pocket money left.

Friday, Saturday and Sunday evenings would be spent at the public house near. Occasionally he would arrive home earlier than usual, and would have liked to have joined in the fun, but no visitor was supposed to encourage him to talk. A chill had entered the room with him, and if he wanted to tell any stories of himself and his rambles, etc., he would be promptly told to 'Shut up and go to bed.' After a time he would realise the position and after wishing us all 'Good night' would disappear.

The story of Helena was not a personal one, for that year a number of us, including his mother, spent a holiday at Shanklin . . .

The sex question was never discussed or only with abhorrence by him, and when the porter told improper stories to the students at the University Bert would just leave them in disgust.

During all the years I knew the family Mrs Lawrence had certainly to be very careful, and there was no margin for luxuries. Sometimes one family would call there on their way home from church and would be given cake and pastry as they had a long way to walk. Afterwards Mrs Lawrence would look rather dismal, for she knew that there would be no more made for another week, but there was no actual poverty. Two of Mrs Lawrence's sisters were in good positions and supplemented her wardrobe, hence the ospreys and the feather boa.

It was always understood that the mahogany furniture and the piano were obtained in the same way. Doubtless the toys at Christmas came from the same source.

One of the sisters had lost her lover in early life, and she wished Bert to have the same names as he had. His mother told us once that as his aunt handed him to the minister to be christened she added the surname, too [i.e. David Herbert Richards Lawrence], and if I wished to vex him, and make him tear his hair, I would call him by the three names.

When he lived at Croydon we exchanged weekly letters, but there was no love-making at all. He was just like a brother, and he would often tell me of the fun he had, playing off one girl

195

against another. Two or three of the girls were madly in love with him, and were jealous of each other gaining ground. It was most amusing to watch them.

If his mother had not been so bitter against one of the girls I believe he would have settled down with her.

BEA.

25 Cf. Lawrence to Edward Garnett, 11 March 1913: 'I've got the pip horribly at present.' (*Letters*, i. 526).

26 There were several farms known to Lawrence in the area north-east of Eastwood. He came to know much the most intimately the Chambers' family home, the Haggs Farm. However in his fiction he drew on the external features of other farms, and Neville here appears to be referring to his portrayal of Felley Mill Farm in *The White Peacock*.

3. The effect of the farm

1 Paul Morel in *Sons and Lovers* is sixteen when he first visits Willey Farm.

2 Nehls gives their dates thus:

Name	Birth	Marriage	Death
Sarah Ann [Oates] Chambers	27 Feb. 1859	? Oct. 1881	8 Jan. 1937
Edmund Chambers	10 Jan. 1863	? Oct. 1881	10 May 1946
Alan Aubrey Chambers	2 July 1882	15 Oct. 1910	20 May 1946
Muriel May Chambers	20 Oct. 1883	1 Nov. 1906	8 July 1955
John Oates Chambers	21 Nov. 1885		15 May 1886
Jessie Chambers	29 Jan. 1887	3 June 1915	3 Apr. 1944
Hubert Chambers	23 Apr. 1888		
Bernard Oates Chambers	4 Feb. 1890	10 Mar. 1921	
Emily Chambers	25 Aug. 1892		22 Sep. 1892
Mary ['Mollie'] Chambers	15 Jan. 1896	27 Nov 1916	
Jonathan David Chambers	13 Oct. 1898	8 Apr. 1926	[1970]

3 The *Young Bert* exhibition at the Castle Museum, Nottingham, displayed four such paintings by Neville as well as still lifes and landscapes by Lawrence. In the catalogue a scene with a windmill is reproduced as plate 104. Lawrence painted it into the album, dated 1904, of Grace Hardwick, a fellow student of his and Louie Burrows' at University College, Nottingham.

4 See appendix B.

5 It is not known precisely at what periods Lawrence wore spectacles. He wrote to Blanche Jennings on 26 Oct. 1908: 'I wonder that my specs. are not moist with tears (Mr Dax has saddled my nose, willy-nilly)' (*Letters*, i. 85).

6 See appendix B.

7 Louie Burrows. See note 20, section 2. Lawrence wrote to Edward Garnett on 30 Dec. 1911: 'My girl is here. She's big, and swarthy, and passionate as a gipsy – but good, awfully good, churchy' (*Letters*, i. 343).

8 No such paintings from his early years appear to have survived.

9 The only place in Lawrence's work where he writes about youthful distress at discovering female pubic hair is in Parkin, the gamekeeper's, marital history in *John Thomas and Lady Jane* (Heinemann, 1972), pp. 225–6, especially: 'But I never knowed afore then as women had hair there. Black hair! An' I don't know why, it upset me an' made me hate the thoughts of women from that day.'

10 Neville may have had in mind for example 'A Prelude' or the descriptive passages of the first version of *The White Peacock*.

11 Approximately one mile north of Eastwood.

12 *Esther Waters* (1894) by George Moore (1852–1933).

13 Louie Burrows. Her family home was at Quorn, a village near Loughborough, Leicestershire.

14 In fixing the date as post-October 1908 by the phrase 'home for holidays', Neville is here concerned to rebut John Middleton Murry's confident assertions about Lawrence's teenage sexual experience; and in his use of 'self-crucifixion' Neville alludes to *Son of Woman* 21: 'He was, and he will say so plainly at the last, a sex-crucified man.' Cf. *Letters*, i. 286.

4. Stages on the journey

1 Cliché from *Hamlet* v. i. 229.

2 Neville appears to be referring again to Murry's comments quoted in section 2, note 19.

3 Lawrence's next serious attack of pneumonia took place after his mother's death in the winter of 1911–12, and Neville could have had this in mind.

4 Moore, *The Priest of Love* 38 identified Ernest's fiancée as Gypsy Dennis, a London stenographer; in *Sons and Lovers* her fictional counterpart bears the name Louisa Lily Denys Western.

5 In his talk, 'D. H. Lawrence of Eastwood, Notts. – early days', ts., Neville specifies that the occasion is the Annual Demon-

stration of the Eastwood and District Band of Hope Union. This was a non-denominational Christian temperance association. The actual event to which Neville here, and Lawrence in *Sons and Lovers*, refers, was reported in some detail in the *Eastwood and Kimberley Advertiser*, for 2 August 1901 (p. 2):

Annual Demonstration [Saturday, 27 July]
Of the festivals which take place in Eastwood during the year – somewhat meagre in number – that promoted by the Eastwood and District Band of Hope Union must undoubtedly be accorded premier place. This annual fete and demonstration took place on Saturday, the lovely Hall grounds again being placed at the disposal of the inaugurators by Mr Lionel Walker-Munro. Following the steps of previous years, and placing an attractive programme before the public, a further grand success evidently seemed assured. Unfortunately the weather was very unsettled, sharp showers falling at intervals, and the attendance suffered in consequence very considerably. Despite the weather there was again a splendid turn-out of children from the various denominations, the procession being quite up to former years. The Old Brinsley Wesleyan Band of Hope and Langley Mill Juvenile Rechabites, having marched to Queen-street, Eastwood, the latter headed by the Eastwood Ambulance Band, a monster procession was formed and marched to the grounds via Nottingham and Mansfield roads, marshalled by Mr Robert Hazledine, as follows: Hucknall Torkard Excelsior Temperance Silver Prize Band, Eastwood Primitive Methodist Band of Hope, Breach Mission Band of Hope, Beauvale P.M. Band of Hope, Eastwood Wesleyan Band of Hope, Eastwood Ambulance Band, Eastwood Congregational Band of Hope, Langley Mill Juvenile Rechabites, Old Brinsley Wesleyan Band of Hope and Hill-top Band of Hope. As regards the gala itself, the maypole, which has for some years been a prominent feature, was discontinued this year, and instead a much larger programme of stage performances was provided, being supplied by Mr Geo. Burton, of Sheffield, and included – Mons. Vilo, the famous juggler; Bros. Deveres, grotesques; Lillian Sivado, aerial gymnast; Bros. Seward, negro comedians; Wheeler and Wilson, acrobats; Hartino, conjuror; Legtric, contortionist; the Dunlops, trick cyclists; and the inevitable Punch and Judy. Both Eastwood and Hucknall Bands at intervals gave excellent selections of music, and judging by the numbers who thronged the stand at every appearance their services were highly appreciated. The children, as usual, sat down to tea in sections in a large marquee. About five o'clock a Temperance meeting was held in the refreshment tent, the Rev. H. Land (Primitive Methodist minister) occupying the chair, and the other speakers were Mr J. B. Thornley (agent of the United Kingdom Alliance) and Mr Chas. Morton, of Nottingham. In

the evening the Eastwood Ambulance Band played for dancing. A word of praise is due to the secretary (Mr J. Smedley) and the following gentlemen, who form the Band of Hope Union Council, and are responsible for the working of the demonstration:— Messrs C. A. Hall, R. Hazledine, J. Hewitt, G. Wilson, W. Sisson, W. H. Gregory, W. Breathwaite, J. Wilcockson, W. Kirk, J. A. Kirk, and G. Wrath.

6 His obituary in the *Eastwood and Kimberley Advertiser* for 18 October 1901 (p. 2) was as follows:

Death of An Eastwood Young Man in London
The death of Wm. Ernest Lawrence, late of Eastwood, took place at Catford, North Kent, on Friday. Deceased, who was twenty-three [years] of age, was conveyed to his home in Walker-street, Eastwood, on Saturday, and interred at the Eastwood Cemetery on Monday. The sad news of his death produced a very sorrowful sensation locally, deceased being well-known. It was only on the Monday preceding the interment that he returned to London after spending the week end with his parents, and on the Sunday evening he attended service at the Eastwood Congregational Church, afterwards proceeding to Kimberley to catch the Nottingham train, where he spent the evening with his brother, going by the first London train the following morning. On Monday he attended at the office as usual, complaining that he had taken cold during the journey, but the following day he was too ill to get up. A doctor was sent for, and he pronounced the case hopeless. A second doctor was called in, but their skill was of no avail, deceased having contracted erysipelas, and pneumonia afterwards set in. As one of his close associates I cannot let this man pass without recording a little of his past life. The memory of his associations amongst us is yet quite fresh in our minds. At the Eastwood library there was no more familiar figure than his, he was a great reader from a boy, and in his early teens he had become acquainted with most of the present day writers and many of the past. His school days were spent at the Beauvale Board Schools, where he showed every sign of a good student, and after passing the standards, he obtained his first situation at the Langley Mill and Aldercar Co-operative Society. After business hours he spent his leisure in reading good books, studying shorthand and practising type-writing on a miniature toy imitation, hoping to obtain a situation eventually in that pursuit. At the age of eighteen the first step was taken towards realising a little of his ambition, when he succeeded in obtaining a situation with the Shipley Colliery Company. His next move was to the Griffiths Cycle Corporation, Coventry, where he acted as correspondent, shorthand writer, and typist, and afterwards with his last employers Messrs. John Holman & Sons, Solicitors, Lime-street, London, during the last four years.

At this office there was a large scope for such ambition as his, and he settled down to work harder than ever, to apply the knowledge he had and to acquire more. His knowledge for a young man was considerable, London's gaiety could not wrest from him his love for work and his keen desire to get on, and after business hours his evenings were spent in the study of French and German languages, a knowledge of which he acquired sufficient to converse and write letters. To undertake so much was too much, but his large mind, his keen desire for hard work, his ambition to make himself thoroughly fitting to fill a high post, to get on and be useful in the world was so great. The senior partner in the firm where he was engaged, said that they looked upon him as a very promising young man and by his death they had sustained a great loss. The interment on Monday was witnessed by a large number of friends and relatives, and as the funeral cortege passed on its way to the Cemetery many blinds were drawn out of respect for the family. The Rev. R. Reid conducted the service in Church, and delivered a most impressive and comforting address. At the grave side the Rev. R. Reid was assisted by the Rev. Geo. Ineson (Moorgreen Congregational minister). There were numerous wreaths from relatives and friends.

– F.M.

7   This incident seems to provide some of the raw material for 'Daughters of the Vicar'.

8   Neville appears to be confused about the dates: his reference to Ilkeston P.T.C. points to the period 1904–5; his reference to haymaking indicates the summer of 1908 (see Lawrence's letter to Blanche Jennings of 30 July – 3 August 1908: *Letters*, i. 65–9).

9   Neville may again have *Son of Woman* 38–40 partly in mind.

10 *The White Peacock*, part II, chapter VIII, 'A Poem of Friendship'. Neville in fact quotes this passage from *Son of Woman* 38–9. He constructs the opening phrase, 'We bathed', which does not appear in the novel, from Murry's introductory sentence which begins, 'They bathed . . .' He then reproduces Murry's text which varies from all editions available at that date in reading: 'He knew' for 'For he knew' and 'against each other' for 'one against the other'.

11 Neville refers to the article cited at the end of section 1, note 1.

12 This was noted by the *Eastwood and Kimberley Advertiser* for Friday 23 December 1904 (p. 2):

> *Colliery Accident*
> Mr Arthur Lawrence, of Walker-street, a miner, was hurt whilst at work down the Brinsley Colliery on Monday. Whilst following his employment Mr Lawrence was struck on the back by a fall of bind, and, falling on a quantity of debris, was badly crushed

internally. Having been medically attended it was found that the injuries were of so serious a nature as to necessitate his removal to Nottingham Infirmary. A pathetic incident in connection with the case is the fact that Mr Lawrence was suffering from a fractured leg exactly a year ago, and was an inmate of the Infirmary on Christmas Day as will be the case this year.

The Lawrences' wedding anniversary also fell on 27 December.

13 Alexander Pope, *An Essay on Man*, Epistle i, lines 94–5:

> Hope springs eternal in the human breast;
> Man never is, but always to be blest.

14 Barber, Sir (Thomas) Philip, 1st Bt. cr. 1960. (1876–1961). Educ. Eton, Trinity College, Cambridge. Had served in the Boer War. High Sheriff of Notts., 1907.

15 Radcliffe and Mickleover were local mental hospitals. A rather different version of this anecdote is recorded by Moore, *Priest of Love* 33.

16 This is reflected in Lawrence's writings; in the play *The Married Man;* as presumably the structural basis for Cyril's sharing a bedroom with George in *The White Peacock;* and (although the attitudes and beliefs expressed in the conversation are developed almost out of recognition) for Birkin's sharing a room with Gerald Crich in *Women in Love.*

17 29 July to 12 August 1911.

18 31 July to 14 August 1909.

19 Lawrence briefly discusses Turner in the 'Study of Thomas Hardy', *Phoenix* 474–6. Lettie and George Saxton dispute the merits of George Clausen in part I, chapter III, 'A Vendor of Visions' of *The White Peacock.*

20 Half-a-crown=2/6=12½p; twenty-two and sixpence=£1.12½p eighteen-pence=7½p. These are technical conversions but, of course, values have changed.

5. Lawrence – 'The Son of Woman'

1 *The London Mercury*, vol. XXIII (no. 137), March 1931, pp. 477–80. The letter is section I of this Memoir.

2 *Son of Woman* was published in April 1931. Neville quotes from Cape's spring announcements.

3 *Son of Woman* 21–2.

4 Some of this correspondence still survives. There is, for example, a letter of enquiry from M. Emile Delavenay.

5 *Now and Then*, a periodical concerning books and authors published occasionally by Jonathan Cape. Spring 1931, pp. 10–12.

6 *News Chronicle*, Friday 17 April 1931, p. 4.

7 Anonymous review in *The Times Literary Supplement*, 16 April 1931.
8 *The Bookman*, May 1931.
9 *Everyman*, 23 April 1931.
10 *Everyman*, 14 May 1931 (p. 505):

> I feel I must write to thank you for your review of *Son of Woman*. As the sister of D. H. Lawrence, I have read most of the reviews of Mr Murry's book, and have been deeply hurt at the terrible misunderstanding of the true Lawrence caused by this book.
>
> I entirely agree with you, that Mr Murry will live to regret having published the book, which to my mind plainly reveals him as unworthy of the friendship he once held. I know that, if my brother had been alive, Mr Murry would never have dared to write anything like this, which seems to be the outcome of hatred and envy – love being the last motive I should attribute to a work of the kind. During one of my conversations with my brother, I realised why his friendship with Mr Murry ended as it did, some years ago, for Lawrence was the soul of honour and truth, and sentimental hypocrisy he couldn't tolerate. He told me he considered it rather horrible the way the memory of Katherine Mansfield was being exploited, just as I think that of my brother is being exploited now.
>
> Why in the name of friendship and sympathy did he go to Vence, at my brother's death, if it was merely an excuse to gather facts for this book? D. H. Lawrence cut him entirely out of his life, and I feel that this may be Mr Murry's revenge.
>
> Why should Mr Murry want to convey to the public the impression of a self-tortured and frustrated man, with no glimpse of the other side? I know of no other person capable of such real happiness as D. H. Lawrence when in a bluebell wood, or milking his cow Susan on the ranch in Mexico, or painting one of the wonderful pictures of his beloved Italian peasants. Another thing Mr Murry overlooks was his marvellous simplicity with people of the working classes. Never did he make them feel ill at ease or inferior, and to his two sisters he was the kindest and most generous brother – sharing all our troubles, and always ready to help in every way.
>
> If only there were a few more with the courage he had to write the truth and what their inward convictions tell them, we should have a better world, and more hope for the future. But the majority have no wish to be crucified as my brother was, and a 'best-seller' is much more important in their lives.
>
> Again thanking you for the best and truest review yet written of *Son of Woman*.
>
> Ada Clarke, Ripley, Derby.

On 23 April 1931, under the heading 'A Book That Should Not Have Been Written' the editor of *Everyman* wrote:

I have found in [Lawrence's] works greater spiritual exaltation than in any other writer of my time . . . [In *Son of Woman*] we do not get a picture of a whole man . . . Three is no hint of happiness. That surely is not the truth about Lawrence. His books show that he rejoiced in man and Nature . . . I confess that I finished the reading of [*Son of Woman*] with dismay. I was not shocked by what I read for Lawrence; for there is nothing shocking to be said of him.

11 Explicit references to Neville by Lawrence in print are few, even now that very extensive life-records and letters have come to light. Unless Neville saw himself and Ada in characters in *The White Peacock*, he is presumably referring to unrecorded historical fact.

12 *Son of Woman* 124.

13 *Ibid.* 38.

14 *Ibid.* 14.

15 *Ibid.* 29.

16 *Ibid.* 385–6.

17 'Autobiographical Sketch', *Phoenix II* 594.

18 *Son of Woman* 361–2. Lady Crystabel and the quotation come from *The White Peacock*, part II, chapter II.

19 *Son of Woman* 362–3. Neville follows Murry, whose quotation has one substantive variant from the first edition (p. 240) 'people' for 'couple', and other punctuational variants.

20 *Son of Woman* 363.

21 *Ibid.* 338, of *St. Mawr*.

22 *Ibid.* 35.

23 This is independently confirmed by May Chambers (Nehls, iii. 584):

> Occasionally the girls discussed him:
> 'Isn't Bert nice!'
> 'Isn't he gentlemanly!'
> 'He never spoons.'
> 'There's never any soft mushy talk where Bert is. You should have heard him rave over a note I showed him from a fellow. It started, "My own sweetheart." I thought it was spiffin', but Bert said it was "drivel and piffle and utter rot".'

Cf. also Lawrence's letter to Blanche Jennings of 15 December 1908: 'I have kissed dozens of girls – on the cheek – never on the mouth – I could not' (*Letters*, i. 99).

24 The reference is to Lawrence's former schoolmaster, George Holderness's family and in particular to his daughter, Edith ('Kitty') Holderness. See section 1, note 21.

25 *Son of Woman* 32–3.

26 *Ibid.* 29.

27 *Ibid.* 23: 'When these obvious identifications have been made, it is easy to understand why the tiresome and unconvincing Lettie is tiresome and unconvincing and her lover Leslie a nullity. She had no original in life. Lawrence had no such sister; and the sister no such lover.'

28 *Ibid.* 63, 75.

29 *Ibid.* 57: 'Nonetheless, it obviously is an account of the happening which underlies the story of *The Trespasser*. Siegfried [*sic*, sc. Siegmund], in that disappointing book, is obviously a composite character; he is partly the married man of Mellors' narrative, and partly Lawrence himself. (For example, the crucial experience of Lawrence's illness at sixteen is given to him.)'

30 Helen Corke.

31 See Helen Corke, *D. H. Lawrence: The Croydon Years;* Helen Corke, *In Our Infancy* (Cambridge University Press, 1975); *The Trespasser* ed. Elizabeth Mansfield (Cambridge University Press, 1981).

32 *Son of Woman* 57. The 'probing' refers to part II, pp. 61–75 entitled 'The Sexual Failure'.

33 *Ibid.* 75.

34 See appendix A.

35 *Son of Woman* 77.

36 *Ibid.* 88.

37 *Ibid.* 88, 363.

38 *Ibid.* 96–7; see also section 1, note 1 above, pp. 184–5, and section 6, note 4 below.

39 *Ibid.* 97. Cf. 'Leave Sex Alone – ', *Pansies* (Secker, 1929), p. 64.

40 *Son of Woman* 97.

41 *Ibid.* 108, 110.

42 *Ibid.* 110.

43 *Ibid.* 111 *The Rainbow*, chapter VI.

44 *Son of Woman*, 49, 55, 72.

45 *Ibid.* 349–51.

46 *Ibid.* 354.

47 *Ibid.* 388.

48 *Ibid.* 333–4; Neville is paraphrasing; Murry actually reports himself as saying, 'You always deny what you actually are.'

49 *Ibid.* 388–9.

6. Lawrence – the son of man

1 *Son of Woman* 143, 173.

2 *Ibid.* 171.
3 *Ibid.* 198.
4 *Ibid.* 95–6. It is noteworthy, considering Murry's subsequent discussion (quoted by Neville pages 125–6, the passage noted 38, in section 5), that in transcribing this extract from 'The Lemon Gardens' in *Twilight in Italy* (Duckworth, 1916), p. 81, Murry has changed Lawrence's 'Man knows the great consummation in the flesh, the sensual ecstasy' into '. . . the sexual ecstasy'.
5 *Son of Woman* 99 (the same continued).
6 *Ibid.* 255–6.
7 I.e. by Murry, *ibid*, 238.
8 *Ibid.* 262. The quotation is from *Kangaroo*, chapter XVII, 'Kangaroo is Killed'.
9 *Son of Woman* 273. The quotation is from *Studies in Classic American Literature* (Secker, 1924), chapter 6, 'Edgar Allan Poe'. 1924 can hardly be called 'the last stage'.
10 *Son of Woman* 320. The quotation is from *The Plumed Serpent*, chapter XVII, 'Fourth Hymn and the Bishop'.
11 *Son of Woman* 348. The quotation is from *Glad Ghosts*. See *The Tales of D. H. Lawrence* (Heinemann, 1934) (hereafter *Tales*) p. 891.
12 *Son of Woman* 348. The quotation is from *Glad Ghosts*, *Tales* 888.
13 *Son of Woman* 350. The quotation is from *Glad Ghosts*, *Tales* 889.
14 *Son of Woman* 357. The quotation is from *David, Complete Plays* 77.
15 *Son of Woman* 373. The quotation is from *The Man who had Died*, *Tales* 1107–8.
16 Psalm 139, verses 8–9 misquoted to echo Murry's comment, *Son of Woman* 44.
17 *Ibid.* 384. The quotation is from the essay 'The Risen Lord', which first appeared in *Everyman*, 3 October 1929; collected into *Assorted Articles, Phoenix II* 571.
18 *Pansies*, Secker, 1929.
19 I.e. endure his fate.
20 Cf. *Letters*, i. 127.
21 *Salammbô*, 1862: a novel by Gustave Flaubert (1821–80).
22 *c.* 8–15 August 1910. See editor's introduction pp. 9–10.
23 Joseph Joachim Raff, 1822–82, Swiss, a prolific composer of symphonies, chamber music, operas, now known only for 'Cavatina', a short, rather slow 'drawing-room piece' for violin and piano.
24 Nina Stewart was a college friend of Lawrence's and a lifelong correspondent of Louie Burrows. See Lawrence's letter to Louie Burrows, 24 July 1910 (*Letters*, i. 172): 'I was thinking

that, if I went to Blackpool I would like to run up to Barrow and see Nina. Do you think it would be proper for two young men to call there? But I think I'll write her a note. Her address is 44 Nelson St, is it not? I hope we may have a good time.'

25 Neville married 4 November 1911.

26 Lawrence stayed with Neville 25–31 March 1912; he had broken his engagement to Louie Burrows 4 February 1912 and, although he met or re-met Frieda Weekley about 17 March, they clearly had not yet formed any plans to elope. (See his letter to Frieda in Metz 6 May 1912: *Letters*, i. 391: 'But if you put up your fingers, and count your days in Germany, and compare them with the days to follow in Nottingham, then you will see, you – I don't mean it – are selling sovereigns at a penny each.')

27 Lawrence's cousin Alvina Reeve, a widow, married Alan Chambers on 15 October 1910.

28 It is not known whether this suggestion was put to Lawrence by a publisher or perhaps the editor of the *English Review*. Lawrence published some sketches of Germany in the *Westminster Gazette*, including 'Christs in the Tirol', 22 March 1913; see *Phoenix* 71–87.

29 The distinction Neville seems to be making is between friends and acquaintances. For 'Leivers' see *Sons and Lovers*. Neville nowhere mentions any fictional name that is not to be found in *Son of Woman*.

30 'Cyril' in *The White Peacock*; Edgar, Miriam, Paul in *Sons and Lovers*.

31 Annable in *The White Peacock*.

32 Alice in *The White Peacock*; Beatrice in *Sons and Lovers*.

33 Carlotta in *Glad Ghosts*.

34 Coutts in *Lady Chatterley's Lover*.

35 Roddice in *Women in Love*.

36 Constance in *Lady Chatterley's Lover*.

37 Crich in *Women in Love*.

38 Emily in *The White Peacock*.

39 Helena in *The Trespasser*.

40 Houghton in *The Lost Girl*.

41 Lettie in *The White Peacock*.

42 Rawdon and Tanny Lilly in *Aaron's Rod*.

43 It may be that Neville alludes to Louie Burrows, but the innuendo is unclear.

44 George Saxton in *The White Peacock*.

45 Aaron Sisson in *Aaron's Rod*.

46 Mellors in *Lady Chatterley's Lover*.

47 Dawes in *Sons and Lovers;* Pynegar is Pinnegar in *The Lost Girl* and *Jimmy and the Desperate Woman.*

48 David in the play *David;* Birkin in *Women in Love.*

49 Although Neville is wrong to identify himself fully and exclusively with the figure of George Saxton in *The White Peacock* (apparently not recognising features from other sources in the composition of George Saxton and features of himself in Leslie Tempest), in view of his description of his political enthusiasms here it is perhaps noteworthy that Lawrence makes George Saxton turn to socialist politics in the latter part of that novel.

50 See note 13 to editor's introduction.

51 *Son of Woman* 300–1. The quotation is from *Studies in Classic American Literature*, chapter 12, 'Whitman'.

Appendix A.   The Rainbow.

1 Secker, 1926; Secker (thin paper edition) 1929.

2 Nehls, i. 558.

3 *Letters*, i. 546.

4 *Letters*, Moore 334.

5 *Ibid.* 328.

6 *Ibid.* 322.

7 *Letters*, i. 546.

8 *Ibid.* i. 550.

9 *Ibid.* i, 381. The first version of 100 pages (now lost) was written between Autumn and late October 1910; the second, of which 353 pages have survived, was written between 13 March and c. 4 July 1911. The third version, completely different from the second, was begun on 3 November 1911, dropped soon because of illness, taken up again on 23 February 1912 and finished on 11 April 1912. This is the version Lawrence calls 'the first draft', presumably because it had reached its final form but would need some revision.

10 Cf. e.g. his letter to Frieda of 9 May 1912 (*Letters*, i. 396): 'And I smoked a pensive cigarette, and philosophised about love and life and battle, and you and me. And I thought of a theme for my next novel.'

11 Memoir, p. 123.

12 See e.g. *D. H. Lawrence: The Critical Heritage*, ed. R. P. Draper (Routledge and Kegan Paul, 1970), p. 102.

13 See *Letters*, i. 369, 371 (*bis*), 375, 381.

14 *Sons and Lovers by D. H. Lawrence. A Facsimile of the Manuscript*, ed. M. Schorer (University of California Press), 1977. The final ms. of *Sons and Lovers* is owned by the Bancroft Library, Berkeley, California. This is the completed novel as Lawrence

wrote and revised it between November 1911 and November 1912. It was known as 'Paul Morel' until October 1912 when the new title *Sons and Lovers* was chosen. For this reason, it should not be confused with the surviving second version of the novel, abandoned in October 1911, which is now owned by the Humanities Research Center, University of Texas, at Austin, and which is generally referred to as 'Paul Morel' to distinguish it from the Berkeley manuscript.